RADICAL JOE

A Life of Joseph Chamberlain

DENIS JUDD

CARDIFF
UNIVERSITY OF WALES PRESS
1993

First published in Great Britain by Hamish Hamilton Ltd., 1977

First edition in paperback published by University of Wales Press, 1993

British Library Cataloguing-in-Publication Data

A catalogue record for this book is available from the British Library.

ISBN 0-7083-1195-4

New material typeset in Wales by Megaron, Cardiff

This edition printed in Wales by WBC Print Limited, Bridgend

*To my family and all those
who helped me to write this book*

CONTENTS

PREFACE

This biography of Joseph Chamberlain aims to provide a full account of the life of one of the most controversial statesmen of modern times, and the founder of a political dynasty whose last representative was Prime Minister at the outbreak of the Second World War. Until recently, Chamberlain has been curiously neglected as a fit subject for a comprehensive, one-volume biography such as this. There was, of course , the monumental, but not easily digested, six-volume *Life* begun by J. L. Garvin in 1932 and completed by Julian Amery in 1969. Other modern studies, admirable as they are, have tended to examine aspects of Chamberlain's career rather than scrutinise his life as a whole. Chamberlain's contemporaries, interestingly, felt no such inhibitions, and his political progress was punctuated at regular intervals by a variety of biographies and assessments, ranging from the adulatory to the bitterly hostile.

I am delighted that this biography of 'Radical Joe' is the first of its kind to appear in paperback, not least because it will make the book more readily available to all of those, including university students, sixth-formers and others at school, who are fascinated by Chamberlain's career and want to make sense of it. I therefore owe a special debt of gratitude to Susan Jenkins, Liz Powell and Ned Thomas at the University of Wales Press for their enthusiasm for the book. Professor Kenneth O. Morgan also played an important part, through his friendly encouragement, in bringing the project to fruition.

It must be said that despite my deep and long-abiding interest in Joseph Chamberlain, and the times in which he lived, the writing of the book was made much easier by the generous study leave I received from the University of North London. Two of my then colleagues, Professor Robert Skidelsky and Dr. Dennis Dean, read the original manuscript and constructively criticised it. A considerable number of librarians and keepers of archives provided me with courteous help, but none more than Dr. Benedict Benedicks at the University of Birmingham Library. I have also enjoyed the friendship and support of many colleagues and fellow historians.

Finally, I have always been fortunate in the support of my family. It was my parents who first encouraged me to study, and whose enthusiasm for the education they had never themselves received, was a vital stimulus to my progress through grammar school and Oxford. They remain equally encouraging to this day. My wife, Dorothy, and our four children, have given whatever help they could to my research and writing, even when it did not directly encompass their own interests. I hope that all of those mentioned above enjoy this new edition of the book.

DENIS JUDD
London, 1993

ACKNOWLEDGEMENTS

The author is particularly grateful to the following for permission to use documents in their possession: the British Library, the Chamberlain Collection, University of Birmingham Library, the Public Record Office, the Bodleian Library, Christ Church College and New College, Oxford, and the Earl of Balfour.

INTRODUCTION

Joseph Chamberlain's public career intrigued his contemporaries, as well as inspiring and antagonising them. During
his lifetime he provoked the extremes of rapturous adulation
and the most punishing abuse; few remained indifferent to his
controversial progress or to his combative political style.

His impact upon the Victorian and Edwardian imagination
was partly the result of his direct, even abrasive, methods, and
partly due to the strong feelings aroused by the causes with
which he become associated. He met the great issues of his day
head-on, and was remarkable for his apparently inexhaustible
capacity to make plans and propose solutions. Indeed some of
Chamberlain's recipes to solve the problems of his time are
uncommonly relevant today: federal 'home rule all round' in
response to the demands of Celtic nationalism; social remedies
on a national and municipal scale to alleviate poverty and
hardship; a thorough re-appraisal of Britain's industrial and
economic capacity, including his own imperial version of the
European Community, in order to maintain and improve living
standards. His single-minded pursuit of a variety of causes,
many of them highly-charged, goes far to explain the hostility
which he aroused, especially when new causes precipitated
those sweeping changes of direction that his enemies took to be
illustrations of unprincipled self-seeking. As circumstances
altered, as new problems emerged, so Chamberlain adjusted his
objectives, though not necessarily his methods.

Posterity has found it as difficult as Chamberlain's contemporaries to fathom his personality and to assess his
achievements. During his career, his detractors saw him as a
political manipulator, supervisor of the Birmingham party
machine and of a local spoils system; a man ambitious enough to
bid for national pre-eminence through his creations, the
National Liberal Federation and the Tariff Reform League. At

worst, he was regarded as an unprincipled nouveau riche capitalist, mouthing Radical slogans in order to win the popular support that would enable him to get his tainted provincial hands upon the highest offices of the state; an ally of 'money-bags' imperialism, the subordinator of Afrikaner independence, and arch-conspirator in the Jameson Raid; the man who connived at his best friend's ruin in the divorce courts, and who pushed his country into an oppressive war in South Africa, and then proceeded to profit from the conflict through companies with whom he still kept business connections; an atheist, a republican, a sinister authoritarian, a race-patriot, a turncoat, a slick opportunist bowing before the changing pressures of public opinion; the man who helped to break up the Liberal party for the sake of a semantic difference with Gladstone over Irish Home Rule, and who twenty years later smashed the Unionist alliance with a scare-mongering and dishonest campaign for tariff reform.

Chamberlain's admirers saw things differently. It was equally possible to portray him as a dedicated reformer, impatient with conventional wisdoms and impelled by a burning desire to root out social inequality and economic distress. A man ever willing to trust the people, revelling in the democratic process and in parliamentary practice, generous to his friends and, though forthright, fair to his enemies. A municipal activist who pushed aside the forces of reaction and self-interest and made a bid to establish Birmingham as a beacon of progress and enlightenment. The visionary who saw in the threat of Irish separation nothing less than the eventual impoverishment of the United Kingdom, and who later directed his countrymen's attention towards the economic and moral potential of Empire. The patriot who despised the politics of drift, and who sought, almost with this last breath, to preach a stirring message of national salvation—a salvation that would result from the drive for national efficiency and from a searching re-appraisal of free trade dogma.

There is another, more realistic, view of Chamberlain's career. It is of a man of obscure, though not uncomfortable origins, who possessing quite remarkable powers of persuasion and analysis, set out to make his country a better place to live in. Lacking the advantages of high birth and assured preferment, Chamberlain was obliged to fight his way to the top through the exercise of his demagogic and organisational abilities. He remained a radical throughout his life: a political radical at the outset of his career, a fiscal and economic radical at the end of it. Even as a municipal reformer and the proposer of the doctrine of 'ransom', however, he was no social revolutionary: his tactics were Fabian, his objectives essentially ameliorative.

For most of his life Chamberlain was a rich man, surrounded by trappings that were often both vulgar and ostentatious. It was doubtless this contrast between his opulent life-style and his well-advertised concern for the poor and the downtrodden that caused so many of his contemporaries to doubt his personal integrity; nor were such misgivings quelled by the ferocious verbal assaults he mounted against wealth and privilege during much of this career.

Chamberlain's capacity for radical reappraisal made him an uncomfortable, though frequently stimulating, colleague, and an alarming and dangerous foe. His instinct to strike at the jugular created a host of political enemies, and yet Lord Salisbury found him a loyal and invaluable ally, despite Chamberlain's earlier derision for the 'class who toil not neither do they spin'.

Ambition was as natural to Chamberlain as life itself. He did not, however, become Prime Minister; the most important Cabinet post that he filled was the previously uncoveted position of Colonial Secretary; his legislative output was almost pitiful, and his achievements in the field of national social reform negligible; he did not transform Britain's relationship with either her self-governing or dependant colonies; the victory in South Africa turned to dust, and tariff reform seemed as far from reach as ever when he died.

Chamberlain's lack of substantial success in his chosen causes was in part due to bad luck and to a tendency to take chances; it was bad luck that Gladstone survived to stay on as Liberal leader for eight years after the Home Rule crisis of 1886, and bad luck that the opening of the tariff reform campaign coincided with a marked up-swing in world trade; Chamberlain chanced his arm in breaking away from main-stream Liberalism, when it seemed to have achieved permanent majority status, and he left the corn tax a hostage to fortune when he went to South Africa at the end of 1902. Perhaps Chamberlain's miscalculations were in some measure the result of deep uncertainties lurking beneath the brash self-confidence of his public image; he lived a life full of tension and conflict, and he was no stranger to depression, introspection and doubt.

Judged by his own exacting standards, Chamberlain's career was essentially a failure. Yet he did more than any other man of his times to create organised politics, and among his bequests to the nation were constituency and national associations, party conferences and party discipline. He left one other legacy—that of his own memory. His political style, the issues with which he grappled, the clangour and excitement of the public debate that he aroused, are real enough, almost tangible, nearly eighty years after his death. If he loved himself, he also loved his country, and with a more abiding passion. His character, as John Morley said, was of a piece—with all its defects and its virtues.

ONE

A LONDON BOYHOOD
1836–54

'As a child Joseph Chamberlain didn't take things easily; he went deeply into them, and was very serious for a boy.'
Miss Charlotte Pace, Chamberlain's first school teacher.

ALTHOUGH JOSEPH Chamberlain was destined to make his private and his political fortune in Birmingham, he spent the first eighteen years of his life in London. He was born on 8 July 1836 at what is now 188 Camberwell Grove in south London. Chamberlain's birthplace was an elegant but unpretentious late Georgian house; it had a basement, a wrought-iron-balustraded balcony outside the tall first storey windows, and, above the second storey, attic rooms.

At the time of Chamberlain's birth, Camberwell was a comparatively quiet and leafy suburb: much of the road to London was still open and pleasant; from the uppermost windows of 188 Camberwell Grove there was a fine view of chestnuts, elms and poplars, and on a clear day it was possible to see the towers of the Palace of Westminster.[1]

Chamberlain's father, also named Joseph (like his father before him), went daily to his wholesale boot and shoe business at 36 Milk Street, Cheapside. The Chamberlains traced back their descent to Daniel Chamberlain, a maltster of Lacock in Wiltshire, who died in 1760. Daniel's son, William, the greatgrandfather of the statesman, had moved to the City of London and set up in business as a cordwainer (a worker in new leather, as opposed to a cobbler—a worker in old leather). By 1836 the Chamberlains had been cordwainers at Milk Street for one hundred and twenty years, and earlier generations had found it convenient to live over the shop.

Joseph Chamberlain was proud of his family's connections with the cordwaining business and with the Cordwainers' Company in particular—six of his ancestors were Masters of the ancient guild, he himself joined it at the age of twenty-one, his four brothers followed him, and his eldest son Austen was later admitted. This

solid, respectable business background was a source of satisfaction
and strength to Chamberlain throughout his life, and on one
occasion he told the House of Commons that 'My family can
boast nothing of distinguished birth and they have not inherited
wealth or anything of that kind. But we have a record—an un-
broken record—of nearly two centuries, of unstained commercial
integrity and honour.'[2]

Religious dissent was also the hallmark of Chamberlain's family.
Through his father's mother he claimed descent from Richard
Serjeant, a clergyman ejected from his living at Kidderminster
after refusing to take the tests stipulated by the 1662 Act of Uniformity. Chamberlain's paternal grandfather was a Unitarian and
so, with the latter's marriage in 1792 to Martha Strutt (the great-
great-granddaughter of Richard Serjeant), two branches of religious, and, by implication, political, nonconformity were united.

Joseph Chamberlain senior, the father of the statesman, was a
rather reserved, severe-faced man of retiring habits. A beadle of
the Cordwainers' Company was to remember him as 'an im-
movable man—nothing could turn him if he had made up his
mind; pleasant and quiet in manner, but not to be moved from
what he said by anybody; you could see it in his face.'[3] In 1834
Joseph Chamberlain senior married Caroline Harben, the daughter
of Henry Harben a London provision merchant dealing chiefly in
cheese. The Harbens, too, were descended from a maltster, from
Southsea. Their family tradition was decidedly more speculative
than that of the Chamberlains: in 1747 Thomas Harben, a Lewes
clockmaker, had bought up the wreck of a Spanish prize ship lost
during the War of the Austrian Succession and had salvaged a
fortune from the Sussex sea and sands; Thomas Harben's son,
also christened Thomas, dabbled in Whig politics, and speculated
unwisely in landed estates—losing most of his fortune as a result.[4]

The marriage of Joseph Chamberlain senior to Caroline Harben
lasted forty years (Joseph dying in 1874 and Caroline a year later).
There were nine offspring, six boys and three girls; of these
children all but one boy lived to maturity. Joseph, the first-born,
was to achieve international stature before the death of any of his
surviving siblings—that of Richard Chamberlain, twice mayor of
Birmingham and M.P. for West Islington, in 1899.

Though nonconformist in religion the members of the Chamberlain family were by no means gloomy, puritanical or bigoted. Their

Unitarianism (a creed which rejects the concept of the Trinity and consequently the divinity of Christ) was broadbased, humanitarian and tolerant. On occasion the Chamberlains found it expedient to conform, or at least to work within the structure of the established church. Thus Joseph Chamberlain's father was at some time a churchwarden at the City church of St. Lawrence Jewry, and when the family settled at 25 Highbury Place in 1845 Joseph was sent to a school in Canonbury Square which was run by the Reverend Arthur Johnson, an Anglican clergyman.

Unitarianism, at the time of Chamberlain's birth, was not a faith given to extreme political or social radicalism; perhaps because of its roots in seventeenth century Presbyterianism. Instead Unitarian energies tended to be devoted to more practical, down-to-earth schemes of reform and improvement; teaching, slum clearance, the provision of greater educational opportunities, the promotion of self-help organisations such as provident societies, an interest in pensions. Birmingham was to provide Joseph Chamberlain with the ideal opportunity to throw the resources of a booming municipality behind such practical reforms, and even at the height of his career, when he had become a world famous and highly controversial statesman, he retained the reputation as a foremost advocate of old age pensions. It could also be argued that his desire to re-order the resources and structure of the British Empire, grandiose and vainglorious as many of his critics believed such an aim to be, was essentially pragmatic, almost pedestrian, owing far more to the art of what was possible and desirable in local political and economic terms than to wild dreams of international aggrandisement and Anglo-Saxon global supremacy.

Unitarianism was, nonetheless, a powerful branch of British Dissent, and attachment to its creed usually implied a broad liberalism—the belief in the removal of civil disabilities for religious nonconformists, support for the Free Trade movement, a dislike of foreign tyranny and of domestic poverty. In short, home-grown Radicalism well became Unitarianism, and Joseph Chamberlain's apparently insatiable appetite for organising change, for questioning traditional assumptions and for challenging widely-held beliefs, sprang directly from his religious background. These qualities were often to make him an uncomfortable political bedfellow, as both Gladstone and Balfour were to discover.

The Chamberlain family worshipped at a Unitarian chapel in

Little Carter Lane, between St. Paul's cathedral and the river. The chapel was a square building, the inside of which was 'furnished with a remarkable neatness, and in point of workmanship is scarcely equalled by any dissenting place of worship in London. The sombre appearance it exhibits appears suited in all ways to the solemnity of divine worship.'[5] Of the congregation, the Hon. W. Porter observed that 'The Carter Lane people are few but united . . . one family in particular, the Chamberlains, have shewn me as much kindness as ever I received in my life. The congregation is composed for the most part of the higher sort of tradesmen, plain, honest and sincere.'[6]

The Carter Lane chapel was plumb in the middle of some of the worst slums in London; families, many living in single rooms, were crowded into wretched, filthy tenements, all too susceptible to disease and what contemporaries called 'moral degredation'. Between the ages of sixteen and eighteen, Joseph Chamberlain became a Sunday school teacher, holding a class for the children from these slums and seeing at first-hand the distressing effects of urban poverty and ignorance upon his unfortunate pupils. Here, too, was fuel for a future explosion of Radical initiative.

Chamberlain's own formal education began when he went, at the age of eight, to a small school in Camberwell Grove kept by Miss Charlotte Pace, assisted by her sister Harriet. His mother had already taught him to read, and he stayed at the school only a year; Miss Charlotte Pace believed in teaching her pupils to read and speak 'distinctly', and she charged fees of eight guineas a year, without Latin, French, and drill, which cost extra. Miss Pace was later to recall that because of the family's Unitarianism she did not 'think [Chamberlain] would learn the Church Catechism, but he certainly took his Bible lesson with the others.' It is evident from the ledgers that Miss Pace kept that Chamberlain must have been familiar with the following works: *The Guide to Knowledge*, *Little Arthur's History of England*, *Rhymes for Youthful Historians*, and *Geography*, mysteriously penned by 'A Lady'.[7]

Miss Pace also recalled the following details of her pupil:

At one time they wanted to get up a 'Peace Society.' I was very much against it, as I felt sure it would stir up quarrels among them; and they were, of course, forbidden to fight. However, like men, I knew they would get tired of it if they had their own way. One afternoon I heard there had been trouble while I had been out, and I sent for the boys to interrogate the offenders. It was just as I had expected. They had been fighting as to who should be the President of the Peace Society, and, of course, Joseph Chamberlain was among them. He didn't like being behind anybody, and when he did fight he was in earnest about it.

As a child Joseph Chamberlain didn't take things easily; he went deeply into them, and was very serious for a boy. He didn't care much for games; he was not so much solitary as solid, industrious, and intelligent, but rather too anxious about his lessons, conscientious and very solemn as a rule. I remember his mother once said to me, 'I find Joseph asks questions which I have great difficulty in answering.'

Mrs. Chamberlain used to come and see me about her son; she was most anxious that he should do well and perform his duties faithfully. She thought much about duty, and I expected her sons to turn out well. They were a serious family, and Mrs. Chamberlain did not wish Joseph to learn or read anything light or frivolous. I remember her very well after all these years; she had a very fine face, quiet and still. I should say that Mr. Chamberlain resembled his mother in looks. I do not remember that I ever saw his father. They were rich City people, and kept much in their own set: in those days people found their friends in the circle of their own Church or Chapel.[8]

Joseph Chamberlain also later recalled his activities in the Peace Society: 'I founded that Peace Society. It was to be a charitable society, and we had a fund of five pence half penny to distribute, of which I contributed the largest share, for I remember my uncle gave me a fourpenny bit. The quarrel was as to what should be done with so large a sum. Eventually, after long consideration, it went to a crossing sweeper near the school, and that was the end of the Peace Society.'[9]

It is interesting that over half a century after his brief schooling at Miss Pace's institution, Chamberlain visited his old teacher who was 'much surprised at his youthful appearance', and 'thought Mr. Chamberlain remembered the neighbourhood surprisingly well.' Chamberlain and his wife sent Miss Pace 'flowers and fruit on several occasions, which I value, not only for the nice gifts, but also, and still more, for the kind thought it shows.' In the autumn of 1899, when Britain went to war with the Transvaal and the Orange Free State ('Chamberlain's War' as his political enemies described it), Miss Pace unerringly put her finger on a significant part of her ex-pupil's public appeal when she said 'I follow Mr. Chamberlain's career with great interest, and I like reading his speeches; he uses simple words, and they are so clear, besides being amusing. And when he has to pounce down on an antagonist he does it so nicely too—just as if he enjoyed it.'[10]

In 1846 the Chamberlains left Camberwell for Highbury in north London. The death of the family's youngest member, 'little Frank', caused Mrs. Chamberlain to associate Camberwell Grove with this sad loss, and her depression may well have been the main reason for moving.[11] The Chamberlains' new home was at 25 Highbury Place, where they were destined to live for nearly twenty years. A contemporary described Highbury Place as 'A fine row of houses, embracing a beautiful view on both sides, and remarkable for its healthy situation. It consists of thirty-nine houses built on a large scale, but varying in size, all having good gardens, and some of them allotments and meadow-land in the front and rear. The road is private, and frequented only by the carriages passing to and fro from the several dwellings situated between the village and Highbury House.'[12]

After the family's move to salubrious and 'fairly rural' Highbury, Joseph Chamberlain was sent to a day school in Canonbury Square run by the Reverend Arthur Johnson, an Anglican clergyman. Chamberlain was later to recall that his old headmaster 'was one of the handsomest men I have ever seen; an excellent teacher, and one to whom I owe much; he was a man of remarkable power and influence.'[13] His Unitarianism apparently unsullied by the Reverend Johnson's schooling, Chamberlain made such good progress at Canonbury Square that when he reached the age of fourteen his headmaster told Joseph Chamberlain senior that the boy knew as much mathematics as his master and was more than ready to move on to another school.

There was one obvious school near at hand: University College School, a mere twenty years old and then nestling alongside its parent institution, 'that godless place' University College, in Gower Street. Chamberlain entered University College School in 1850, and stayed there for two years. The School provided a most congenial environment for someone of Chamberlain's background, since it provided a liberal, unsectarian education without religious instruction. The headmaster Dr. Thomas Hewitt Key pursued high standards of scholarship, set no great store on athletic achievement, and, remarkably in an age notable for scholastic flogging, had dispensed with corporal punishment. University College School was a haven for boys from Nonconformist and Dissenting families. There was a strong Unitarian contingent, and the names of Kenrick, Martineau, Nettlefold, Preston and Harben, all representing families connected with the Chamberlains, can be found in the school register. Some of the masters were also Unitarians, and the statesman John Morley attended the school shortly after Chamberlain's time there.

Joseph Chamberlain's two years at University College School were marked by substantial academic achievements: in the school honours list for 1851–2 he was honourably mentioned in the Sixth Latin group; he gained the second prize in Sixth form French, and the first prize in the Mathematics Sixth; in the Sixth Mechanics and Hydrostatics he was joint first.

His brothers Richard and Arthur also attended the school. Richard, in particular, achieved far more popularity than Joseph, whose single-minded pursuit of learning did not endear him to many of his school fellows, one of whom was later to recall that 'Even at an early age he [Chamberlain] possessed a good deal of individuality and a strong will, and always wanted to take the lead in anything that was going on among his companions. He had little taste for boyish sports, and made but few acquaintances amongst his schoolfellows. He was, however, always fond of study.'[14]

There is no doubt that Chamberlain's powerful intellect was skilfully stimulated and fed at University College School. His education there not only awakened an interest in science and technology but also gave him a life-long passion for absorbing new ideas in a wide variety of areas—the arts, history, English and French literature.

In November 1902, Chamberlain, then Colonial Secretary, with the Boer War six months behind him, reminisced over his school days when unveiling a memorial tablet to old boys of the school who had died in the conflict in South Africa:

I can remember many of the incidents of my school life, and I entertain always the most kindly sentiments and regard for my old schoolfellows and my old teachers. I can call up to-day, as if it were yesterday, the portly form of Professor Key, most kindly of Head Masters, marching solemnly to call to order a somewhat unruly class. I can recall my dear old friend Professor Cook enforcing his mathematical instruction with the oft-repeated assertion, that never in the long course of his life had he met with boys so bad as we were, and that to attempt to get into our heads the mysteries of algebra was like firing a cannonball into a mountain of mud. Yet this terrible comparison did not prevent him from exhibiting on many occasions the greatest pride and delight in the proficiency of his scholars. I remember also Professor Merlet, that quaint and genial Frenchman, endeavouring to instil into our British understandings the beauties of Molière, and in the excitement of his recitals acting the parts he read as if he had just come from the boards of the Française. I remember all this and more, and I remember my schoolmates, and rejoice that so many of them have subsequently achieved distinction. These were the late Professor Jevons, Mr. Justice Charles, Sir Ralph Littler, whom we are pleased to see here to-day; Mr. Prevost, Governor of the Bank of England; Sir Edwin Durning Lawrence, also present, and my friend—for he has always been my friend—Sir Michael Foster, one of the most distinguished of our men of science. Well, I have said enough to explain why, though I have in some measure lost touch with your work, I could not resist the call that was made on me, even in the midst of exceptional pressure, to come once more among you, and to say how proud I am, that in a great crisis of our national history our old school should have done its duty. . . .

It is here that our characters are fixed, and it is impossible that our course in life should not be materially directed by our experience at school. In my time the school was a good one, and the education, so far as it went, was excellent and thorough. I have many times felt my gratitude to it. There was only one thing which they did not teach well then—in fact, I am not certain that they taught it at all then. I hope they teach it to you now, and that is the geography of the British Empire. It is said, that one of my predecessors, on being first appointed, went to his office, and said that as he was now Secretary of State for the Colonies, he should like to know where the Colonies were. I am glad to think that in these recent years not only has communication between ourselves and our children across the seas been much more frequent, but our mutual knowledge of one another has increased, and with it our mutual sympathy. You boys who are now beginning your careers should bear in mind the responsibility which hereafter will fall on you, for you are the heirs of a great Empire and the citizens of no mean city. I thank the Principal for his kindness in seconding this vote. He has told you that, though I had no university education, I am now the Chancellor of a university; but I am something more than that. Other men take degrees after much labour and many examinations. I am a Doctor of Laws of four great universities, and I am thankful to say that on no occasion was I examined. That shows you what you may possibly do in the future, though I do not recommend you to try to achieve academical honours by the short cut which I have adopted.[15]

If Chamberlain had proceeded from school to University College, 'academical honours' would have been his for the taking. But, despite his mother's wishes, his father refused on principle to send him to University College (Oxford and Cambridge did not then admit Nonconformists); the principle was one of equity, for Joseph Chamberlain senior argued that since he could not afford to send all his sons to university, the eldest should not enjoy this special privilege simply by right of seniority. That Chamberlain's father felt such financial constraint is strange in view of the fact that in 1846 the family business made a profit of £1,284; perhaps he was displaying a businessman's appropriate caution over future profits. On the other hand, he was prepared to offer Joseph (and his other sons) a settlement of £200 if he would train for the Unitarian ministry, an offer which none of the Chamberlain brothers took up.

So, in 1852, Chamberlain left the academic atmosphere of Gower Street for the family's wholesale boot and shoe business in Milk Street. It is a matter for speculation whether this abrupt ending of his formal education was in any sense a disadvantage in his subsequent career. Certainly his public activities bear witness to a remarkable clarity of mind and to a formidable intellectual energy. His political opponents were keenly aware of the sharp cutting-edge of both his tongue and his pen; doubtless they were thankful to have been spared conflict with a mind rendered (arguably) even more nimble and dextrous by a university education.

Chamberlain was not prone to self-pity, but John Morley wrote of him, in volume one of his *Recollections*:

> Yet he was sorry that he had missed chances for wider beginnings in the humaner letters. When in later years he paid his first visit with me to Jowett at Oxford, and I had taken him round the garden walks, antique gates, and 'massy piles of old munificence', he said to me in a fervid accent, 'Ah, how I wish I could have had a training in this place.' Yet he came to be more widely read in books worth reading than most men in public life, and there was no limit to his interest in art, modern history, imaginative letters and all they import in politics. As it was, he drew round him at Birmingham a remarkable circle, and in after-dinner conversations with them in his library there was an activity of mind, a discussion of theoretical social views in terms of practical life, an atmosphere of strenuous and disinterested public spirit, all far superior for effective purpose to the over-critical air and tone of the academic common-room.[16]

Chamberlain spent two years in the Milk Street business, during which time, it could be claimed, he learnt far more of the world and of the ordinary men and women that peopled it than any undergraduate could have done.

Working with his father could have been no easy matter. Old Mr. Chamberlain was frugal, sedate, punctual and precise. Mrs. Russell Martineau, his niece, recalled that 'His religion to him was the life within the life. When anyone was first introduced he would sometimes say at once, "Yes, sir, Joseph Chamberlain and a Unitarian." If they swallowed that it was alright.'[17]

The future statesman worked strict hours in Milk Street; the business only closed during weekdays on Good Friday and Christmas Day, and even then letters were brought round to the family residence by an old employee. Chamberlain put on a workman's apron and learnt the ancient craft of cordwaining at his father's benches; he was also instructed in book-keeping and business practice. Working so intimately among shoe-makers, he must have been influenced by the Radical and Chartist views so characteristic of the trade. No doubt he also came to appreciate how bitterly many of them resented the 1832 Reform Act as a mere collusion between the aristocracy and the middle clashes, and how they hated both Whigs and Tories, and still hoped for a massive extension of the franchise. It would perhaps be too much to claim that the genesis of Chamberlain's municipal radicalism can be traced to those two years in Milk Street, yet his daily contact with working men must have played its part.

There were, of course, other influences at work in the early 1850s. The introduction of Free Trade had been warmly welcomed by the Chamberlains, and in 1850 they mourned the death of Robert Peel—the statesman who had given the doctrine political substance. With the 'hungry forties' set firmly behind it, the nation seemed destined to exploit and enjoy the industrial and commercial supremacy that had been breathtakingly demonstrated at the Great Exhibition of 1851. At the same time, Free Trade seemed to spawn free institutions throughout the Empire; as the bonds of the old mercantilism were snapped one by one (the Corn Laws, the Navigation Acts, the Sugar Acts), responsible government burgeoned in the colonies of white settlements, in British North America, Australia, New Zealand and the Cape.

At home, middle-class Dissenters, like the Chamberlains, pressed for the complete removal of legal and religious disabilities; they welcomed the repeal and lowering of customs duties in Gladstone's budget of 1853, and welcomed even more the prospect of the lowering and eventual abandonment of income tax.

In foreign affairs, the Chamberlains, avid readers of the *Daily News*, supported the convictions of Palmerston rather than those of Radicals like Cobden and Bright. Palmerstonian foreign policy was characterised by a relentless pursuit of British interests on a global scale; sometimes these interests coincided with liberal causes and sometimes they did not. The deepening crisis in the Near East, where Russia seemed bent on dismembering the ramshackle Turkish Empire, allowed a happy conjunction of national interest and liberal principles: Tsarist autocracy could be viewed as a menace to European liberties, and Russian expansionism posed an apparent threat to British strategic and commercial interests in the Eastern Mediterranean and the Near East. When Britain entered the Crimean War in 1854, therefore, the Chamberlains had no truck with John Bright's Peace Society, nor with *The Times* (described by a rival journal as 'The Russian organ of Printing House Square'); they backed Palmerston, who, as belligerent as ever from his unlikely and unaccustomed duties at the Home Office, wanted to 'make an Example of the Red-haired barbarians.'

The Chamberlains, in their support of Palmerston's pro-war stance, were at one with countless other middle-class families in Britain—whether Nonconformist or Anglican. The family's leisure activities were similarly those of contemporary middle-class house-holds. The younger Joseph Chamberlain was an avid reader, devouring contemporary fiction, and being particularly fond of the novels of Charles Dickens. The Chamberlains bought *Pickwick*, *Martin Chuzzlewit* and *David Copperfield* as they came out in parts. It became something of a family joke that Joseph was once so engrossed in *Pickwick* that he absent-mindedly consumed the contents of a silver basket full of biscuits set upon the dining table of his uncle Bailey, continually reaching out with one hand while holding the novel in the other.

Chamberlain's love of contemporary fiction was matched by his passion for amateur theatricals. Together with his Harben cousins he would write, produce and act in a variety of theatrical diversions, either in the drawing rooms of the respective families or, more frequently, in his uncle Bailey's warehouse in High Holborn. Chamberlain was, it seems, the life and soul of these occasions: he wrote comedy, farce, and once a tragedy in rhyming couplets over which his cousins trembled, declaring it to be as fearful as the ghost stories he so often told them. A programme compiled by the young Joseph Chamberlain has survived; it is an indication of his own inventiveness as well as of an evidently strong youthful loyalty to the crown—note the 'Theatre Royal' and the final flourish of 'Vivat Regina':

THEATRE ROYAL, HIGH HOLBORN
This evening, Tuesday, January 31st 1854
Will Be Presented The Drama Of
'PERFECTION'

Sir Lawrence Paragon	MR. BENJAMIN HARBEN
Charles Paragon	MR. STANTON PRESTON
Sam	MR. JOSEPH CHAMBERLAIN
Kate O'Brien	MISS CHARLOTTE BAILEY
Susan	MISS FRANCES BAILEY

To Be Followed By
'DONE ON BOTH SIDES'

Mr. Whiffles	Mr. Charles Bailey
Mr. John Brownjohn	Mr. Joseph Chamberlain
Mr. Pygmalion Phibbs . . .	Mr. Stanton Preston
Mrs. Whiffles	Miss Emily Bailey
Lydia	Miss Frances Bailey

Doors open at 8 o'clock: performance to commence at half-past
VIVAT REGINA

Chamberlain also took great pains with his acting, learning his lines as he travelled from Highbury to Milk Street and astonishing passers-by with his histrionic gestures and declamations. His theatrical talents, so spontaneously expressed and so assiduously fostered, were to stand him in good stead in his later political career when as Radical orator and then as Unionist statesman he held audiences spell-bound and his enemies prayed, almost invariably without success, for him to fluff his lines.

It was not merely amateur theatricals that Chamberlain shared with his cousins. There were family suppers, monthly six o'clock family teas, and shared seaside holidays. Deal, Margate, Eastbourne and Brighton were the seaside resorts patronised by the families. At Brighton, Chamberlain once shocked his cousins by proposing a game of ringing the bells of boarding houses and asking for somebody: 'Thinking of their other cousins, they decided to ask for "Nettlefold". Whereupon they went knocking and ringing, Joe showing a great command of feature. On some doorsteps they met a sour reception from harassed landladies, but presently one was so kind that they were conscience-smitten and repented.'[18]

During his two years in the Milk Street business, Chamberlain continued to mix hard work with the pursuit of decorous pleasure: he played chess with his father, attended lectures on chemistry and electricity at the Polytechnic, and frequently visited the Great Exhibition in Hyde Park. Amid the exhibits in Hyde Park was an American patent for the production, by steam machinery, of a revolutionary woodscrew with a pointed end. This screw could be pushed into wood with a light hammer tap or even by a firm thumb; it thereafter acted as its own gimlet, boring into the wood when turned by a screwdriver. Hitherto the iron screws for fixing

woodwork were blunt-ended, requiring a hole to be drilled by a
gimlet before they could be driven home.

Chamberlain's uncle John Sutton Nettlefold (who had married
Martha Chamberlain, sister of Joseph senior) manufactured woodscrews in Birmingham by the old method. He saw the American
invention in Hyde Park and appreciated its potential as a money-
maker. For two years he hesitated over the patent; to buy it meant
a substantial capital outlay; not to buy it might mean the ultimate
ruin of his business. In 1854 John Nettlefold took the plunge and
bought the United Kingdom rights on the patent. He found he
needed £30,000 both to buy the patent and to begin the manufacture of the new woodscrew. He asked Joseph Chamberlain
senior to invest money in the project. Chamberlain senior thought
the matter over; he visited Nettlefold's works at Birmingham; he
decided to invest capital in the venture.

But who would represent the Chamberlain family in Birmingham? Chamberlain senior had little inclination to shift north; but
there was another possibility, and Mr. Chamberlain put it plainly
when he announced 'We will send Joe.' There was no appeal
against the decision, and, it seems, no inclination to appeal in the
first place.

In the late autumn of 1854, the young Joseph Chamberlain, aged
eighteen years, boarded the train for Birmingham. It was, arguably,
the contemporary equivalent, in terms of business opportunity, to
a modern executive flight to the Gulf of Bahrein. The Crimean
War had begun some months earlier and Birmingham's industry
had been stimulated as a result. The city's factories vibrated with
energy and its furnaces belched forth flame. It was, in short, the
place where a young man could hope to make his fortune and,
perhaps, an undying name for himself.

TWO

THE BIRMINGHAM BUSINESSMAN
1854–66

'No man who made any kind of reputation in our Society has failed to make it in after life.'
Joseph Chamberlain, reminiscing in 1896 of his early years as a member of the Birmingham and Edgbaston Debating Society.

WHEN CHAMBERLAIN arrived in Birmingham in 1854 the city's industries were strikingly varied, an amalgam of ancient crafts and new, profitable enterprises. In the centre of the city could be found the long-established jewellers, gunsmiths and brass-workers, while on the periphery new industrial areas were being established at Smethwick, Witton, and Small Heath—after 1861 the home of the Birmingham Small Arms Company. Squalid streets characterised the older parts of the city, while at Edgbaston and Handsworth suburban villas were being built for the wealthy and the successful. New railway lines linked the old Birmingham with its peripheral industrial areas, and, in the 1870s, the tramways marked out the development of the city streets.[19]

Standing four-square in the geographical centre of England and Wales, Birmingham enjoyed a profitable proximity to the Black Country—producer of the vital raw materials of iron and coal. Four main trades dominated the city's industrial life: brass goods, jewellery, buttons and guns. About 8,000 men worked in the brass industry, slightly fewer in jewellery and some 6,000 in both gun and button manufacturing. As well as supplying the home market, Birmingham's main products were shipped in abundance overseas: cheap muskets to West Africa, buttons, in magnificent variety, to Europe.[20]

But brass was the chief staple of the city, and in the 1860s W. C. Aitken, a local manufacturer, wrote, 'What Manchester is to cotton, Bradford in wool and Sheffield in steels, Birmingham is in brass; its articles of cabinet and general brass foundry are to be found in every part of the world; its gas fittings in every city and town into which gas has been introduced, from Indus to the Poles—on the railways in every country and on every sea, its locomotive and marine engine solid brass tubes generate the vapour which impels the locomotive over the iron road, and propels the steam boat over the ocean wave.'[21]

In addition to brass and the other chief manufactures, Birmingham made steel pens, iron and brass bedsteads, wire, and woodscrews. Most of the city's products were made in small factories employing less than twenty men, employers and employed often working side-by-side. There was no such thing as a monolithic, highly centralised and well-regulated industrial structure; the present day assembly lines of Longbridge would have seemed immense, impersonal and unacceptably rigorous to mid-Victorian Birmingham workingmen.

In many ways, Birmingham's industry was half way along the slow, evolutionary path from cottage-based to large factory-based production. There was ample opportunity for the exercise of entrepreneurial skills: particularly important were the 'factors' whose activities ranged from putting out work, to organising different stages of manufacture for a particular product. Subcontractors (or 'butties') hired labour, often making substantial profits for themselves, and feeling themselves independent of the employers of labour. Nor should it be supposed that the mid-century Birmingham worker was metaphorically chained to his workbench. Although the factors sometimes ruthlessly forced down piecework rates, the workingman often failed to come to work on Mondays and Tuesdays, preferring instead to concentrate his labour into the remaining three days of the week.[22]

Birmingham's workers, in fact, felt a considerable degree of independence—an independence sometimes inconveniently recognised by those employers who charged their operatives for the gas or power that they used in their work. There were several reasons for this independence of spirit. One was the comparative security of employment resulting from Birmingham's steady economic progress; the city had avoided anything like a major slump. Another reason lay in the very multiplicity of small workshops and factories; a disgruntled craftsman, even (though less certainly) an unskilled labourer, could move on to other employment near at hand. These free-ranging opportunities meant that an ambitious artisan stood a very real chance of making progress, of becoming a 'factor', or eventually the owner of a workshop. Such circumstances may also explain why Birmingham, in mid-century, lacked a really vigorous trade-union movement.

The relatively democratic character of much of Birmingham's industrial society should not, however, be allowed to disguise the more brutal and squalid qualities of the city's life. Small factories often meant overcrowded and depressing working conditions. Employers and 'factors' could more easily bully and browbeat small work forces. St. Mary's Ward was notorious for its appalling housing and the violence and drunkenness of its denizens. Moreover, as the new suburbs were built, employers tended to move away from their factories, and instead of living over the shop, more and more chose to live in Edgbaston and Handsworth.

When Chamberlain first settled in Birmingham he took rooms in Frederick Street in Edgbaston. From there it was half a mile to the firm's offices in Broad Street, and Chamberlain walked there and back each day. He began to learn the commercial side of the business, sitting on a high stool among the clerks. He seems to have been both proficient and popular in those early days— certainly less dour than when a pupil at University College School. Chamberlain was quickly promoted and moved 'upstairs' as a principal to share a room with his cousin Joseph Nettlefold, son of the Nettlefold senior whose initiative had brought the Chamberlains into the new-fangled screw manufacturing trade.

The young Joseph Chamberlain and the young Joseph Nettlefold were soon to form a vitally creative partnership for the firm, Nettlefold and Chamberlain. Joseph Nettlefold was soon to prove his worth as a mechanical engineer and factory organiser, while Chamberlain took control of the management and sales side of the firm's activities.

The company, with its offices in Broad Street and its works in Smethwick, prospered within a few years of Chamberlain's arrival. There is no doubt that much of this success was due to Chamberlain, though there is more to it than is revealed by the bland judgement of the firm's cashier, 'Money was made very rapidly after Mr. Joseph came.'[23] Joseph Nettlefold senior had merely bought the United Kingdom patent rights to the new screw manufacturing process; equivalent rights were held in the United States, France, Russia and the German states. There was, more-

over, competition in the home market from established screw
manufacturers, none of whom would welcome their latest and
most threatening rival. Capital expenditure was, at first, bound to
be heavy as the new machinery was bought in.

Chamberlain lost no time in facing and surmounting these
difficulties. His early years in Birmingham reveal with striking
clarity his extraordinary energy, his capacity for mastering detail,
his sound business judgement, and above all his flair and style.
The rashness and impetuosity of which he was to be frequently
accused during his political career, seems to have been held firmly
in check in his business dealings. Instead there is the impression of
a hard-working, sober, though perhaps increasingly dominating,
young businessman.

Arriving punctually at his Broad Street offices at nine o'clock
in the morning, he only left at six in the evening and, quite
frequently, even later. One of his earliest, and most daunting, tasks
was to break into the French wood screw market. The way in
which he succeeded in this task provides ample evidence of his
business methods. To begin with, he had already acquired a sound
knowledge of French at University College School, but he took
considerable pains to improve his fluency, both by reading French
literature and, for a time, arranging for a Frenchman to breakfast
with him and to converse at the same time. He was always careful
to quote in decimalised weights and measures for French dealers,
and ensured that French consumers should have their screws
packaged in the traditional blue paper. Nettlefold and Chamberlain
came to dominate the French market.

But there were markets elsewhere. Chamberlain established a
flourishing trade with Ireland, which he visited several times as his
own commercial traveller. It was even said of him that he was
bound to return from holidays to Switzerland or Germany with a
full order book. By the time Chamberlain retired from the firm in
1874, the company was exporting screws, either directly, or through
agents, to Russia, the United States, Italy, Poland, Spain, France,
Malta, India, New Zealand, Japan, Germany, Canada, Belgium,
Switzerland and Australia. In the home market the Admiralty and
the Great Western Railway were regular customers.[24]

Between 1866 and 1874 Chamberlain kept at his Broad Street
office a detailed account, in his own hand, of the firm's business
transactions. A century and more later this notebook shows quite

plainly that Chamberlain the salesman was as clear-minded, force-ful, competent and masterful as he was later to be in his political life. An extract from the notebook, chosen at random, goes some way to illustrate this:

March 14 (1867)	Wakefield showed his cost book including all expenses in the Screw business to present date & amounting to £1650. Also calculations showing cost of

100 gro. 1.1/2 10 to be for wire 3 bdles.		19.	6
Wages including paper & string together	1	0	7
	2	**0**	**1**

He expected to sell at 62½% Net. to Ironmongers. Had heard that Bradleys made 6000 gro. per week & their wages were £75 per week. The Diffce in price made a difference of £75 per week to them & they had paid Ludford off £1100, had had abt. £2000 in Attwoods bank & had added £1500 with the machinery. W. offered to sell for £1250 + £200 if premises were not taken say £1450.
J.C. offered £1000 Cash as the outside sum.

March 15   J.T. Wakefield called in Broad St. & Said his Birmh. friend had called & offered to pay £200 as caution money for the intended company which he proposed to form by private circl.
(This appears to be the agent for the Promoter mentioned in previous conversation). He showed a letter from Gardiner offering to build machines for £20 each Cash. Self acting. Said also that Gardiner told him Bradley's made 6000 gross per week. Offered to sell for £1400 without premises or £1200 if N. & C. would take lease. J.C. refused & W. left promising to write his decision in the course of a week.

March 20   J.T. Wakefield offered to sell for £1300 without prems. or £1100 with the lease. J.C. refused but offered to submit to J.H.N. an offer to pay £1000 with lease or £1100 without.

March 25   Field A. & Co., Mr. Marichew called to ask that

payment of goods had in latter part of Quarter shd.
be postponed to the middle of May instead of being
made middle of April. Interest at 5% to be charged
& £3000 Cash to be paid at once & other payments
to go on all the time as usual – this is as received fr.
the U.S.
Possible settlement of this qr's a/c would be made
earlier but certainly not later than 15th May. J.C.
agreed.[25]

The commercial success of Nettlefold and Chamberlain was
achieved at the inevitable cost of ruining many of the small manufacturers of the old blunt-ended screw. Deep animosities were
aroused in Birmingham and elsewhere, and accusations that
Chamberlain had used threats and sharp practice in his drive to
establish a near-monopoly in the trade were very much alive in the
early 1880s when Chamberlain was in Gladstone's second Cabinet
as President of the Board of Trade. In November 1884, a H. R.
Grenfell wrote a letter to the *Daily News* in which he accused
Chamberlain of class-warfare by his attack on Lord Salisbury as a
member of a class 'who toil not neither do they spin'. Grenfell went
on, '[Chamberlain] is reported (I know not how truly) to have
made a large fortune in a monopoly secured by most questionable
dodges, and to have realised that fortune by investing it in securities
which will in future give no anxiety or labour.'[26]

Rebuttals swiftly followed. One came from the Reverend R. M.
Grier, vicar of Rugeley, who wrote a letter to the *Daily News* on
15 November 1884:

Up to a recent period I believed the story so industriously
circulated about the way in which Mr. Chamberlain realised his
wealth, and when a friend of his challenged the truth of it I had
no doubt that it could easily be verified. I was quickly, and I need
hardly say agreeably, undeceived. Having made careful inquiries
both of his friends and opponents in Birmingham, I could find
no foundation whatever for the attacks which have been made
upon him as a man of business. I had been given to understand
that copies of a threatening circular to the small screw manufacturers, whom he is supposed to have deliberately ruined, were
extant, and could be produced. I could not discover one. His
firm, I learned, had always stood high among the people, and

more especially the working-men of Birmingham, for honesty and straightforward dealing, and all that could be truly said against it was that other firms had suffered indirectly through its success. This, I think, can hardly be imputed as blame to Mr. Chamberlain. For him, however, I hold no brief. His method of carrying on political controversy is not always to my taste, and I am the servant of a Church to which he is not thought to bear any goodwill. I write in the interests of truth.[27]

Ten days later, A. Stokes and Company, screw and rivet manufacturers of Green Street, Birmingham, also wrote to the *Daily News* on Chamberlain's behalf, quoting from their own experience of being approached by his firm with a view to amalgamation:

Having seen in the newspapers various absurd and false statements concerning Mr. Chamberlain and the screw trade, we, as a representative firm of the screw trade in Birmingham, feel bound, in common fairness to Mr. Chamberlain, to state the simple facts of the case, and state the esteem in which Mr. Chamberlain is held by the oldest members of the trade in Birmingham in reference to the important and extensive transactions connected with his name; and our firm having been established in the trade for nearly half a century has had every opportunity of knowing the details of all those transactions and their results, and we unhesitatingly affirm, that Mr. Chamberlain's actions were highly beneficial to those connected with the trade, and beneficent to those whose businesses were purchased on such liberal terms; also to those who, like ourselves, remained in trade as well as his own firm.

And we affirm that Mr. Chamberlain revived that which was then a declining trade, and we are pleased to offer him our thanks for what he then did, and for the successful manner in which he and his firm competed with Continental makers. And we gladly bear testimony to Mr. Chamberlain's great abilities, and the courteous and honourable manner in which he conducted those great transactions, and we are pleased to state that those who, like our firm, were brought into contact with Mr. Chamberlain in reference to the purchase of their business, were treated in a most liberal and honourable manner, though the negotiations did not in some cases result in completion of the purchase.

And all reports as to threats to crush out the smaller makers

are false and absurd, and must be made by persons ignorant of
the facts and wilfully malicious.[28]

There is, alas, no testimony from the smaller firms that were
destroyed or mopped-up by the growing industrial power of
Nettlefold and Chamberlain. Perhaps all that can properly be said
is that even if those firms that were taken over were not threatened
in the way that Chamberlain's detractors claimed, they may well
have received offers that were 'impossible to refuse'.

Contemporary criticism was also made of Chamberlain's alleged
indifference to the welfare of his workmen. Again, there is no hard
evidence of such an attitude. On the other hand, it is easy to see
that such rumours could have proved useful to both the right and
left of Victorian politics: Tories, before the Liberal split of 1886
at least, had good cause to fear the powerful appeal of Chamberlain's
radicalism; after 1886 he was hated by many erstwhile Radical and
Liberal supporters as an ally of Conservatism. It is, above all,
difficult to see the young Chamberlain, Unitarian, Sunday school
teacher, and high-minded municipal reformer as a hard-faced
oppressor of his work force. There is, on the contrary, a good deal
of evidence that he flung himself with zeal behind the civic causes
of Birmingham's Unitarian community.

Based first of all at the New Meeting House, but later at the
Church of the Messiah, built on arches over the canal at Broad
Street, Chamberlain taught literature, history, French and arith-
metic in Sunday school. He was first president of the school's
Mutual Improvement Society; he read from his beloved *Pickwick
Papers* at Penny Reading sessions; he even taught at a night school,
after leaving his office. He also helped to found a Working Men's
Institute at Small Heath, calling up the Reverend Henry Solly
from the Carter Lane church in London to advise him. A Benefit
Club, separate from the Institute, was founded with his backing
to make provision for his workmen against sickness and misfortune.[29]

The Unitarians of Birmingham, like so many of the city's nonconformist groups, were fired by the civic gospel, preached so
forcefully from a score of pulpits. The Church of the Messiah,
which Chamberlain attended, was the place of worship for a
number of Unitarian families forming an elite group within the
Birmingham commercial community—families like the Nettle-

folds, Kenricks, Martineaus, and, as h...
gradually moved up to join him, the Cha...
gospel was preached as clearly to them as to th...
George Dawson's Church of the Saviour or a...
Congregational Church where Dr. Robert Dale argu...
city must assume its full social responsibilities and that m...
politics were a noble Christian mission. Instructed, as he must...
been, to work to clothe the naked, feed the hungry, and teac...
the ignorant, there is no cause to doubt the young Chamberlain's
genuine desire to do his civic duty. It was a duty, moreover, that
fitted snugly into the pattern of Birmingham radicalism.

This radicalism had been given its civic character by the formation, in December 1829 of 'The Political Union for the Protection
of Public Rights'. Founded by Thomas Attwood and a dozen of
Birmingham's gentlemen and tradesmen, this organisation was
soon transformed into the 'General Political Union' which aimed
to unite employers and artisans in a movement for radical reform.
The eighth clause of the Union's constitution put its objects
clearly: 'To collect and organise the peaceful expression of public
opinion, so as to bring it to act upon the legislative functions in a
just, legal, and effectual way'.[30] Later, under the leadership of the
Quaker manufacturer Joseph Sturge, Birmingham produced the
Complete Suffrage Union to 'unite two dissevered classes' and to
promote 'a happy union of all classes for the purpose of securing
their full and efficient representation in Parliament'.

The fact that Birmingham, before the Great Reform Bill of
1832, was not represented in Parliament lent a sharp cutting-edge
to the activities of Attwood's Political Union in its early days. As
the Bill hung perilously between life and death, a quarter of a
million men from the Political Unions of Birmingham, Staffordshire, Warwickshire and Worcestershire met at Newhall Hill on
7 May 1832; they chanted 'the Bill, the whole Bill, and nothing but
the Bill', and sang the hymn of the Unions, which ended with these
sentiments:

> God is our guide! no sword we draw;
>   We kindle not war's fatal fires.
> By union, justice, reason, law,
>   We claim the birthright of our sires!
> And thus we raise from sea to sea
>   Our sacred watchword, Liberty![31]

Reform Bill was eventually
...royal assent, two members
...olefield, were elected to the
...gham realised another ambi-
...ration; this, together with the
...stablished the local political
...e Street Commissioners could
...ublic will as expressed by the
...ommissioners finally lost their

...rrival in Birmingham, however,
...warted in a number of ways. For
...ad scarcely opened the floodgates
or ...ral working-class male remained
overwhelmingly ... d. Since the country's urban
population grew rapidly during the second third of the century
(Birmingham was no exception, its population expanding from
147,000 to 300,000 between 1831 and 1865) there was bound to
be a renewed clamour from the swollen cities for more parliamentary reform.

Birmingham's response to these demographic and reforming
pressures was, until the late 1860s, muted. The town's councillors
preferred the Gladstonian principles of public frugality to those
of open-handed municipal reform. Reform, after all, was likely to
cost ratepayers dear. Chadwick's classic *Report on the Sanitary
Conditions of the Labouring Classes* did not galvanise Birmingham's
local rulers; plans to build a sewage farm foundered on the skilful
opposition of Thomas Avery (of the scale-making firm), and
untreated sewage continued to flow directly into the river
Tame.

Although dirt, disease, and mean housing continued to character-
ise the older parts of Birmingham, the city fathers could dip their
hands into the municipal pocket on occasion. In 1860 the council
decided to build the monumental Birmingham Reference Library,
and to develop the public lending libraries. There was also the
Birmingham and Midland Institute, a project which Charles
Dickens publicly backed during his visit to the city in January
1853, and which he later supported by giving some of his celebrated readings. Music festivals were a great feature of Birmingham
life, and in 1846 Mendelssohn came to conduct the first per-

formance of his *Elijah*. A new municipal art gallery was also established.

Self-help, however, was the dominant theme of Birmingham's activities. Profits from its music festivals were put towards the building of a General Hospital, and Lajos Kossuth, the Hungarian liberal, received £750 from Birmingham's citizens when he visited the town to a rapturous reception after his flight from his homeland in 1849. In June 1860 the town was due to receive Queen Victoria on an official visit, and the young Joseph Chamberlain has left, in a letter to his mother, a clear account of Birmingham's preparations: 'Last Monday [William] Kenrick met me in Birmingham and we walked together through the route the Queen's procession was to take on the morrow to see the preparations, decorations etc. These were exceedingly good—all the main streets had subscribed together in order to obtain some general and uniform system of ornament. . . . Several very good arches were erected along the route—one especially deserved notice—built by the Gunmakers and appropriately adorned with swords, guns, pistols, ramrods etc.'[32]

Chamberlain, in his first years in Birmingham, participated fully in the town's social and cultural life. Shortly after arriving, he was elected a member of the Birmingham and Edgbaston Debating Society on 29 November 1854. A fortnight later he took part in his first debate, the motion being 'That the character and conduct of Oliver Cromwell do not entitle him to the admiration of posterity'. As a descendant of the ejected Richard Serjeant, Chamberlain spoke warmly in defence of the Lord Protector, only to see the motion lost by fifteen votes.[33]

Membership of the Birmingham and Edgbaston Debating Society was much to Chamberlain's benefit. In the short term, it brought him into contact with men who did not belong to the Unitarian, business circle which provided him with his introduction to Birmingham society. In the long term, it helped to make an accomplished public speaker of him.

Despite his childhood acting experiences, despite the reputation of his later years, Chamberlain was evidently not a born orator. His speech making was, at the outset of his membership of the society, stiff, over-elaborate and obviously learned by rote—though clear. A contemporary later recorded these impressions of Chamberlain's early public speeches:

It was impossible not to be interested, edified, and often amused by the intelligence, point, and smartness of his speech. At the same time there was, especially in the earlier days of his career, a certain setness and formality of style that suggested that his speeches were anything but the inspiration of the moment, but had been made beforehand and were being read off—the result of painstaking study, care, and elaboration. . . .

One incident that came under my notice certainly went far to corroborate this view. I refer to the occasion of a little semi-public dinner at which Mr. Chamberlain was put down to propose a certain toast. He proceeded for a time in his usually happy, characteristic manner, when all at once he came to a full stop! We all looked up, and he looked down, embarrassed and confused. He apparently had lost the thread of the discourse he had so carefully woven; he could not pick up the dropped stitches; and if I remember rightly, he sat down, his speech not safely delivered. . . .

He was a man to inspire admiration and confidence. There was always a promptness and 'all thereness' in his nature, with a decided touch of self-reliance, and I may even say audacity. In fact, without intending any reflection upon him, he might perhaps appropriately take as his motto, 'L'audace, l'audace, toujours de l'audace'.[34]

Chamberlain from 1858 onwards filled all of the offices of the Debating Society by turn. In 1859 he became secretary, and wrote reports in his already characteristic small, neat handwriting. From the reports of the year 1859–60 we learn that the Society had 150 members, and that the average attendance was forty-seven which represented a twenty per cent increase over the preceding year. Among the motions debated were the following:

'That it is advisable to make bribery at elections a penal offence both for the briber and the party bribed.'
'That Trades Unions are injurious to the interests of both masters and work people.'
'That Lord John Russell's Reform Bill is unsound in principle and weak in detail and can only be regarded as an expedient for checking agitation on the subject.'

'That the Idylls of the King by Alfred Tennyson are unworthy both of him and of his subject.'

'That the mental capacities of both sexes are equal.'[35]

By 1859 Chamberlain seems to have emerged as a self-assured, witty speaker. He already wore the eyeglass so gratefully noted later (together with the orchid in his lapel) by political cartoonists. In July 1869 *Aris' Gazette* recorded that during the Society's annual summer dinner at the Lyttelton Arms, Hagley, he proposed ' "The Artopsariacoluthic Members" (or followers of the loaves and fishes) explaining in a speech which elicited constant laughter and applause that the members in question were those who always attended the annual (free) supper of the Society, but did not think it necessary to be present at the ordinary meetings.'[36]

In 1896, at the height of his political powers, Chamberlain reminisced, as President of the Society, during its Jubilee year:

We were rather a Radical body [he said]. In our case the prevailing Liberalism of our time occasionally landed us in difficulties, since we could not always find sufficient speakers to defend the more moderate opinion; and I remember on one occasion, when we were unable to agree as to the disposal of £7 odd, which the Treasurer had unexpectedly disclosed to us, we unanimously approved of the suggestion of the Hon. Secretary (whom I see before me and whom I now know as Mr. Alderman Johnson), which was that we should buy a Tory with it! . . .

No man who made any kind of reputation in our Society has failed to make it in after life; and there are not many citizens who have since distinguished themselves in connection with our town who did not serve an apprenticeship first in connection with our Society. . . .

It is a great pleasure to me to go back to those times and to recall the incidents to which reference has been made. Mr. Saunders reminds me of one that I had forgotten when he spoke of the occasion on which I was asked to propose the health of 'The Silent Members,' and described me as an audacious debater who taunted those gentlemen with their silence and urged them to take a more active part in the proceedings of the Society.

How changed the times and circumstances!

I belong to another Debating Society. I should like to propose

'The Silent Members' there. But I am no longer audacious, and I am sure I should not taunt them with their silence.

I can recall also another incident which you may think characteristic.

I met a gentleman who was to be proposed as member the same night, and we were talking about what was to us an important event. He said, 'I mean to make use of the Society—I mean to speak every night.' I said, 'I have no such idea; I think I shall be a silent member and never open my mouth.' That gentleman never spoke. I spoke the first night, and I believe I spoke on a good number of occasions afterwards.

I say the incident is characteristic because it shows even in those early days I was an inconsistent person. But I owe a great deal to the Society, and I am delighted to know that it is as prosperous as when I left it. I am touched with the kindness with which I have been received. . . . Although since the times of which we have been speaking I have been engaged in large affairs and been interested in many subjects, it is quite true, as my friend Mr. Bunce has said, that my affection is always with Birmingham; and the life of this Society is associated with the life of Birmingham during the last fifty years. You cannot separate the one from the other. The Society is, I think I may say, peculiar to those who have made Birmingham what it is— the most independent, the most original of cities of the Empire. . . .

. . . I am a believer in the uses and advantages of Debating Societies: there friendships may be cemented and sympathy created. . . . And I am convinced they tend to promote a spirit of inquiry, widen the bounds of knowledge, quicken and broaden the intellectual activity, and cultivate that gift of clear speaking which is in our democratic and representative system a necessary force and a potent influence for progress. . . .

I am content to take the etymological definition of eloquence: 'speaking out'—speaking plainly, simply, fully, forcibly. And that is within the reach of any man of ordinary ability who will take the trouble to acquire the art.[37]

Apart from Chamberlain's charming, almost naïve, confession of inconsistency (what a gift to his political foes in 1896!), there is much of interest in this text. There is, of course, no gainsaying the Radical spirit of the Society during the 1850s and 1860s, yet it was hardly a home from home for working-class members and it remained almost exclusively the preserve of representatives of the city's professional, industrial and commercial élite. Radicalism, moreover, had many mansions, and Chamberlain, as befitted his Unitarian background, emerges as something of a moderate during his active membership of the Debating Society.

While serving as secretary in 1859, for example, Chamberlain wrote to the Lord-Lieutenant of Warwickshire urging him to allow the Society to form from its own ranks a company of Rifle Volunteers. The request was duly refused, and Chamberlain wrote in plain terms to the Lord-Lieutenant assuring him that he had lost the services of a fine company of men. The Society, in fact, proceeded to form its own non-official Rifle Corps. There is no reason to suppose that the proposed Rifle Company, or the non-official Corps, was meant to form the vanguard of a Birmingham-based revolutionary insurrection! On the contrary, the plans smack of the solid, established, middle-class virtues of patriotism and the love of law and order.

At a less parochial level, Chamberlain showed little sympathy with the views on foreign policy of Birmingham's newly elected M.P. the Radical and pacifist, John Bright. Swept out of his Manchester seat in 1857 by the strong Palmerstonian tide that flowed in the first post-Crimean War general election, Bright was found a Parliamentary refuge in Birmingham—but only on condition that he dropped his opposition to the suppression of the Indian Mutiny. Ill-health delayed Bright's first speech to his new constituents for more than a year. At last, in October 1858, he spoke at the Town Hall. The young Chamberlain heard this speech, and was later to recall, 'I heard all of Bright's Birmingham speeches. I had the sincerest admiration for his efforts on behalf of all legislative reforms. But I did not from the first agree with his foreign policy, which was practically a "peace at any price" policy.'[38]

The Birmingham and Edgbaston Debating Society soon set aside two nights to debate the motion 'That this Society strongly condemns the principles enunciated in the speeches recently made by Mr. Bright in Birmingham, and also the spirit in which those speeches were delivered.' Chamberlain spoke on the second night, in the theatre of the Old Philosophical Institution in Cannon Street, not at the Society's usual venue of the 'Hen and Chickens'.

He attacked Bright's Quakerish convictions that non-intervention should be the touchstone of the nation's dealing with foreign states, and that aristocracies were responsible for war itself. The motion was lost by one vote. Not long afterwards, Chamberlain met the illustrious orator at a dinner party given by one of Birmingham's leading citizens George Dixon. After dinner, Bright spoke, among other things, of his belief that Gibraltar was a 'memorial of shame' and should be handed back to Spain. Chamberlain, a mere twenty-two years old, argued stoutly with Bright who subsequently told his host that he was glad to find young Liberals who could think for themselves.[39]

The young man's reaction to Bright's pacifism is an early revelation of that intermingling of the principles of reform at home and a firm hand abroad that is so characteristic of Chamberlain's career. In 1858 he espoused domestic change and the brusque and provocative qualities of Palmerstonian foreign policy. Half a century later, Chamberlain had become irrevocably associated with the call for social reform at home and a resolute and business-like ordering of Britain's imperial and trading affairs. Between the two stances there is the time-span of fifty years, but scarcely a whisker in matters of principle. Scratch the surface of Chamberlain in his various guises as municipal reformer, Little Englander, and expansionist Imperialist and what is revealed is a fervent patriot, a dedicated nationalist.

There is, however, more to Chamberlain's early years in Birmingham than business success and apprentice oratory. His cultural activities reveal a remarkably enquiring mind. In February 1861, for example, he wrote to his mother that 'Last Monday I was at an interesting lecture on the Remains and Traces of the pre-historic races.'[40] His notebooks, a set of neat manuscript volumes, show the extent of his reading: history from Caesar to the reign of George II, and varied pickings from literature—Milton, Words-worth, Michelet, Gibbon, Elizabeth Barrett Browning, Clarendon, Cervantes, Dryden, Froude, Carlyle, Tennyson and George Eliot. There is even a collection of amusing anecdotes, many culled from newspapers, and all numbered and indexed so that they can speedily be put to use in the service of the Debating Society. Indeed, much of his other reading is equally for a specific purpose—for the instruction of his Sunday school pupils. It is characteristic of Chamberlain that he stored up such information in an almost calculated fashion, to be digested and retained for future use; nor is it surprising to find that whenever he used a quotation publicly, at least in these early days, he ticked it off, adding the place and date of use.

The impression of Chamberlain is the late 1850s is overwhelmingly that of a serious, almost priggish, young man, absorbing information from a wide variety of sources, and beginning to demonstrate the forthright self-confidence, and the capacity for direct and arousing communication that was later to stand him in such good stead. There are the occasional flashes of warmth, too, as in his letters written to his mother during his hard-walking, rock climbing Alpine holidays of 1857 and 1860. In August 1857 he wrote, from Moulanvers, near Chamonix, in what is the first letter of his to be preserved:

Dear Mother,

Here we are on our route to the Jardin and after 6 days averaging 9 hours walking in each, exclusive of all halts, in first rate spirits and not the least tired. I hope you will have already received my 10 pages from Zermatt as it will give me no gratification to have written so much merely for the inspection of the Post Office Authorities. Since then 'I have lived' i.e. I have actually crossed 3 glaciers. . . .

Such a view! [from the edge of Mont Cerrin] Far as the eye could stretch—from the ground at one's feet to the horizon—one vast expanse of snow covered mountains, some of the loftiest in Europe—snow-fields and glaciers. . . .

I am brown as mahogany nearly but am at present sadly disfigured by very bad lips made sore by the cold wind. Love to all. . . . I delight in the prospect of meeting you all well.

Ever yours,
Joseph.[41]

Three years later he writes from Zermatt, complaining that his face and lips are swollen by the cold winds, and adding a wry postscript: 'I forgot to say that I have made a valuable correction to a commonly received scientific statement that which says that the skin comes off once in 7 years. No such thing! The skin of the face and neck comes off in 7 days like a very bad thin brown paper in strips an inch long and $\frac{1}{2}$ inch broad. The new skin is very red and tender and is chosen as a delightful recreation ground for juvenile flies.'[42]

Chamberlain's family was still, naturally enough, of great importance to him. As often as he could he returned to London, and the house at Highbury. There he enjoyed convivial evenings with cousins, aunts and uncles, and visitors; there was no Nonconformist abstinence there, no stinting of food and drink and cigars, no lack of lively and noisy conversation, though all these good things were sometimes mingled with a formality, a stiffness which Chamberlain's aunt Ellen Preston (née Harben) described in a letter written in 1857 in anticipation of the family celebrations of young Joseph's twenty-first birthday:

> I have bought Fergusson's *Handbook of Architecture*, 2 vols., for Joe and have sent it this evening to be ready for the morrow. I wonder how Caroline [his mother] will get on. . . . The longer I live the more convinced I am of the horrible unreal state in which our conventionalities place us—there will Caroline be, anxious about eels and entrées, when, behind all that, her mother's heart is welling up with love and thoughts too deep for words, full of hope and aspirations for her first-born, and full too of the recollections of the day when the young man, now *nearly* fulfilling all a mother's heart could wish, lay by her side a baby. I can fancy your Uncle Joseph offering best cuts and passing the Madeira, while a more costly liquid glitters behind his dimmed glasses.[43]

In October 1860 Chamberlain proposed marriage to Harriet Kenrick, the daughter of Mr. and Mrs. Archibald Kenrick, Unitarians of Berrow Court in Birmingham Harriet accepted him, and they were married in July 1861 at the New Meeting House in Birmingham. The courtship was not one of romantic impetuosity, marked by flights, denials and the exchange of passionate letters. As befitted the representatives of two of Birmingham's more prosperous Unitarian families, the relationship was based on a sensible compatibility of interests and background, and fostered by contact at religious meetings, dances and domestic entertainments.

The couple prepared thoughtfully for their marriage, though in February 1861 their future domestic harmony seemed threatened by a plague of grand pianos and Chamberlain wrote to his mother:

It seems we are to suffer from an 'embarras de richesses'—a profusion of grand pianos, since I have to announce that Harrie has been offered another and would have been offered a fourth had not Arthur's intentions become known. . . . I also hear that Mrs. Kenrick intends giving us a cheffonier (is that the way the thing is spelt?) on her account. Are not these handsome presents? It is a pity we can't furnish a room entirely with pianos as our drawing room would be done for us.[44]

Chamberlain and Harriet were both twenty-five when they married. There seems no reason to doubt their happiness, which was destined to last for a little more than two years. Harriet gave birth to a daughter Beatrice, and on 16 October 1863 a son, Joseph Austen Chamberlain was born. As if to fulfil her presentiment that she would die in childbirth, Harriet fell ill two days after the birth, and, within a week of the successful delivery of her son, died. Chamberlain, not much given to the outward show of emotion, wrote, in conventional yet heartfelt terms, three weeks after her death: 'There seemed to be such immense resources of happiness in store for us in the future that I know now there was only one blow which could possibly have dispersed them all and taken every interest in this life away for a time. . . . As I write all this, and think that I am never to know and feel her love or delight in her ways here again, I declare it seems almost impossible to live.'[45]

But live he did, devoting more of his energies to the booming fortunes of Nettlefold and Chamberlain. The family business in Milk Street had been rendered insignificant by the continuing success of the screw-making enterprise in Birmingham, and, a little before Harriet's death, old Joseph Chamberlain sold up and moved to Moor Green Hall from there to branch out into metal manufacturing himself. Mrs. Chamberlain accompanied him, and Mary Chamberlain, who soon married William Kenrick, the brother of Harriet.

Chamberlain and his young children went to live with his Kenrick parents-in-law at Berrow Court, where he had already learnt to cherish the magnificent orchids grown there. To contemporaries he seemed much the same; alert, high-spirited, 'allthere' as his Birmingham friends put it. He was, after all, adept at mastering his feelings no matter how strongly or deeply they possessed him. In 1866, when he reached the age of thirty, he was strikingly successful in his work, yet, outside a modest circle of friends and acquaintances, obscure. In fact he was on the threshold of a public career that would propel him like a fiery comet across the turbulent political skies of Victorian Britain.

THREE

'STRANGE DOINGS':
CHAMBERLAIN AND REFORM
1867–73

'Is it not possible to form a band of "irreconcilables" to smash up this gigantic sham called a Liberal party, and to secure reorganization on a new basis?'

Joseph Chamberlain to Captain F. A. Maxse, June 1873

IN OCTOBER 1865 the Prime Minister, Lord Palmerston, died two days before his eighty-first birthday. Palmerston's death removed a symbolic figure from British political life: the way was now clear for electoral reform, and for the rise to supremacy of Gladstone—whom Palmerston privately thought would ruin the Liberal party and end up in the madhouse.

There had been widespread and growing agitation for a second electoral reform bill in the year of Palmerston's death. In Birmingham, John Bright pleaded eloquently for reform, and the town's Liberal leaders set up the Liberal Association from which was to grow the formidable political machine that was destined to dominate local politics and, transformed into the National Liberal Federation, to galvanise political activity in other English cities.

Chamberlain joined the Birmingham Liberal Association at its foundation, though not in any office, these being taken by established local stalwarts like P. H. Muntz, Chairman, and the Mayor George Dixon, Treasurer (both soon to represent the city in the House of Commons) and John Jaffray, Secretary, who was proprietor of the *Birmingham Daily Post*.[46]

The demands of the reformers seemed amply justified. Britain's population had more than doubled since 1801, and the period following the 1832 Reform Bill had seen a remarkable increase in England and Wales, as well as a substantial internal migration from the countryside to cities and to colliery districts. The population of England and Wales in the early 1860s was more than twenty million, that of Scotland over three million, while the Irish population, still declining in the shadow of the 'hungry forties', was a little less than five million. But the census of 1861, on which these statistics are based, had also shown that for the first time there was an excess of urban dwellers over the rural population—an excess dramatically converted into a majority of seventy-five per cent by the time of the 1901 census.[47]

The spectacular growth of the great Victorian conurbations of London, Birmingham and the West Midlands, Manchester, West Yorkshire, Liverpool, Newcastle and Glasgow, threw into sharp relief the urgent need both to redistribute Parliamentary seats and to extend the franchise to a sizeable proportion of urban males at the very least.

In 1866, a year after Palmerston's death, Lord John Russell's Liberal administration presented a Reform Bill to the House of Commons. The Bill, backed by both Russell and Gladstone, was by no means revolutionary. If it had been passed it would have enfranchised 400,000 men, about half of them working class; the borough electorate would have risen from thirty-six per cent of the total male occupiers of property to fifty-one per cent; in England and Wales one man in four would have had the vote compared with one man in five.[48]

The Bill was quite plainly an attempt to add a modest number of working-class men to the electorate while at the same time ensuring the continuing political supremacy of the governing élite. Radicals disliked the Bill for its failure to concede household suffrage or the secret ballot, while conservative supporters of the government like Robert Lowe and Lord Elcho denounced it as a step towards the dismantling of the social order and the destruction of property rights.

These divisions in the ranks of the government's supporters gave Disraeli and the Conservatives ample opportunity to out-manoeuvre their opponents. The 'Adullamites', led by Lowe and Elcho, provided the Conservatives with the fifth column they needed and in June 1866 the government was defeated by eleven votes on an Adullamite amendment to the Bill. Russell wearily decided to resign and on 26 June Lord Derby was invited by the Queen to form a minority Conservative administration.

The summer and autumn of 1866 seemed amply to bear out Gladstone's defiant words, spoken when the government had been defeated by the Adullamite amendment in June, 'You may bury the Bill that we have introduced but . . . [you] cannot fight against the future. Time is on our side. The great social forces which move onwards in their might and majesty . . . those great social forces are against you; they are marshalled on our side.' Though it was perfectly legitimate for contemporaries to doubt Gladstone's commitment to democracy in its fullest sense, they had every reason to react warily to his growing taste for demagoguery, for, as he claimed, powerful social forces were indeed mustering for a massive show of strength.

The working men of Britain had claims for reform that went far beyond shows of brute strength such as the notorious Hyde Park riot of May 1866 when Matthew Arnold had watched dismayed as demonstrators tore down railings and trampled on the flower beds. Widespread British working-class support for the North during the recently ended American Civil War had been seen by many observers as a sign that the British working man could disentangle moral issues from material ones; after all, the slave-owning Southern Confederacy supplied the raw cotton so vital for the mills of Lancashire, and the Northern blockade had cut off this commodity. The triumph of the Union, moreover, seemed to show that democracy was sufficiently stable and efficient to surmount so massive an internal challenge. Garibaldi's successes in the cause of Italian nationalism had also provided encouragement for British Radicals. It was furthermore possible to argue, as did John Bright, that British working men, through their membership of co-operative and friendly societies, were acting responsibly and also creating substantial links with capitalism and the established social and economic order.[49]

The National Reform Union and the Reform League had both been founded in 1864. But whereas the former was based in Manchester, partly on the foundations of the old Anti-Corn Law League and aimed to mobilise both the middle and working classes for reform, the latter swept up former Chartists as well as active trade unionists into a militantly proletarian movement pressing unashamedly for manhood suffrage. Both organisations organised massive demonstrations in British cities in the period 1866-7.

In Birmingham, on 27 August 1866, there was a tremendous public demonstration for reform. The Mayor of Birmingham marched with a quarter of a million men at his back, to Brookfields outside the town. There the demonstrators listened to addresses delivered from six platforms; in the evening, at the Town Hall, Bright delivered an impassioned speech, awakening memories of the brave days of 1832. The Birmingham demonstration of 27 August was a remarkable show of middle and working-class cooperation: the factories and works were shut (including Nettlefold and Chamberlain), and artisans and employers marched side by side to Brookfields under the banners of reform.

Joseph Chamberlain attended the demonstration and heard Bright speak in the evening. His sense of strong political commitment can clearly be traced to this time, and he was later to recall the excitement of these experiences: 'They were great meetings in those days, 1858–66. The men poured into the hall, black as they were from the factories . . . the seats then used to be removed from the body of the hall, and the people were packed together like herrings.'[50]

The passing of the Reform Bill of 1867 opened the way for a remarkable extension of democracy in the boroughs. Disraeli's acceptance of a Radical amendment proposing household suffrage (the famous 'leap in the dark' of the future Lord Salisbury's anguished description) nearly doubled the electorate from some 1,430,000 to 2,470,000. This move enfranchised almost a third of adult males, increased the borough electorate by 140 per cent and made the artisan class the largest group among urban voters. Disraeli accepted the amendment on the calculation that it would put an end to the reform issue, isolate Gladstone, would do the Conservatives no harm in the boroughs (which tended to be Liberal strongholds anyway) and might well do them good in the counties.

The General Election of November 1868 produced the expected Liberal majority; in the event, 110, as opposed to seventy in 1865. It is difficult to estimate the impact of the Reform Bill upon the results, since the Liberals made most of their gains in Scotland, Wales and Ireland. Certainly the election aroused great public interest, and the number of contested seats rose to about half of the total.

In Birmingham the election was both a triumph for law and order and also for Liberal party organisation. The danger of public disorder had been clearly demonstrated by the Irish riots of the previous year, provoked by the bitter, anti-Catholic rhetoric of John Murphy, a delegate of the London Protestant Electoral Union. The 8th Hussars were called in to help the police, but eventually Protestant rough-necks wrecked the Irish quarter in Park Street and burnt down houses. Joseph Chamberlain visited the scene of the disturbances the next day, noticing that 'The roofs were gone, the fronts of the houses also; the remains of the fires were still to be seen.' An old man later recalled:

'I remember as 'ow a man I knew were a-standin' at 'is door.
' "Go in," says the soldiers.
' "Not I," says 'e.
' "Go in," they says again.
' "Not I," says 'e. "I'm a-standin' at my own door."
'Then they takes and cuts 'is ear clean off. Yes, they was very strict in those days!'[51]

Though the General Election was marked by the traditional tumult at the hustings, the 'Brummagem Frankenstein', so beloved of cartoonists, turned out to be a relatively well-behaved creature, perfectly willing to listen to instructions. The Reform Bill had given Birmingham three Parliamentary seats, and it was quite conceivable that the minority Conservative vote could secure one or even two of these if Liberal voters failed to distribute their two votes apiece sensibly among the three Liberal candidates. The Birmingham Liberal Association, working through its ward committees, indeed ensured that the Liberal vote would be given evenly to all three of the party's candidates. The results were a breakthrough for local party organisation and pointed the way to the 'caucus' system and to the eventual power of the National Liberal Federation:

George Dixon (Liberal)	15,098 votes
P. H. Muntz (Liberal)	14,614 votes
John Bright (Liberal)	14,601 votes
Sampson S. Lloyd (Conservative)	8,760 votes
Sebastian Evans (Conservative)	7,061 votes.

This crushing mobilisation of voting strength was a watershed between the previous, somewhat slipshod way of garnering votes and the new businesslike methods pioneered by Francis Schnadhorst as Secretary of the Birmingham Liberal Association after 1873, and Joseph Chamberlain. As the results of the November election were announced from the hustings, cards with black edges were distributed among the crowd; they read:

Sacred to the Memory of
SAMPSON S. LLOYD and SEBASTIAN EVANS, L.L.D.,
who departed their political life on Tuesday, 17 November 1868,
having fallen victims to that dread disease Public Opinion,
accelerated by the action of the 'Vote-as-you're told Committee'.
They were interred at the hustings, Town Hall, November 18th,
amid the woeful lamentations of their chapfallen supporters.

Chamberlain had taken an active part in the election campaign.
In June 1868, for instance, he chaired a meeting of the Edgbaston
Liberal Election Committee at a public dinner at the 'Plough and
Harrow' hotel. Chamberlain made a speech which is worth quoting
in part, not because of its excellence (indeed it is much more
clearly formal and careful than excellent) but because it is his first
speech to be recorded in any fullness. In his remarks Chamberlain
complimented George Dixon, already an M.P. for Birmingham,
who was present at the dinner, and went on to say of John Bright,
'For my own part I must say that, while I have always appreciated
the power of Mr. Bright's oratory, I have never thought it so great
as in some of his recent speeches, in which he persuaded, implored
and warned his hearers to do a tardy act of justice and to redress
grievous wrong.' He dismissed the Conservatives, hoping to
disguise themselves as Constitutional Associations, with the words
'So long as the Liberal party continue in their [sic] present robust
health and in their present position they will probably be able to
swallow several Constitutional associations without suffering!'
Chamberlain concluded by calling for party unity, and urging
Liberals to make 'Measures, not men . . . their motto.'[52]
    A year later Chamberlain was again prominent in the local
campaign to support Gladstone's Irish Church Disestablishment
Bill against the delaying tactics of the House of Lords. On 15 June
1869 a meeting called by the Liberal Association was held at
Birmingham's town hall to debate the issue. The mayor, called
Holland, was chairman, and, as was then the practice, Conservative
speakers were represented on the platform and their supporters in
the body of the hall. Chamberlain had been chosen to second the
resolution supporting the Disestablishment Bill. It was a testing
occasion upon which to make his début, at thirty-three years of
age, as a town hall orator: Birmingham meetings were not re-
nowned for their quiet, good manners, and the clash of Liberal

and Conservative interests could well degenerate into physical violence.

When Chamberlain's turn to speak came, the meeting was already so tumultuous that it was noticed that J. S. Wright, who had, by repute, the loudest voice in Birmingham, could only be heard a few feet from the platform. It was Chamberlain's task to second, amid a cacophony of cheers, counter-cheers and heckling, the motion that the Irish Church Disestablishment Bill ought to become law since it had received large majorities in the House of Commons and was in accordance with the national will as expressed at the recent General Election. For the first time it is possible to discern the style of the later Joseph Chamberlain in this speech with its uninhibited attack on the House of Lords, its hard, rational, challenging qualities:

It is only just [he said], that those who have to discuss the Bill should have full opportunity of judging what is the national will on this question. When, however, they are in full possession of the conclusion to which the great majority of their fellow-countrymen have come, if they should see fit in contradiction to those conclusions to try again at this time—and it will be a final attempt—to stem the tide of popular opinion, the people of Birmingham will have to consider in the next great meeting within these walls whether an institution which again blocks the way to progress is entitled to their continuous respect.

It was scarcely likely that they would sit tamely by and see their efforts frustrated by the obstinacy or bigotry of one hundred or two hundred persons, however highly placed they might be. The majority in the Commons of one hundred and fourteen represented the wishes of six million people. The sixty Peers opposed to them in the Lords represented three things. Some of them represented the oppression of feudal lords in times gone by, when people were expected to be grateful for being ruled by the aristocracy. In the second place, some of them represented the great wealth acquired by the possession of land in the vicinity of large towns—*e.g.* Manchester and Birmingham —which land enriched its proprietors without care or labour on their part. And, lastly, they represented, and very imperfectly too in many cases, the brains, the intelligence, and the acquirements of ancestors long since dead, who unfortunately had been unable to transmit to their descendants the talents by which they had risen. It was of such men as these that the greatest member of the House of Lords who ever sat in that body—Lord Bacon—related that it was customary to say in his time that they were like potatoes—the best part was underground.

One might respect the Peerage very much and have an esteem for certain members of it; but when it came to estimating the opinion of one unknown nobleman as equivalent to the opinion of hundreds of thousands of his fellow-subjects, it was an estimate impossible for the people to hold while they retained any vestige of self-respect.

It was impossible that the House of Lords should not see in the history of the last few months proof that the House of Commons was in accord with the people.

It reminds me of an anecdote of a farmer and his barometer. It was somewhat out of order, and it perpetually stood at 'Set Fair,' though it rained incessantly for three days. But then even the patience of the farmer was exhausted, and he took the barometer and beat it against the steps of his house, and said to it, 'Now won't you believe your own eyes?'

All over the country the people had approved Mr. Gladstone's Irish policy; yet the Peers were waiting, and their Conservative friends professed themselves dissatisfied.

In the words of that great statesman Mr. Gladstone, after the time was come and the case was proved action was still to be deferred, though in this case justice deferred was justice denied.

I venture to hope that the effect of this and similar meetings will be that the House of Lords will be advised in time, will take counsel of the most intelligent and most able of the Tory Peers, and avert, for this time at least, the spectacle of a conflict between the peers and people.[53]

After Chamberlain had spoken, the meeting began to disintegrate; Conservatives felt that they were being cheated of a fair hearing and, after an hour and a half of futile activity, charged the platform and ousted the mayor from the chair. The police were called in to protect the mayor, and, as free fights broke out in the hall, the motion was put to the meeting, and carried. Despite the ugly ending of the affair, Chamberlain could be well pleased with his performance which had given him welcome prominence in the eyes of Birmingham Liberals.

It was a prominence that he was to build on substantially through his activities in the National Education League and as a Birmingham town councillor. Chamberlain was elected to the council for St. Paul's ward, in West Birmingham, in November 1869 thus beginning a career in municipal politics that would soon bring him both the mayoralty and a national reputation. That reputation, however, was forged, at least in the beginning, by the heated controversy surrounding the work of the National Education League.

The League grew out of the Birmingham Education League, established in 1867 by radicals anxious to collect information concerning education and to disseminate pamphlets drawing the attention of the public to the nation's shortcomings in the educational field. Chamberlain was a founder member of the Birmingham Education League, but the inspiration came more from Devon-born Jesse Collings, self-made businessman and destined to be one of Chamberlain's closest political allies, when he remarked to George Dixon that if the town 'could have an Education Society on the right lines, the very stones in the street would rise up and join us.'[54]

Educational reform was an eminently suitable cause for someone of Chamberlain's background and convictions. In the first instance the early investigations of the Education League showed that of some four and a quarter million children of school age, two million (mostly in the great urban areas) did not go to school at all, and a further million went to uninspected and, therefore, arguably inefficient schools. This was clearly incompatible with the civic gospel espoused by Chamberlain, and others, that it was as much the duty of the state to see that children were adequately educated as to see that they were fed. It was also possible to argue persuasively, as did Matthew Arnold, that proper schooling would ensure the triumph of 'culture' over 'anarchy'; or, as did John Stuart Mill, that liberty itself went hand in hand with education. Admirers of the victorious American Union, or of efficient, expanding Prussia, were also quick to draw equations between the success of those nations and their superior systems of public education.

It is doubtful, however, whether statistical proof of educational inequality interwoven with the pious warnings of progressive intellectuals would have been sufficient to galvanise the stones in the streets of Birmingham, or indeed anywhere else. What gave the Education League much of its passion and appeal was the extent of government aid to Church of England schools, and the close relationship thus implied between church and state. In England and Wales elementary education was the responsibility of voluntary bodies, of which the Church of England was overwhelmingly the most important. By the late 1860s some 1,300,000 children attended government aided schools, which meant that because of the Church's paramount position in voluntary education the vast majority of these pupils received Anglican religious instruction as part of the curriculum.

This example of the long-established relationship between the state and the established church was bound to give deep offence to Nonconformists, especially as the political restrictions on non-Anglicans had been swept away decades before, as had (more recently) similar discrimination affecting entry to the universities. As part of the drive to emancipate Dissenters from the final traces of their earlier second-class citizenship, Chamberlain and others were determined to campaign for free, secular and compulsory elementary education.

One of the major obstacles to be overcome, however, was the very nature of the Liberal party itself, for though the vast majority of Dissenters were Liberals (of one sort or another) by no means all Liberals were Dissenters. Gladstone, Prime Minister since 1868, was a zealous High Churchman who wanted to preserve the role of religion in popular education; John Stuart Mill disliked the prospect of compulsory education by the state; many Whigs disapproved of secular instruction.

All this explains why educational reform was an explosive issue, very likely to assume the dimensions of a bitter political confrontation. A confrontation, moreover, that would not merely set Liberal against Conservative, but also Liberal against Liberal. Chamberlain was determined to turn the education issue into an appeal to the interests of the working classes and to the enthusiasm of Radicals. Through a popular campaign he hoped to bring irresistible pressure upon the Liberal party leadership, and thus to play a part in heading off a violent confrontation between established society and the fast-multiplying urban poor.

Chamberlain's own views on educational reform were formulated as early as 1867 when he prepared, in draft, the aims of a brain-child, the 'National Society for the Promotion of Universal Compulsory Education':

PRINCIPLES

1. That it is as much the duty of the State to see that the children are educated as to see that they are fed.

2. That the right to education ought not to be restricted by any Religious Tests.

3. That the enjoyment of this right ought not to depend on the caprice of charity or the will of parents.

OBJECTS

1. To collect and disseminate information as to the state of Education in Great Britain.

2. To publish and defend the principles of the Society by means of Public Meetings, Lectures and the Press.

3. To urge on Government the duty of immediate legislative action.

It follows from these premises that the action of the Society will be extended to secure:

1. Free Education, at all events in cases where parents are unable to pay.

2. Unsectarian Education in all cases where new schools are established or supported by the National Treasury. . . .

These new Schools should be supported by local rates largely supplemented by Government Grants. The management should be local under Government inspection.

These schools should be unsectarian. The nation cannot justly be called on to support schools which are in part devoted to the propagation of sectarian views.

Lastly the establishment of these schools should be imperative in districts insufficiently supplied. The education of the poor must not be suffered to depend on the chance circumstances of their neighbourhood to a charitable squire or clergyman.[55]

These clear and progressive objectives of Chamberlain were by no means universally acceptable to the membership of the Birmingham Education League. He decided, therefore, to extend its scope and to form a National Education League; a circular, setting out the objects of the League, was sent to prominent educationalists and other likely sympathisers. Chamberlain's active role in the transformation of the Birmingham League into a national body was not merely the result of his convictions; it also reflected the fact that he was, in a sense, a major 'shareholder' in the venture, for, of the original £7,000 subscribed in Birmingham, he put up £1,000, his father another £1,000 and the Kenricks (Chamberlain's in-laws) £2,500. Of the preliminary subscription total, therefore, Chamberlain, his father and his in-laws provided well over half.[56]

The new technology had made Chamberlain rich, and he was now able to use some of that wealth, in effect, to buy himself a controlling position in the National Education League. By 1870 he was acting President (in place of George Dixon) and Chairman of the powerful Executive Committee. The conjunction of money, a controversial cause, extraordinary innate ability, and a remarkable capacity for mastering the techniques of political management and public persuasion was to be the making of Chamberlain's career.

In October 1869 the National Education League held its first conference in Birmingham. Its membership included two and a half thousand 'persons of influence' (including forty M.P.'s) and nearly four hundred ministers of religion. By 1870 the League, modelled on Cobden's great Anti-Corn Law League, had spawned over a hundred branches—mostly in the cities and towns, and drawing in trades unions and various working men's organisations; its funds amounted to more than £60,000, and over a quarter of a million pamphlets and leaflets had been printed. The League made plain its desire to promote a school system supported by local rates and government grants; schools aided by local rates must be under the management of local authorities subject to government inspection; such schools should also be free and non-sectarian, and attendance should be compulsory. These objectives mirrored very closely the proposals outlined by Chamberlain in 1867.

At the 1869 Conference, Chamberlain made the first of the speeches that were to attract national attention and mark him out as a leader of considerable promise:

I believe we may say that, directly or indirectly, from eight hundred thousand to one hundred thousand working men have at these meetings in Birmingham given their support to the platform of the League. They had a personal interest in this matter. For it is not merely a question whether this country shall continue to maintain its position among the nations, or whether it shall lag behind in civilisation and leave the victory in industrial and intellectual progress to other nations; but for you it is also a question of the future of your own class, and perhaps of your families; and you have to say whether they shall enjoy the advantages which education confers, or whether they shall remain in the position to which ignorance will condemn them even if they do not enter into the ranks of pauperism and crime.

I should be the last to deny or depreciate the enormous sacrifices which have been made by many of the clergy to establish and maintain schools. But I say that on their own confession their motive has been, not the education of the people as a thing which is good in itself, but the maintenance of the doctrines of the Church of England. I say that, even if they had been a great deal more successful than they have really been, it is the worst kind of Conservatism to say that because a thing is good of its kind it shall not be supplanted by something which is better and more complete.

If denominational education is to be extended in England, how can you in justice refuse denominational education in Ireland (*i.e.* Roman Catholic education)? And then you will have this glorious anomaly in our splendid constitutional system; you will have the State spending money on mutually destructive objects; and the patient people will be called upon in one breath to swallow the poison and the antidote and to pay the bill for both!

But if this matter of education is taken up by the working classes, as we hope and believe it will be, and if it is made part of their political programme, then our success is certain, and we may yet live to see the glorious time when, prizing knowledge as her noblest wealth and best production, this Imperial realm, while she exacts allegiance, will admit the obligation, on her part, to teach those who are born to serve her; and thus only shall we maintain our position as a great nation and guard and protect the highest interests of every class of the community.[57]

Early in 1870 the Liberal government put forward their proposals for an Elementary Education Bill. W. E. Forster, the minister responsible, immediately became the target of a flurry of Non-conformist attacks, for the Bill proposed to preserve the Church schools within the national educational structure and, indeed, to put them on the rates; there was to be no universal system of school boards, nor was education to be free or compulsory.

On 24 February 1870 the executive committee of the National Education League, with Chamberlain in the chair, decided to appeal to the Prime Minister on the grounds that sectarian teaching on the rates was unacceptable. Chamberlain sent out an inflammatory circular to all League branches urging them to hold public meetings, draw up petitions and send representatives on a delegation to Gladstone on 9 March. He told George Dixon on 26 February that 'The fight will be on the religious question. . . . My hope is that we may make such a show as will justify you in talking out the Bill. I don't believe Forster will give way on the religious point, and we will fight tooth and nail against the Bill if this clause is preserved.'[58]

A week later Chamberlain wrote again to Dixon, conjuring up a vivid picture of Nonconformity disregarded by an ungrateful government: 'If Forster forces his Bill through the House there will be a tremendous revival of the agitation for the disestablishment of the English Church. Very strong feeling was expressed against Mr. Forster, who was accused of gross ingratitude to the Dissenters who assisted so greatly in securing the present government majority, and it was asserted amid cheers that the present Education Bill was a distinct betrayal and contradiction of the principle involved in the Irish Church [Disestablishment] Bill.'[59]

On 9 March the Education League delegation, a very large one by the standards of the time, descended upon 10 Downing Street. It was Chamberlain's first meeting with Gladstone. The Prime Minister, flanked by Lord Ripon and Forster, waited inside to receive the delegates, four hundred from the Leagues' branches and forty-six M.P.'s. George Dixon introduced the delegates and then handed over to Chamberlain to summarise the League's objections to the Bill. In the light of the future stormy political relationship that was to develop between Chamberlain and Gladstone, this first encounter is interesting to analyse. The Prime Minister was, at sixty years old, the holder of the highest office in politics, and secure in his family's position in Liverpool's commercial aristocracy, his Oxford classical education, his proven public capacity, and his association with the great landed families of Whig persuasions. Against him is Chamberlain, thirty-four years old, spokesman for the industrial masses, representing Dissent and, perhaps, a new Radicalism.

Chamberlain spoke cogently and plainly, laying particular emphasis upon what he called the 'permissive sectarianism' of the Bill. His fellow-delegates repeatedly applauded him. It was an impressive performance, and an eye-witness was later to recall that 'The manner in which he secured the earnest and rapt attention of Mr. Gladstone while purposely ruffling the temper of Mr. Forster was not easily forgotten.'[60]

For his part Gladstone acknowledged that the League took 'great objection to several of the provisions that are contained in the Government Bill. But at the same time I listened with great comfort and satisfaction . . . to the declaration of Mr. Chamberlain . . . who did not hesitate to state that he thought in other matters, outside the limit of your objections, the Bill may fairly be regarded as a noble measure.'[61]

Perhaps convinced by the delegates' arguments that changes in the Education Bill were essential, Gladstone agreed, during the second reading, to make some amendments in the proposed legislation. After considerable debate, a mangled, compromise Bill emerged. It differed from the original measure in a few important respects: voluntary (i.e. Church) schools were not to be put on the rates, but were instead given increased support from central government funds; this provision flowed from the Cowper-Temple amendment which stipulated that in rate-aided schools there should be non-denominational religious teaching. The net effect of the amendment proposed by Cowper-Temple (an evangelical Anglican and Chairman of the National Education Union, a rival to the National Education League) was to remove Church schools from rate-payer control and to bolster them against financial pressure by government grants.

There was no joy here for Chamberlain and the Education Leaguers, but the Bill passed the Commons with Conservative support—132 Liberal M.P.'s voting against their government and a further 133 abstaining. Chamberlain was incensed and on 16 July wrote bitterly to George Dixon from Whitby where he was holidaying with his family:

—I wish our side would fight like the Conservatives—the Bill would then have been doomed long ago. The Tories are never afraid of being factious and it is a great advantage to them. . . . It [the Bill] is not National Education at all—it is a trick to strengthen the Church of England. . . .

We are preparing a circular and manifesto to our branches, and on the answer to that and on the Resolutions which may be passed at the next meeting of the Executive will depend the scope and character of our future action.

My feeling is that we must strengthen ourselves in the House of Commons at all risks. I would rather see a Tory Ministry in power than a Liberal Government truckling to Tory prejudices. . . .

I expect to return to Birmingham in a week and bring my caravan (nine souls in all) back with me. Meanwhile, I hope to form a branch here and give the Prime Minister's son [Herbert Gladstone, M.P. for Whitby] some trouble at the next election.[62]

Convinced that the government had betrayed an important section of its supporters, Chamberlain threw himself into a national campaign to whip up opposition to the Education Act. His case pivoted on the Act's controversial clause 25, which empowered school boards to pay the fees of poor children attending voluntary schools. It could easily be argued that this clause enabled school boards, if they so wished, to subsidise church schools. Given Liberal voting strength in the large boroughs this prospect need not theoretically have posed many problems for Dissenters; in practice, however, the school boards were elected on the principle of a cumulative vote and this produced, in 1870, a majority of churchmen on the Birmingham and Manchester Boards.

The Birmingham débâcle is particularly interesting in view of the electoral triumph in 1868 of the 'Vote as you're told committee'. What went wrong? C. E. Mathews, a local ally of Chamberlain's, put it down to the fact that 'By grasping improperly at the whole fifteen seats we only got six. That mistake gave Mr. Chamberlain the opportunity of showing what could be done by the bold and fearless leader of a minority. What historic fights took place on the Board—fights in which Chamberlain, Dale, Dawson, and Vince all greatly distinguished themselves!'[63]

The lesson was immediately learnt and in the 1873 elections to the Birmingham School Board a Liberal majority was elected and

Chamberlain became chairman. The efficient handling of this election was a further, significant, step in the establishment of the political machine that was to dominate Birmingham politics and to make such an impact nationally through the National Liberal Federation.

From his strong position as Birmingham councillor and member of the School Board, Chamberlain had fought a dogged fight against the implementation of clause 25 between 1870 and 1873; he had the backing of four-fifths of the Birmingham town council, and eventually reached a compromise whereby the Church majority on the School Board agreed to make payments from the rates only to denominational schools that were linked with education for industry.

As chairman of the School Board between 1873 and 1876 Chamberlain attempted to circumvent the religious controversy by the creation of a Religious Education Society to provide voluntary teachers in each denomination. When this stratagem showed signs of failure, an agreement was reached whereby the Bible was read daily in denominational schools, but without commentary. Chamberlain became a superb practitioner of political skills during these years. C. E. Mathews recalled that 'he showed [as chairman of the School Board] a different and even a superior kind of capacity.' Another observer commented, 'There is nothing, perhaps, to compare with these debates in the archives of any other provincial majority. In tactics, in the arrangements in private council of the plan of the battle, and above all in the scheme concocted on the spur of the moment to avoid checkmate on a sudden and unexpected contingency—in these things Chamberlain was supreme.'[64]

While Chamberlain was making a name for himself in municipal politics, and gaining confidence as a Radical with a growing national reputation, both his business affairs and his family life flourished. Nettlefold and Chamberlain continued to boom: in 1865 Birmingham produced 130,000 gross of woodscrews weekly of which Nettlefold and Chamberlain manufactured 90,000 gross—more than the total national output in 1850.[65] By the early 1870s the firm had not only achieved a near-monopoly in the domestic market, but had seized a major part of the world trade from American rivals. Much of the credit for this spectacular success must go to Chamberlain (only a partner in the firm from 1869) for

his ability to out-manoeuvre his rivals, his failure to make mistakes
of any weight, and his skill at rationalising production.

He avoided industrial conflict by generally providing high wages
and good conditions of employment. But strikes were sometimes
threatened and then he was apt to open negotiations by adopting
the posture of 'a lion rampant', following such shows of aggression
with reasonable talk, and, eventually, reaching a settlement.

When in 1874, following the death of Joseph Chamberlain
senior, Chamberlain and his two brothers decided to sell out, some
£600,000 was paid to them. After appropriate family settlements,
Chamberlain was probably left with £120,000 or a fifth of the
total. This gave him the wealth he needed in order to devote his
energies full-time to politics; the sum did not make him inordinately
rich compared with some of his contemporaries, though by modern
standards he could be considered a millionaire.

In 1868 Chamberlain married for the second time. His bride was
Florence Kenrick, a close cousin of his first wife Harriet. The bond
between the Chamberlain and Kenrick families was thus strengthened. Two letters written by Chamberlain while on honeymoon
reveal a good deal about the private man. The first written at the
Derwentwater Hotel, near Keswick in the Lake District, was sent
to his sister-in-law Carrie Kenrick (the sister of the dead Harriet
Kenrick) who was looking after Chamberlain's young children,
Beatrice and Austen:

> [The inn] is a homely little place, and fresh air, good living
> and the change and rest told on me and knocked me up. I was
> 'drefful bad' on Tuesday with a fearful headache and (Shall we
> say?) cholera. I laid up on Wednesday—took things easily
> yesterday and today am nearly well only shaky. . . . The weather
> continues splendid but is now very hot. . . . The Portugal
> laurels are in flower—roses spendid, especially a yellow rose (is
> it Banksia?) which is a mass of blossom. I have not seen any very
> rare ferns—we do not intend to collect until we get to Bowness.
> All the wild flowers are luxuriant and as usual, in fine air, a
> darker colour than with us—the fox-gloves especially are very
> rich and deep. . . .
> Florence is quite well, thank goodness, though sorely tried
> by midges, as we have hitherto always contrived to forget the
> specific which I provided in the tincture of Pyrethrum roseum.[66]

This letter bears witness to Chamberlain's deep interest in botany; an interest that had flourished amid the well-tended gardens at Berrow Court, the home of Harriet Kenrick's parents. It is also interesting that Chamberlain saw quite plainly that 'the change and the rest' had knocked him up; his prodigious energies, at first devoted to the family business but now being turned more and more towards local and national politics, apparently needed a freer range than that provided by a homely, isolated honeymoon environment. Like Gladstone, he thrived best on work; like Gladstone, he became an extraordinary prolific letter writer and speechmaker, and a political activist in the fullest sense of the term. His son Austen later recalled how his father, 'never rested. To his last day he seemed too young to leave things as they are.'[67]

Enclosed with the letter to Carrie Kenrick is a letter to Austen Chamberlain, then five years old, which contains a measure of paternal tenderness, a warning against over-eating, and two references to being 'a man':

My dear Boy,

I like yr. letter very much and still more to hear that you are growing up a brave man. I wish I could have a bathe in the sea with you—it will be so jolly this hot weather. What fine games you are having—with tea in the garden 3 times and iced water and all sorts of good things.

Mind you don't make yourself ill with all those sugar plums and keep the coloured eggs to show me. I send some letters very prettily coloured which you can give to Auntie. One of them is 'Oh! you goose'. So you may keep that for yourself. And then there is a bee—mind he does not sting you.

My nose is not so red as it was, thank you, but I am getting very brown and when you come home from the sea, we will look who is brownest, you or Beatrice or Papa. I am afraid all the radishes will be gone before that time and there will be none for me. Write to me directly you have had your first bath in the sea and tell me how you behaved and if you were frightened or if you enjoyed it like a man. Good-bye—love and kisses

from Papa[68]

Florence Chamberlain, though at first rather reserved and diffident, came to play a full supportive role in the marriage. It was, however, a clearly supportive role; there was no question as to who was master in the household. Until her death in childbirth in February 1875, the second Mrs. Chamberlain devoted herself to furthering her husband's career and making his life as comfortable as possible: she studied botany in order to share his interest in gardening, she became a dutiful 'platform wife', she read his speeches and articles as he prepared them and even compiled an index of the reports of his written and spoken words.

There were four children from Chamberlain's second marriage: Neville (the future Prime Minister) born in March 1869, and Ida, Hilda and Ethel. Austen was later to write of Florence Chamberlain that 'Between them [her own children] and us [her stepchildren] she made no distinction, and amidst all the cares of the growing family and of my father's public life . . . she always found time to play with us, to read to us, and to watch over us with all a mother's love.'[69]

The Chamberlains moved to Southbourne, a long, low house with a large conservatory, in the then open country of Edgbaston. There, and at his friend C. E. Mathews's house at Oakgate, he showed the same delight in, and talent for, amateur theatricals. Southbourne also became famous (or infamous in the eyes of local Tories) for its 'tobacco parliaments', informal social affairs which took place two or three times each week, and which went far to resolve certain problems facing Birmingham's local politicians. John Morley who (like Sir Charles Dilke in 1869) had by 1873 become friends with Chamberlain, recalled the armosphere at these Southbourne gatherings:

> Seriously as they applied themselves to their topics, gaiety was abundant. . . . Nobody could be more readily and cheerfully silent than their host, nobody a more narrowly attentive listener. He had a certain testing, half-ironic, yet never supercilious glance, that kept men to their point. Swift in debate, he was not in the least affected with the barren spirit of contradiction. . . . He could be as secret as anybody when he pleased, or when secrecy was a binding duty towards other people. But he was an open man, a spontaneous man. I have always thought him, of all the men of action that I have known, the frankest and most direct, as he was, with two exceptions [Gladstone and Parnell?] the boldest and the most intrepid. This instinct was one secret of his power as a popular leader. When he encountered a current

of doubt, dislike, suspicion, prejudice in some place or some section of his party, his rule and first impulse was to hasten to put his case, to explain, to have it out. . . . Right or wrong in his conclusions, in thought or reasoning, or decision or act, nobody was keener in clearing a question of its lumber.[70]

Though still predominantly active in Birmingham politics and as a leader of the National Education League, Chamberlain now began, in the early 1870s, to broaden his appeal, to mobilise working-class and Radical support for change other than that connected with the hated Education Act. At the same time the Education League adopted a much tougher approach to the government.

At its third annual meeting in October 1871 the League (now boasting 300 branches) agreed to withdraw support from any Liberal candidate in Parliamentary elections who was unwilling to pledge himself to a repeal of clause 25 and other offensive sections of the Education Act. As a result, League candidates were actually put up at several by-elections where, to the joy of the Conservatives, they opposed official Liberal candidates. By January 1872 the League's Executive Committee, led by Chamberlain, came out bluntly for the establishment of universal school boards controlling all existing schools and providing secular instruction only (religious education was to be provided out-of-hours).

But Chamberlain had by now come to share John Bright's view that the Nonconformist revolt over education was unlikely to break up the Liberal party, or indeed to force it to accommodate the Dissenters' grievances. Between 1871 and 1873, therefore, he began to construct a programme that would redress Radical demands for 'free schools, free land, and free church'.

Through a heavy programme of public speaking, and through organisations like the Liberation Society, Chamberlain began to press for an improvement in the conditions of rural workers— advocating, for example, cheaper land prices, thus making small-holdings more readily available, and the extension of the vote to the land workers, who were then trying to organise through the Agricultural Labourers' Union for better pay and conditions of work.

By June 1873 Chamberlain was prepared to break down the structure of the Liberal party alliance. Writing to his friend Captain

F. A. Maxse he asked, 'Is it not possible to form a band of "irreconcilables" to smash up this gigantic sham called a Liberal party, and to secure re-organisation on a new basis?'[71]

In September 1873 Chamberlain published his first article in the *Fortnightly Review*. Entitled 'The Liberal Party and its Leaders', it contained a startling attack upon Gladstone's leadership, and gave substance to Chamberlain's proposal to Morley on 19 August 1873 that:

> The object just now should be to state as clearly as possible the programme of the party of the future, and to make a party thereby. At present there are only individual Radicals, each specially interested in some part of the whole, but with no connected organisation or idea of united action. There are Leagues and Associations and Unions but no party; and there never will or can be till we choose out the most important of all the questions debated, and weld them into a connected scheme which all or most of us may accept as our programme. . . . My hope, therefore, is that the reforms and changes we require will be accepted some day as part of the whole platform of the party to whom the future belongs, and whose victory, when it comes, will involve the acceptance of a new political system . . . there are the germs of an heroic struggle which shall excite enthusiasm and devotion.[72]

The subsequent article in the *Fortnightly Review* proposed four 'F's' as the programme of the future: 'Free Church, Free Schools, Free Land and Free Labour'. The latter was a more recent addition to the earlier battle-cries, and referred to the rights of trade unions, though Chamberlain himself disapproved of union picketing. In his article Chamberlain argued that:

> This programme may seem advanced. . . . But no one of ordinary foresight and intelligence will doubt that every item of it will be secured before twenty years have passed away. . . . Every electioneering agent knows that during the last two years there has been a total absence of this necessary enthusiasm on the Liberal side and that they have found the most absolute indifference as to the result of the contest. . . . If we are to have a temporary return to Tory practice, the conservatives and not the liberals are the people to carry it into effect. It is fatal to the

sincerity and honesty of politics that men should sit on the Treasury benches to do the bidding of a triumphant Opposition. . . .

Mr. Mill has written 'whoever feels the amount of interest in the Government of his country which befits a freeman, has some convictions on national affairs which are like his life blood, and which the strength of his belief in them forbids him to make the subject of compromise or postpone to the judgement of any person however greatly his superior.' Of this kind are the differences which now separate Mr. Gladstone's Government from those who in time past have been its earnest supporters and to whose labours and sacrifices that Government owed its strong position . . . their efforts will perhaps be better appreciated when the results of the ingratitude and contempt with which they have been treated become manifest in the approaching General Election.[73]

This was indeed a programme, and an approach, to shake the existing political establishment, and Chamberlain was its chief architect. Before he could devote his energies full-time, and on a national scale, to this 'New Radicalism', however, he undertook further weighty civic duties, for in November 1873 the Liberals won the Birmingham municipal elections and Chamberlain was appointed mayor.

FOUR

MAYOR OF BIRMINGHAM
1873–6

'The Town will be parked, paved, assized, marketed, Gas-and-Watered and *improved*—all as the result of three years' active work.'
Chamberlain to Jesse Collings, June 1876

CHAMBERLAIN'S VICTORY in St. Paul's ward during the municipal elections of November 1873 was a narrow one, reflecting the determined fight put up by his Conservative opponent, who denounced him as a 'monopoliser and a dictator'. His enemies certainly had good cause to fear the elevation to the mayoralty of a man who was an active member of the School Board, and was also bidding fair to turn the Liberal party upside down and to fashion out of the ruins a coherent Radical opposition to the Tories. During the election campaign Chamberlain was execrated as a conspirator, a republican and, in essence, an atheist. A cartoon was exhibited in New Street showing him addressing a working-class audience with the words, 'Now, me lads, let us be equal, and I will be your King.'[74]

The Liberal election machine, however, had a clean sweep in both the municipal and School Board elections thanks chiefly to the Prussian-like efficiency of Francis Schnadhorst, the Birmingham Liberal Association's local organiser. Chamberlain wrote exultantly to John Morley on 19 November 1873, after the School Board elections, 'We have given the Beer and Bible Tories a smashing defeat—polling 291,000 votes to their 195,000.'[75] The Liberal Association had campaigned in this latter election on the effective and uncomplicated slogan, 'The People above the Priests.' It was now up to Chamberlain, as mayor, to satisfy the needs of the people in matters other than education.

At his back he had the solid support of the Liberal Association. Organised politics, on the Birmingham model, were to spread throughout the English political system, but there were early criticisms that Chamberlain was misguided in fighting local administrative issues in party-political terms. His enemies accused him, moreover, of introducing a Tammany Hall spoils system, and it was even claimed that street sweeping was a job reserved for Liberal loyalists.

Chamberlain had no inhibitions about the wholesale introduction of party-political conflict into municipal government. For one thing, he could argue that the problems facing Birmingham required action not apathy, and that the political battle for domination of the town council and the School Board had shaken citizens from such apathy. For another, the democratic structure of the local Liberal Association had the effect of actively involving quite large numbers of working men (many recently enfranchised by the 1867 Reform Act) in municipal politics: elected ward committees themselves elected a central representative committee; this central committee met eight or nine times a year, its most important function being to choose Liberal candidates for Parliament and for the School Board. Above the central committee was an executive committee of 100 members, which was in turn managed by a committee of eleven.

Although the various committees contained representatives from a broad cross-section of local society, the Liberal Association was not a perfectly egalitarian structure. The central committee was an unwieldy body, containing 400 members in 1868 and over 2,000 within a few years. The executive committee itself was cumbersome, and real power tended to rest with the committee of eleven. As in so many other Liberal Associations, this meant that a civic élite emerged, composed for the most part of businessmen and Nonconformist leaders. Among the latter, who lent warm support to the civic reformers though not eligible to sit on the town council, were Dr. Dale of the Congregationalists, Charles Vince of the Baptists, and Dr. Crosskey of the Unitarians. George Dawson, though not attached to any denomination was, in Dr. Dale's words 'the prophet of the new movement.'[76]

The man to transform George Dawson's prophesies into real achievements was, however, Joseph Chamberlain. Re-elected mayor in 1874 and 1875 his tenure of office was only ended by his successful candidature for the House of Commons in June 1876. These years were the dawn of the 'Golden Age' of Birmingham's municipal development.

Dr. Dale was convinced that Chamberlain's mayoralty was of great significance: 'Mr. Chamberlain gave himself to the work with

a contagious enthusiasm. . . . He used his social influence to add
strength to the movement. He appealed in private to men of ability
who cared nothing for public life, and he showed how much they
might do for the town if they would go into the Council; he insisted
that what they were able to do it was their duty to do. He dreamt
dreams and saw visions of what Birmingham might become, and
resolved that, he for his part, would do his utmost to fulfil them.'[77]

Chamberlain's mayoralty was marked by the Corporation's
purchase of local gas and water concerns, by the ambitious improvement scheme proposed in July 1875, and by the general attempt to
raise the standard of the town's cultural and recreational amenities.
Chamberlain's drive to push through these programmes of municipal socialism, or more crudely, 'gas and water socialism', was
made possible by the conjunction of a number of favourable
circumstances. Perhaps chief among these was his own business
experience and flair, allied with the capacity to cajole and persuade,
and above all to present his proposals cogently. A colleague was
later to recall: 'His speeches at this time in the Council were clear,
well arranged and persuasive. He took much pains to attach the
members of the Council to himself and to persuade them to his
own views, raising their self respect and gradually introducing a
higher tone. As his influence and following increased, his policy
in this respect remained the same. Though somewhat dogmatic,
his satire, if keen, was never malicious as is alleged.'[78]

The deputy chairman of the first Birmingham Gas Committee
who witnessed Chamberlain's negotiations with the Birmingham
Gas Company (which was bought out, together with the Birmingham and Staffordshire Gas Company), later wrote: 'I consider Mr.
Chamberlain the most able negotiator I have ever met. He always
discerned the line of least resistance, and advanced along it,
concentrating his force on the vital points to be secured, while
surrendering, where necessary, unimportant advantages. There
was no guesswork in his methods; he secured exact information,
carefully prepared his plans, and in a word, knew exactly what he
wanted and how to get it.'[79]

A further advantage possessed by Chamberlain was his capacity
to use the local press in support of his aims. This technique, later
utilised upon the national political stage, did not always work to
his advantage, and in December 1880 and April 1881 he felt
obliged to assure the Prime Minister, Gladstone, that he was not

responsible for leaks to the *Standard* concerning aspects of the government's policies towards Ireland.[80] In the days of his mayoralty, however, Chamberlain had the ear and the support of J. T. Bunce, editor of the influential *Birmingham Daily Post*, and, 'Through the columns of the most powerful newspaper in the midland counties the new ideas about municipal life and duty were pressed on the whole community.'[81]

Chamberlain's reforms were also greatly assisted by the work of the Local Government Board established by Act of Parliament in 1871, and by the Public Health Acts of 1872 and 1875 which enabled corporations to take over gas and water concerns. *allowed change*

But nothing would have come of Chamberlain's municipal ambitions without the Liberals' domination of the local government machine. Chamberlain himself claimed that the Town Council, like the Duke of Wellington's army, would 'go anywhere and do anything'. He referred again to his powers in a letter to his close friend and political ally Sir Charles Dilke in January 1876: 'I have been very fully occupied with local affairs—having now almost despotic authority here, & being able to carry out innumerable schemes, which I hope will result in the advantage and improvement of the town. Anyhow, I have committed the Corporation to a capital expenditure of nearly 5 millions in the last 12 months—so it is kill or cure.'[82]

Chamberlain's first great project was to set up a municipal gas supply. Other municipalities in England and Wales had already undertaken similar measures, but Birmingham critics of the scheme would have to be convinced that an increase in the municipal debt from £500,000 to £2,500,000 would be worthwhile. Chamberlain argued forcibly that the take-over would eventually be profitable to the Corporation and would not involve an inevitable rise in gas prices. He turned on a sceptical member of the Town Council and accused him of wishing 'to throw away future large profits for the sake of present small gains. I cannot accept that as my line of policy; it is not the way in which I have been in the habit of conducting my own private business.'[83]

The two private gas companies were bought out for £1,953,050, 18s. 11d. The Town Council voted for the step by a majority of fifty-four to two, and a meeting of ratepayers also approved the scheme. There were, however, doubts that municipalised gas would be as profitable as Chamberlain claimed when he told a

meeting of ratepayers that 'if they will take his bargain and farm it
out to me, I will pay them £20,000 a year for it, and at the end of
fourteen years I shall have a snug little fortune of £150,000 or
£200,000.'[84] In the first year of its operation municipalised gas
made a profit of £34,000, and by 1879 Chamberlain could show
that the following sums had been made available for Birmingham's
improvement through the profitability of gas: £80,000 for rate
relief, £50,000 to the reserve fund, and £35,000 to the sinking
fund. The price of gas, moreover, had not risen; indeed, it had
been twice reduced during the first three years of the project.[85]

The corporation's purchase of the local waterworks, on the other
hand, could not be expected to yield considerable profits. Chamberlain put it succinctly when he presented the case for a Parliamentary Bill to enable the Corporation to acquire the waterworks to a
House of Commons Committee: 'We have not the slightest
intention of making a profit. . . . We shall get our profit indirectly
in the comfort of the town and in the health of the inhabitants.'[86]

A better supply of water for Birmingham's citizens was urgently
needed. Out of a population of some 300,000, about 150,000 were
dependent upon well water, much of which was polluted with
sewage. In any case, the Water Company's piped water only ran
on three days of the week; for the rest there were the tainted well
water and the water carts, both of them a serious risk to health.

The provision of an adequate, pure, and cheap supply of water
gave Chamberlain the perfect opportunity to further implement the
gospel of civic reform. When in December 1874 he spoke before
the Town Council in favour of the compulsory purchase of the
water system (failing a sale by agreement) he insisted that 'all
monopolies, regulated monopolies, sustained by the State in the
interests of the inhabitants generally, should be controlled by the
representatives of the people, and should not be left in the hands
of private speculators.' He went on to deplore the rising death-rate,
especially among children, from contagious and preventable
diseases; most of the wells which supplied the poorest sections of
the community were contaminated. He went on to refer to the
cases of poor people convicted of stealing water: 'They might as
well be convicted for stealing air. I have sometimes wondered why
the supply of air is not regulated by the Legislature and handed
over to some Company with a dividend limited to 10 per cent!'[87]

There was not one vote against Chamberlain's proposals to the

Town Council. The waterworks were taken-over on 1 January 1876, the Bill permitting the Corporation to acquire them having received the royal assent (together with the Gas Bill) in August 1875. The private water companies eventually received a sum of £1,350,000 to be paid over twenty-five years in annuities of £54,491. Having taken the 'power of life and death' out of private hands, Chamberlain went on to convince the Council that 'whereas there should be a profit made on the gas undertaking the water should never be a source of profit; all profit should go in reduction of the price of water.'

This was pure municipal socialism, although Chamberlain, even at this stage of his career, must be seen as a practical, reforming Radical rather than a socialist. He disliked top-heavy bureaucratic organisations and centralised authority, preferring instead to encourage local communities to shoulder the political responsibilities to which over-ambitious individuals might otherwise aspire. Despite his own ambitions, and the dynamic thrust of his personality, Chamberlain took pains to base his claims to authority upon the democratic process. Thus in June 1874, after laying the cornerstone of the new Council Chamber (prior to his mayoralty the Council had met in the 'Old Woodman' public house) he said:

> I have an abiding faith in municipal institutions; I have a deep sense of the value and importance of local self-government. Our Corporation represents the authority of the people; through us you obtain a full and direct representation of the popular will, and consequently any disrespect to us, anything which depreciates us in the public estimation, necessarily degrades the principles which we represent, strikes through us at the Constitution itself, and lowers our authority and public usefulness. It behoves us to find fitting accommodation for our local Parliament.'[88]

Having made gas and water safe for democracy, Chamberlain turned to other schemes for improving the quality of life in Birmingham. There was, of course, the money to do it; not merely through the rates and the profits from municipalised gas, but also from the Corporation's ability to raise loans at very favourable rates of interest. In municipal finance, as in other fields, nothing succeeded as well as success itself.

Chamberlain's assault on the town's squalor and poverty must, however, be seen in a wider context. Impatient with the Liberal party's leadership, scornful of the Whig connection, and aspiring to lead a cleansed Radical alliance against the Tories, Chamberlain also had his eye on a national audience when he proposed local reform. In October 1874, speaking in Birmingham, he struck out at the root cause of Victorian Britain's social problems:

> I am a Radical Reformer because I would reform and remove ignorance, poverty, intemperance, and crime at their very roots. What is the cause of all this ignorance and vice? Many people say that intemperance is at the bottom of everything and I am not inclined to disagree with them. I believe we hardly ever find misery or poverty without finding that intemperance is one of the factors in such conditions. But at the same time I believe intemperance itself is only an effect produced by causes that lie deeper still. I should say these causes, in the first place, are the gross ignorance of the masses; and, in the second place, the horrible, shameful homes in which many of the poor are forced to live.[89]

In July 1875 Chamberlain put before the Council an ambitious improvement scheme which involved a massive programme of slum-clearance in the centre of Birmingham. In squalid streets like Coach Yard, Bull Street, Cherry Street, Rope Walk, and Lower Priory, stench, misery, ignorance, disease and early death were commonplace. The death-rate was, in fact, double that in salubrious Edgbaston, and Chamberlain estimated that each year Birmingham suffered 3,000 preventable deaths and 18,000 preventable illnesses. The annual cost to the town, in terms of medical expenses, loss of wages and so forth, he reckoned at £54,000—or three or four-fold the yearly average cost of the improvement scheme. He put his case before the Town Council in his now typical clear-cut and hard-hitting manner:

> We want to make these people healthier and better; I want to make them happier also. Let us consider for a moment the forlorn and desolate lives the best of these people must live, in courts like those described. It made my heart bleed when I heard the descriptions of Mr. White [town councillor for the ward in which some of the worst districts lay] and others of the dreariness . . . and the lack of everything which would add

interest or pleasure to the life that obtains among that class. . . . I know for a fact that there are people there almost as ignorant of what is going on around them as if they lived in a lonely and savage island. . . . Some would even lose themselves in New Street. There are people who do not know that there is an existence on the other side of the Town Hall; people who are as ignorant of all that goes to make the pleasure, the interest, the activity, and the merit of our lives, as if they were savages in Ceylon, instead of being Englishmen and Englishwomen in the nineteenth century enjoying all the blessings of civilization.'[90]

Having thus revealed the bleeding heart of a convinced environmental reformer, what was Chamberlain going to do about it? As in the case of his gas and water schemes the recent legislation of central government provided him with vital support. The Artisans' Dwellings Act became law in 1875, carried through by Disraeli's ministry. Chamberlain had been one of the municipal leaders consulted during the preparation of the Bill by Cross, the Home Secretary. The Act encouraged municipalities to undertake slum-clearance by enabling them to borrow the necessary finance at low rates of interest; the corporations could also become freeholders of the land acquired under the Act.

Chamberlain proposed to drive a grand new road, Corporation Street, plumb through the overcrowded and wretched slums in the centre of the town. Nearly fifty acres of property were to be brought into municipal ownership. Naturally enough, the slum landlords protested bitterly against the Corporation's assumption of compulsory purchase powers, arguing that the Artisans' Dwellings Act was intended to be used for sanitary improvements only. Chamberlain swept such protests aside, and later dealt firmly with another difficulty which arose when the Commissioner supervising the Local Government Board's inquiry into the scheme threatened to be obstructive over the issue of compulsory purchase. On 10 April 1876 Chamberlain appealed directly to the President of the Local Government Board, Sclater-Booth, and was able to tell his loyal henchman Jesse Collings:

The improvement scheme is I hope safe. The Commissioner on the second day's inquiry said something I did not like about not giving us compulsory powers between New St. and Bull St., so I talked of throwing up the scheme and mightily frightened some

of the great property owners, who were standing out for ex-
orbitant profits. . . . But today I have been to London and had a
private interview with Sclater-Booth, who has promised to
throw over the Commissioner and give me all I want! Hurray
for the Tories!'[91]

The improvement scheme, however, was the most difficult
undertaking of Chamberlain's mayoralty. Though the Corporation
raised the money needed to purchase the land (aided by an Improvement Trust Fund of nearly £60,000, towards which Chamberlain
contributed £10,000 himself) the Improvement Committee came
to the conclusion that it would be too expensive to rehouse the
slum-dwellers in municipally built accommodation. The land was
therefore let out on seventy-five year leases as a business proposition; Chamberlain would not accept the principle of ninety-nine
year leases, arguing that the shorter terms would not substantially
affect the finances involved and the property would revert that
much sooner to the Corporation.

For all the ballyhoo that accompanied it, the improvement
scheme was not a complete success. Many of those who had in-
habited the slums were not rehoused in the old areas, though
accommodation was eventually provided in the suburbs. The
scheme, moreover, lost the corporation a net £300,000—a sum
equivalent to 3d. on the rates. Chamberlain did not consider this
loss a serious one, remarking that as he looked to getting ultimately
a shilling rate out of gas he did not fear the cost. In one respect,
however, the scheme was an undoubted triumph for the civic
gospellers, for the death-rate of the inhabitants of the improved
quarter dropped from 53.2 per 1,000 during the period 1873–5 to
21.3 per 1,000 from 1879–81.[92]

Chamberlain's mayoralty was distinguished for activities other
than his determined assault upon unlit and badly paved streets,
contaminated water, inadequate sewers, and slum tenements. He
also tried his utmost to bring some light where there was darkness,
to promote culture against potential anarchy. It was not merely
that he secured an assize for Birmingham, it was much more an
attempt to give all citizens a share in a cultural and recreational
collective estate.

He therefore flung public and private funds behind a systematic
programme of municipal improvement: the central and the branch

libraries, the art gallery and various collections were enlarged and enriched; municipal swimming baths, new parks and public gardens were opened, many new schools were built. Chamberlain was quite ready to dip into his pocket, telling Jesse Collings in April 1875 that he was offering £1,000, through the Free Libraries Committee of which Collings was chairman, to the art gallery to enable them to purchase objects of industrial art for permanent exhibition.[93] Chamberlain neatly summed up his philosophy towards the improvement of amenities when he opened Highgate Park in 1876: 'It is simply nonsense to wonder at the want of refinement of our people when no opportunity is given to innocent enjoyment. We are too apt to forget that the ugliness of our ordinary English existence has a bad influence on us.'[94]

By the time Chamberlain had reached the third year of his mayoralty he had indeed given some substance to his earlier pledge that 'By God's help the town shall not know itself.' In June 1876, and on the point of taking up his seat in the House of Commons, he told Jesse Collings: 'I think I have now almost completed my municipal programme and may sing *nunc dimittis*. The Town will be parked, paved, assized, marketed, Gas-and-Watered and *improved*—all as the result of three years' active work.'[95]

The significance of Chamberlain's whirlwind period of office as mayor did not, however, simply lie in the municipal improvements he left behind him, and upon which he was to keep so watchful an eye. His practical contribution to Birmingham's physical and moral well-being, the dynamic style of his politics, was to provide him with a power-base that later might have raised envious eyebrows among the Democratic party bosses on the other side of the Atlantic. Birmingham was to become Chamberlain's personal political fief, repaying him with a loyalty that transcended the contortions and shifts of his public career.

In under three years, therefore, Chamberlain had made a profound impact upon the fabric and the imagination of Birmingham. His appearance must have helped him to promote an image of efficiency and respectability. Contemporaries noted that he seemed extraordinarily youthful (scarcely old enough to be married some said); though short of stature, he was slim, with a fresh, clean-shaven face. He took care to dress well, and in those days he was described as wearing 'a black velvet coat, jaunty eyeglass in eye, red neck-tie drawn through a ring, very smart indeed.'[96]

Yet in private he had suffered another tragedy, for on 14 February 1875 (St. Valentine's Day by a cruel irony) his second wife Florence died suddenly having given birth to their fifth child the day before; the child died within hours and was placed in the same coffin.

Chamberlain, usually so active and sprightly, staggered under this blow. He wrote gloomily to Dr. Dale in reply to a letter of condolence: 'You may know . . . how completely identified in tastes and opinions my wife and I have been. She shared every thought and plan I had—there is not a fibre in my whole being which has not been roughly torn asunder. You can judge how desolate and solitary I feel and how dark and difficult my future life seems to me.'[97] He set down, amid his grief, his feelings, so that one day his young children by Florence could read them and understand:

> . . . within the last few days I have read again what I wrote shortly after Harrie's death about her life and character; and I am struck with its resemblance to what I now write and feel about Florence. . . . In the perfect communion and intercourse I have had with these two, I have known the highest form of human happiness—by their deaths I have twice been called on to bear the keenest pain and intensest sorrow.[98]

Although Chamberlain did not usually allow his private feelings to surface for all to see, those who were close to him witnessed the grief which gripped him after Florence's death and which was intensified in September 1875 by the death of his mother. In a little over a year and a half he had lost his father, his second wife, a new-born child, and now his mother. These bereavements destroyed Chamberlain's religious beliefs at their foundations. In December 1875 he wrote to his friend John Morley: 'It is a hideous business, and our conception of its end and meaning is thoroughly unsatisfactory. We may be right—I fear we are—and I refuse to try and buy comfort by forcing myself to insincere conviction—but still I thoroughly abhor the result at which I have arrived, and I think it a grievous misfortune to have been born into such a destiny.'[99]

Chamberlain's years as mayor of Birmingham did not have the effect of so immersing him in municipal activity that he ceased to attract the attention of the public at large. On the contrary, his municipal reforms were further evidence of the growing authority and experience of one of the most advanced Liberals in the country. The official visit of the Prince and Princess of Wales to Birmingham in November 1874 (exactly a year since Chamberlain had become mayor) had the effect of bringing the mayor considerable publicity—most of it favourable.

At first sight, the visit of the future King Edward VII and Queen Alexandra to radical Birmingham, with its allegedly republican mayor, might seem to be a little like venturing into the lion's den. But how much of a republican was Chamberlain? In fact, there was nothing of the blood-stained Communard about him; he cherished no desire to die upon the barricades, or indeed to encourage others to die upon them.

His early republican reputation sprang chiefly from his attending an Electoral Reform Congress in London in November 1872 as a delegate from three organisations: the Birmingham Liberal Association, the Central Nonconformist Association, and the Birmingham Republican Club. Chamberlain later explained this event by saying, 'It is true I agreed to appear as a delegate, but I was not a member of the [Republican] Club, which was of no importance in Birmingham, and their proposal that I should represent them was made without my knowledge. I was attending the Congress on behalf of the Birmingham Liberal Association.'[100] Certainly Chamberlain's speech at the Congress contained no reference to republicanism.

The republican label stuck, however, and on 6 December 1872 Chamberlain tried to set the record straight while proposing the health of Queen Victoria (appropriately enough) at a dinner held in St. Paul's ward, Birmingham. The speech revealed his respect for republicanism as the most rational and enlightened system of government; he was also at pains to equate republicanism with equality of opportunity. Chamberlain's words are worth quoting in full since they explain how a sympathy for republican principles was perfectly consistent with his own advanced Liberalism:

I have been taxed with professing Republicanism. I hold, and very few intelligent men do not now hold, that the best form of Government for a free and enlightened people is that of a Republic, and that is the form of Government to which the nations of Europe are surely and not very slowly tending. But at the same time I am not at all prepared to enter into an agitation in order to upset the existing state of things, to destroy monarchy, and to change the name of the titular ruler of this country. I do not consider the name a matter of the slightest importance. What is of real importance is the spread of a real Republican spirit among the people. The idea, to my mind, that underlies Republicanism is this: that in all cases merit should have a fair chance, that it should not be handicapped in the race by any accident of birth or privilege; that all men should have equal rights before the law, equal chances of serving their country.[101]

Chamberlain was, in fact, quite prepared to see the monarch as representing 'the popular authority, the popular will, and the supremacy of law and order.'[102] The royal visit to Birmingham, therefore, was marked by great popular enthusiasm and an impeccably courteous reception by the mayor; thousands of spectators flocked in from the Black Country and other neighbouring regions, and the trees near the royal route were full of agile sightseers. The Prince and Princess of Wales inspected Gillot's pen factory, and the Princess electro-plated a vase at Elkington's; they were entertained to lunch by the mayor and mayoress in the rooms of the Society for Artists, since the Council House was not yet built.

So warm was Birmingham's welcome to the royal couple that Chamberlain was able to make a telling point in his address to his guests:

This town has long been distinguished, and not without cause, for the independence of its citizens, and the freedom and outspokenness with which all opinions are discussed; and this fact gives value to the welcome which has been offered, and stamps the sincerity of the wishes which are everywhere expressed for the continued health of their Royal Highnesses.[103]

Privately Chamberlain observed that his critics seemed to have forgotten 'that a man might be a gentleman as well as a Republican, and that even an advanced Liberal might not be unmindful of the duties of hospitality and the courtesy which everyone owes a guest.'[104]

The national press wholeheartedly agreed that Chamberlain had acquitted himself admirably in his reception of the royal couple. *The Times* said, 'Whatever Mr. Chamberlain's views may be, his speeches have been admirably worthy of the occasion and have done the highest credit to himself. . . . We do not know that we have ever heard or chronicled speeches made before Royal person-ages by Mayors, whether they were Tories or Whigs, or Liberals or Radicals, which were couched in such a tone at once of courteous homage, manly independence and gentlemanly feeling—which were so perfectly becoming and so much the right thing in every way as those of Mr. Chamberlain.'[105] The *Saturday Review* and the *Spectator*, both journals accustomed to attack Chamberlain, were warm in his praise. A Tenniel cartoon in *Punch* showed the mayor as the 'Brummagem Lion' kneeling benignly before the Princess of Wales to have his claws clipped; this represented an exaggerated view of Chamberlain's political ferocity, but the verses that accompanied it reflected relief and respect for the radical mayor:

> Like a gentleman he has comported himself in this
>   glare of the princely sun;
> Has just said what he ought to have said and done
>   what he ought to have done;
> Has put his red cap in his pocket, and sat on his
>   *Fortnightly* article,
> And of red Republican claws or teeth displayed
>   not so much as a particle.[106]

In a word, the royal visit to Birmingham did Chamberlain nothing but good, and less than a week later he was re-elected mayor amid great enthusiasm.

Chamberlain had not ceased his national campaigning on the education issue, or for a re-fashioning of Liberalism, when he became mayor. Indeed, the reference in the *Punch* doggerel quoted above to 'his *Fortnightly* article' was highly topical, since in the October edition of the *Fortnightly Review* (edited by John Morley) Chamberlain had published his follow-up to his provocative 'The Liberal Party and its Leaders'. This second article also attracted widespread national comment, and is a remarkable example of the way Chamberlain could raise hackles even though he was as yet without a Parliamentary seat. In the article he once more hit out at the Liberal party establishment:

It is highly improbable that the opposition will cross the floor of the House for some years to come. . . . The advanced Liberals

... form an important element in the Liberal Party. .... Without
them it would be difficult to distinguish the party of the moderate
Tories who do not practise their principles from the party of the
moderate Liberals who have no principles to practise. .... If it is
really the desire of the country that nothing more should be done,
then Conservatives are the proper persons to carry out its
wishes. ....

The Liberal party will never regain power on terms like these.
Much as Mr. Gladstone is honoured and respected it is not for
his credit or for ours that we should take him back as we recover
a stolen watch—on the condition that no questions are asked. ....

We are compelled occasionally to turn aside from the con-
templation of our virtues and intelligence and wealth, to recognise
the fact that we have in our midst a vast population more ignorant
than the barbarians whom we profess to convert, more miserable
than the most wretched in other countries to whom we attempt
from time to time to carry succour and relief.[107]

By carrying the radical attack to the Tories and right-wing
Liberals, Chamberlain was consciously bidding for support from
the rural labouring class as well as the urban artisans. If the ad-
herents of Joseph Arch's newly formed Agricultural Labourers'
Union (to which Chamberlain subscribed £5 a week) could be
marshalled behind a new party of progress this would shake even
further the Liberal establishment.

Chamberlain was by now clearly conscious that his Nonconformist support needed to be broadened and that the National
Education League itself provided too narrow a platform for his
ambitions. In March 1874 Chamberlain had told Dilke, 'I don't
think the [Education] League will do. It must be a new organisation
although our experience & acquired information may be useful.'[108]
Two days earlier Dilke had said, 'What about your idea of widening
the basis of the League. If it were done now—I could get all the
trades unions in to a joint movement—with you for its head.'[109]
Even earlier, in August 1873, Chamberlain had put the problem to
Morley, commenting that 'If we get any compromise from the
government [regarding the Education Act] that we can possibly
accept, it will probably be well to dissolve the League, leaving its
still unaccomplished work to be taken up as part of the large
question.'[110]

The experience of running a few Education League candidates against official Liberals in the unexpected General Election of January 1874 had also convinced Chamberlain that on the one hand there was impatience with the party leadership over the education issue, but also comparatively little working-class enthusiasm for the particular cause.

Gladstone's resignation from the party leadership in January 1875 did not lead to any fundamental shift in official Liberal attitudes. Chamberlain saw Gladstone go with equanimity; he would not have supported W. E. Forster at any price; Lord Hartington was, in his eyes, the best of a bad bunch—and Hartington became leader, though as a Whig, and thus on the right wing of the party, he was hardly likely to satisfy the demands of the advanced Liberals.

One way of influencing events in the way he wished was to become a member of Parliament. Between January 1874 and June 1876 Chamberlain ran twice for the House of Commons and maintained a vigilant watch for suitable seats.

His first attempt to win a seat was hardly a happy one. When Gladstone precipitated the General Election of January 1874, Chamberlain was invited to stand as the Radical candidate for one of the two seats in Sheffield. The invitation arose out of the tangled state of the Liberal party there: the Sheffield Radical, Henry Wilson, disgusted with the 1870 Education Act had broken away from the local Liberal Association and had formed a splinter group—the Sheffield Reform Association. Impressed by Chamberlain's first article in the *Fortnightly Review* of October 1874, Wilson invited the newly-appointed mayor of Birmingham to Sheffield to meet the rebels of the Reform Association, who subsequently adopted him as their parliamentary candidate.

When the election came it was characterised by a bitter, savage and disorderly campaign. There were four candidates: J. A. Roebuck, the veteran Liberal who had often been a thorn in Palmerston's side; A. J. Mundella, the sitting member; the Sheffield Liberal Association's candidate, A. J. Allott; and Chamberlain, standing in the Radical interest and as the nominee of the Reform Association.

Chamberlain had to face a variety of abuse during the campaign. He was accused of atheism and republicanism; of sham radicalism; of being a rich monopolist eager to trample on his workers' rights.

Dead cats were hurled at him at the hustings, and once a red herring hit him on the forehead. Roebuck made a bid for the Anglican and anti-temperance vote with the compelling slogan of 'stand by your National Religion and your National Beverage'.

When the poll was declared Roebuck and Mundella headed it with 14,193 and 12,858 respectively; Chamberlain came third with 11,053 votes, and Allott received a derisory vote of 621. There is no doubt that Chamberlain was vexed and humiliated by his failure. As the power behind the National Education League, as a man well on his way to becoming one of the best known of the advanced Liberals, he must have expected better treatment at the hands of the electors of radical Sheffield.

Though for the next two and a half years he devoted himself energetically to his work as mayor of Birmingham he still toyed with the idea of a parliamentary seat. Despite several visits to Sheffield, he at last came to the conclusion that he should not stand there again. In March 1873, less than two months after his Sheffield defeat, he wrote to Dilke: 'In confidence do you know anything about Northampton? [Where a by-election was due] If Gilpin resigns and Bradlaugh does not stand I shall possibly go there. I was asked before but refused to stand against Bradlaugh. I don't want to try again till I have finished my Mayoralty but if such an opportunity occurred I must take it when it comes.'[111]

Bradlaugh, the battle-hardened humanist and free-thinker, did stand and Northampton receded from Chamberlain's range of options. But in the same month Dilke suggested Bolton where he thought the sitting M.P., Cross, was likely to be unseated on petition. He went on, 'I think that with Home Rule you could carry the Irish—and if you did you could win the seat.'[112] In November 1875 Dilke, luxuriating in a holiday in Japan, wrote 'I have heard out here a little more of Leeds, and it seems there will be a vacancy.'[113] To have provoked a letter from Dilke from Japan 'where the maidens say "Ohio" to you most pleasantly' plainly indicates Chamberlain's strong desire to enter the House of Commons. In May of the same year another friend had been concerned over Chamberlain's parliamentary prospects, although on this occasion Jesse Collings had urged him, for the sake of the programme of municipal reform, not to stand at the Norwich by-election.[114]

In May 1876 Chamberlain's perfect chance came when George

Dixon at last decided to retire from his Birmingham seat—badgered into this step, some said, by Chamberlain's local supporters. Thus provided with an opening (and at some cost in terms of a good deal of resentment from Dixon, who subsequently found his way back into the Commons), Chamberlain felt obliged to tell Collings of his doubts, which it must be supposed, were genuine enough: 'What a fool I am to go to Parliament and give up the opportunity of influencing the only constructive legislation in the country for the sake of tacking M.P. to my name. Upon my word I think sometimes that both Birmingham and I will have cause to regret this step.'[115]

Chamberlain was returned unopposed for Birmingham on 17 June 1876. The three-week period that elapsed between his nomination for the seat and his election is remarkable for the anxiety and the surprising lack of poise that marked his deportment. On the same day that he was nominated he publicly denounced Disraeli, the Prime Minister, as 'a man who never told the truth except by accident; a man who went down to the House of Commons and flung at the British Parliament the first lie that entered his head.' Chamberlain was obliged to issue a prompt and full apology. He was, moreover, easily irritated, and could not sleep or eat properly.

His depression and anxiety were perhaps the result of municipal burdens, or the result of illness—for he was now prone to attacks of gout, and as early as January 1876 had told Dilke, 'I am laid up with the gout—which I always thought was reserved by a just providence for Tories exclusively.'[116] Possibly he had set so much store on entering Parliament, despite his disclaimers, that the imminent realisation of his ambitions disturbed his peace of mind. Doubtless the humiliation at Sheffield still rankled. Even when he was safely elected, he approached his first address to his new constituents with trepidation: 'I . . . funked my speech in Bingley Hall more than I have feared anything for a long time past.'[117]

On 9 July he wrote a deeply depressed letter to John Morley:

You are quite right in thinking that the reaction would come. It has come, and I have been thoroughly wretched and depressed. I have broken with my old life, and have as yet no interest in, or hope of, my future—everything reminds me of what might have been and recalls my present loneliness. I can neither look back

nor forward with any satisfaction, and I have lost the dogged
endurance which has sustained me so long. This life is a d——d
bad business for me, and I wish I were out of it.[118]

Chamberlain, despite his reputation as an assured and adroit
public figure, was clearly a profoundly unhappy man as he stood
on the threshold of his parliamentary career. Having resigned the
mayoralty, and uncertain of the role he might play in the House of
Commons, he was prey to an uncharacteristic uncertainty and to
self-pity.

His lament of loneliness should also be taken seriously. He was
the father of six children, but there was no wife to look after them.
Chamberlain had, as Beatrice Potter later testified, positive qualities
of 'energy and personal magnetism, in a word masculine force to
an almost superlative degree.'[119] He remained a widower from
1875 to 1888. In 1876 he had only just begun that period of personal
solitude. Chamberlain's sexual energies could only find full release
through marriage; his somewhat reserved private character, his
public reputation, and the conventions of the time, all made
sexual activity outside of wedlock unthinkable. The death of
Florence, therefore, still imposed upon him serious personal con-
straints and disabilities and it is clear that as he prepared to undertake a vitally important new stage in his career, these disadvantages
were extra-keenly felt.

The new member for Birmingham, however, had to take his
seat. The date set was 13 July, and John Bright and Joseph Cowen
(the Radical member for Newcastle) were to introduce him to the
House of Commons. It was the start of a parliamentary career that
was to last until 1914, the year of his death.

FIVE

MEMBER OF PARLIAMENT
1876–80

There is literally no Liberal & no Radical party in the House of Commons.

Chamberlain to Walter Wren, April 1878

WHEN CHAMBERLAIN took his seat in the House of Commons in July 1876 he committed the gaffe of keeping on his hat while waiting on the cross benches to take his oath. The Birmingham *Town Crier* in its bogus 'Diary of a New Member' gave an imaginary account of Chamberlain's feelings:

July 15th. Kept my hat on in the House when I went there. Other people did the same. It seems to be the only sign of difference between the Members and doorkeepers. Seems I was wrong; you don't wear your hat until you are sworn. Felt strongly disposed to swear off-hand; but there is a form provided, which you are obliged to follow. It is longer than it need be, and not so expressive as a voluntary form might be made. Mr. Bright and Mr. Cowen took me to see the Speaker. . . . We shook hands, and I went through the formality of the oath. Then I took my seat, put on my hat, and felt as if I had been in the House for a twelvemonth.[120]

In fact, Chamberlain felt distinctly ill-at-ease at the outset of his parliamentary career. His Radical and republican reputation, his recent abuse of Disraeli, and his attacks on the Liberal leadership, made many other members cool, if not openly antagonistic, towards him. A day or two after being sworn-in he wrote to Jesse Collings that 'The atmosphere is strange, unsympathetic, almost hostile', though he 'was very kindly received by the Radicals and many other members whom I knew.'[121]

Within a fortnight, however, Chamberlain had decidedly found his feet. He had dined peaceably with Forster and Lowe, and greatly relished his extensive contact with his close friends Dilke and Morley (though the latter was not yet a member of the Commons).

He had also, with almost indecent haste, tried to organise a small Radical splinter group to prod the Liberals in the House. On 27 July 1876 he wrote to Dilke announcing that, 'We met last night & settled a programme & general course of action. Notice of Bills & resolutions to be given next Thursday. . . . I think there is every chance of our union being productive of useful practical results, but it is agreed that our arrangements shall remain strictly private for the present. Omne ignotum pro magnifico.'[122]

Chamberlain's remarkably early bid to set up a parliamentary Radical action group was, in his imagination at least, a step towards founding the new party that would gobble up the advanced Liberals and subsequently bear the burden of meaningful opposition to the Tories. It was a move which reflected clearly his ambitions, his fundamental self-confidence and his sense of urgency. The bid was, however, doomed to failure. Joseph Cowen's membership of the group ended with his refusal to back the anti-Turkish, Bulgarian atrocities agitation of 1876–7. Cowen's departure removed one of the ablest of the younger Radicals from the group. Some time later, on 11 April 1878, Chamberlain wrote despondently to Walter Wren:

> Since I have been in the House I have twice joined in efforts to establish a small party that would be willing to give and take, and work together towards some general common objects. On both occasions the attempt has ended in utter failure.
>
> The only remedy for this state of things lies with the constituencies. When the majority in the country has made up its mind what it wants, and wants it very much, they will send to the House of Commons men with sufficiently definite opinions & with earnestness to form a new party.[123]

His early experiences in the House of Commons certainly confirmed Chamberlain in his low opinion of Liberal party organisation. He told Wren that, 'There is literally no Liberal & no Radical party in the House of Commons. Those who call themselves Radicals are as much divided amongst themselves upon questions of cardinal importance as they are separated from the Whigs. In fact, speaking for myself, I have more hope of Lord Hartington [leader of the Liberal party] than of many of my fellow members who sit below the gangway.'[124]

The divisions within the party were all the more infuriating in view of the difficulties encountered by the Conservative government under Disraeli's leadership. The Balkan and Near Eastern crisis, arising out of the Russo-Turkish war, gave the opposition the chance to pillory Disraeli as a supporter, by implication, of the Bulgarian massacres of 1876. As Gladstone shook himself out of his retirement to launch a ferocious campaign against the government's alleged indifference to the massacres, Chamberlain wrote to Dilke in December 1876, 'I think the Govt. is in a hole. They can't escape humiliation on this Eastn. business. Unfortunately our own party is in a hopeless condition & would be at one another's throats if there was the least chance of their getting into power.'[125]

The Bulgarian atrocities, however, gave the Liberal party a moral cause around which to rally as best they could. Nonconformists, the provincial press, and the respectable middle classes could all unite in their abhorrence of the abominable Turk and of the brash jingoism of the supporters of Disraeli's 'oriental' policy. In Gladstone the Liberal conscience found a passionate spokesman and pamphleteer anxious to drive the Turks 'bag and baggage' out of Europe.

Chamberlain seems to have seen the Bulgarian agitation chiefly in terms of his own immediate political priorities: an explosion of public indignation would enable Radicalism to gather more support by identification with moral rather than with bread and butter causes. Radicalism would also benefit from clinging to Gladstone's coat-tails as he thundered out his denunciations of Disraeli and the Turks. Chamberlain was, moreover, prepared to have Gladstone back as leader of the party, though such a move might well delay the fulfilment of any leadership ambitions he may have entertained. He told Dilke in October 1876, 'I don't believe I am more Gladstonian than you, but at this time I can't help thinking he is our best card . . . if he were to come back for a few years (he can't continue in public life for very much longer) he would probably do much for us and pave the way for more.'[126]

So Gladstone was to be used as an unwitting architect of the new Radicalism, and could then be expected to retire gracefully from the restructured political landscape. The irony of this calculation of Chamberlain's was to lie not only in Gladstone's tenacious hold on his political career (he did not retire as an M.P. until 1895 and was Prime Minister at the age of eighty-five), but also in the mutually damaging collisions that were to occur between them in the future.

For the time being, however, Chamberlain, after his savage attacks on the Liberal leadership, appeared to be effecting a détente with his party's former chief. To cement this growing understanding and, more important, to make use of Gladstone's reputation in the country in the Radical cause, Chamberlain decided to associate him with the formation of the National Liberal Federation.

The public excitement generated by the Bulgarian horrors, and the anxieties felt over the first signs of economic depression, helped to make the time ripe for the founding of a federation of the nation's various Liberal Associations. Chamberlain wanted to make Birmingham, not London, the centre of the proposed federation, thus enormously strengthening his own hand against the power-mongering 'Whigs and Whips' in the metropolis. If, furthermore, the Birmingham model could triumph as the blueprint for the federation's organisation then the Liberal party would benefit from an increased association with the working class, for on the Birmingham Liberal Association's central committee of 600 Chamberlain claimed that three-quarters were working men.

On 6 February 1877 Chamberlain told John Morley that he was about to dissolve the Education League 'announcing at the same time the formation of a Federation of Liberal Associations with headquarters at Birmingham and the League officers as chief cooks. I think this may become a very powerful organisation, and pro-portionately detested by all Whigs and Whips.'[127] Less than a month later he expressed to Jesse Collings his anxieties that the Liberal Associations of Manchester and Leeds would, by claiming equal representation on all the committees of Federation, 'seriously hamper our action'.

The next thing was to coax Gladstone to Birmingham to sanctify the formation of the Federation. On 16 April 1877, Chamberlain invited Gladstone to attend a meeting to be held on 31 May 'on the occasion of an important Conference of Liberal Associations formed on the model of the Birmingham Liberal Association.' He con-tinued persuasively:

I venture to think that Birmingham has some claim on your kind consideration as it is of all towns in the kingdom the one which has [been] for many years past the most consistently and thoroughly Liberal. It was the first to move last year in the almost universal protest against the misgovernment of the Turkish provinces; and the vast majority of its inhabitants have followed with hearty sympathy & admiration your course in reference to this matter.[128]

Despite these and other blandishments (including the prospect of a tour of Birmingham's schools, factories and municipal improvements) Gladstone did not agree to attend the meeting until the middle of May. Even then there were a number of difficulties to overcome concerning the arrangements: Birmingham Liberals wanted to change the date of the meeting from 31 May to the day before; Chamberlain wanted Gladstone to arrive by an earlier train than the one he proposed in order to get a comfortable dinner at Southbourne, 'not a scramble'; would Gladstone not like to see the Enfield factory with its 'curious machinery'?

These negotiations over arrangements are interesting as representing an early clash of wills (admittedly over fairly trivial matters) between Chamberlain and Gladstone. It is a reflection of Chamberlain's keen desire to associate his distinguished visitor with the project afoot that Gladstone won on all counts: the date of the meeting stayed as 31 May, Gladstone arrived on the train he preferred, and saw only what he wanted to see. Chamberlain conceded by acknowledging that Gladstone must not over-tax his strength, and added 'The working classes [are] anxious to show their appreciation of your services & character by giving you an almost Royal welcome.'[129]

On 31 May Gladstone spoke before a terrifyingly large crowd of nearly 30,000 in Bingley Hall. Evincing no great enthusiasm for the proposed National Liberal Federation, believing it to be a result of the 'power of the purse', Gladstone nonetheless gave the organisation a brief blessing before plunging into an attack upon Turkish misrule.

The Bingley Hall meeting accordingly passed a resolution condemning Turkish misgovernment culminating in the Bulgarian massacres; it then went on to support a second resolution, proposed by Chamberlain, that a 'Federation of Liberal Associations' should be established to allow the people a proper expression of their views on parliamentary legislation.

Chamberlain had got his national organisation. What was the significance of the newly created National Liberal Federation? Chamberlain had put it blandly when he told Gladstone that 'it is the inauguration of an effort to secure greater unity of aim & action on the part of Liberal organizations; and also to make these bodies more thoroughly representative of all sections of the party.'[130] These were noble and necessary aims, yet there were, on all sides, criticisms of the Federation.

For one thing, it was very much the creature of Birmingham Radicalism, a fact reflected in the agreement that the executive and general committees would meet in the town, and by the dominance of Birmingham men in its offices: Chamberlain as President, Schnadhorst as paid Secretary, Collings, Harris and Powell Williams on the executive committee. This goes far to explain the coldness of Manchester Liberals towards the scheme, and their subsequent, unsuccessful, attempt to set up a national organisation of their own. For another, it posed a distinct threat to the Whiggish right of the party who saw it, quite correctly, as a take-over bid by the agents of democracy and those advocating the fuller participation of the masses in political policy-making.

The Tories, aided and abetted by a *Times* leader, dubbed the new organisation a 'caucus', thus hoping to smear the National Liberal Federation by association with United States machine politics and, some said, corruption. The abusive word stuck, and the term 'Liberal caucus' passed into current usage.

Was Chamberlain trying to Americanise British politics, to introduce a 'spoils system' as his detractors claimed? In Birmingham, as previously shown, opponents of the ruling Liberal organisation felt that non-Liberals might not even aspire to be street-sweepers. Was such a thing contemplated on a national scale? The answer to this is clearly in the negative; Chamberlain did not aspire to buy working-class votes by bribery, though he certainly hoped that radical reforms, passed through Parliament in the proper manner, would encourage workers to vote for the party that had introduced such reforms.

As to the charge that Chamberlain sought to 'Americanise' British politics there is more to be said. To begin with, Chamberlain argued that there was much to admire in United States public life: after all, he claimed, in an article in the *Fortnightly Review* of November 1878, the Americans were fortunate in having no land problem, no church problem and no foreign policy. Furthermore if he could be accused of promoting a party platform that was exactly what he believed was needed to stop the 'politics of drift', and the stumbling concentration upon one great problem at a time. An agreed party programme, santioned by a democratic national organisation, would put an end to drift. There is also no doubt that the National Liberal Federation, especially after the 1880 General Election which returned the Liberals to power and made Chamberlain a Cabinet minister, acted as a whip for government policies, bringing recalcitrant M.P.s into line through constituency pressure.

In all these ways, whether basing himself on the American model or not, Chamberlain played a vital part in tightening-up party discipline, and ensuring that, firstly, a party programme should exist, and, secondly, that it should reflect democratically expressed constituency opinion. Despite the fact that Gladstone successfully carried the bulk of the National Liberal Federation with him after he split with Chamberlain over Irish Home Rule, the organisation undoubtedly altered the character of British political activity, and this was no mean achievement for its chief architect.

It is worth noting that a number of accusations levelled against Chamberlain at this time resurface later in his career, particularly during the tariff reform campaign of 1903-6. The Tariff Reform League was viewed (like the National Liberal Federation) as a Chamberlainite bid for a take-over at constituency and subsequently at a national, level. The League's propaganda methods, its canvassing techniques, the reproduction of Chamberlain's speeches on gramophone records, were all considered to be symptoms of 'Americanisation'. The Tariff Reform League's promises to working-class voters ('Tariff Reform means work for All!') were similarly seen as a form of electoral bribery. Between the formation of the National Liberal Federation, however, and the launching of the tariff reform campaign there was to be a gap of nearly forty years. Chamberlain had, in any case, other preoccupations in the late 1870s.

One of the most important of these was to make a mark in the House of Commons. Chamberlain delivered his maiden speech on 4 August 1876, less than three weeks after taking his seat. The opportunity arose during a debate on Lord Sandon's Bill to encourage full attendance at elementary schools. Clause 25, that red rag to the Nonconformist, Radical bull, was once more at issue, since the government had accepted an amendment making the clause compulsory, not optional. Chamberlain felt obliged to intervene. It was a crowded House, and as he rose to speak, Disraeli, frail and elderly upon the Treasury bench, lifted his eyeglass to scrutinise the new member. Chamberlain, according to one observer, immediately 'struck the conversational key and tone of argument which characterises the present House of Commons'. The speaker himself 'felt as cool as if at the Town Council.'[131] He spoke concisely and distinctly for twenty minutes, drawing on his experiences on the Birmingham School Board, and concluding with some matters of principle:

> A great deal had been said about the right of a parent to have the choice of schools. Let hon. Gentlemen opposite carry that principle to its logical conclusion and apply it to the rural districts, instead of leaving 10,000 or 12,000 country parishes with only Church schools. The right of conscience, he thought, was becoming a geographical expression. In the towns it meant the right of every one to get his religion taught at the expense of every one else, while in the country it was the right of the Church to drive the children into her schools and enforce the payment of a rate more obnoxious than the old church rate, because it was levied not merely for the maintenance of the fabric of the Church, but for the teaching of her principles and doctrines. He looked with alarm at the probable effect of the proposed Amendment. It would throw into the election of Boards of Guardians all the discord and confusion that frequently attended school board elections, and would not tend to bring about the perfection of religious instruction that was desired. As a general rule Boards of Guardians refused to appoint Roman Catholic chaplains in work-houses, and he thought it probable that they would use every legal means to avoid contributing towards the cost of educating Catholic children in the Catholic faith. In conclusion, he felt bound to say that the Amendment raised a most important principle—a principle which had agitated this country in past times, and which would agitate it again. He deeply regretted it should have been brought forward at the eleventh hour, and he considered it would justify even a factious opposition on the part

of hon. Gentlemen on his side of the House. The clause would lead to future opposition, which, he believed, would be detrimental to the cause of education. He thanked the House for having listened to him so attentively.[132]

Having made his parliamentary début, Chamberlain spoke on a considerable number of subjects during the next three and a half years. This was in addition to a great deal of public speechmaking, a programme which in December 1876 caused him to tell Dilke that he could not spare the latter a day at the beginning of January since he had 'half a dozen speeches to make on Free Church, Temperance, Local Museums & Heaven knows what'.[133]

His House of Commons speeches were equally varied. In domestic matters he kept a close watch on educational issues: pressing for free public elementary education, supporting Lord Randolph Churchill's plea for a select committee to consider Irish endowed schools, criticising examination arrangements which stipulated that a child must attend school 250 times before sitting an examination, deploring the interference of the Education Department in the activities of School Boards, and supporting the employment of female teachers.[134]

Chamberlain supported the extension of the franchise in Irish boroughs in order to bring Ireland into line with the rest of the United Kingdom in this respect. His advocacy that the hours of polling should be extended in British boroughs to benefit working men was, however, unsuccessful. He also argued, during the committee on the Public Works (Consolidated Fund) Bill the value of the great municipal authorities being able to borrow money at low rates of interest. The County Government Bill provoked his criticism that 'instead of simplifying the constitution [it] had actually complicated it'.

Two other domestic issues caught Chamberlain's attention: the first, concerning the vexed question of the licensing of alcohol, touched one of the abiding preoccupations of the Nonconformist vote—temperance; the second, related to flogging as a means of maintaining army discipline. The licensing controversy contained a good deal of electoral advantage for Chamberlain, the flogging issue far less.

Total abstinence from alcohol held no charms for Chamberlain, who drank and ate with great freedom for most of his life. On the other hand, his tidy and precise mind deplored the vagaries and abuses of the current traffic in intoxicating beverages. Still drawing heavily upon his Birmingham experience, he proposed, during the early months of 1877, to take the drink trade out of private hands (with full compensation) and to make the municipal authorities responsible for its regulation. He wanted to reduce the numbers of public houses, to encourage them to sell food and non-alcoholic drinks, and to make them decent places. Gladstone listened to his proposals with enthusiasm, but nothing came of them. He had, however, demonstrated his integrity to the Nonconformist and respectable middle-class vote, and the temperance cause enabled him to embark on a vigorous bout of public speaking.

Chamberlain's trenchant opposition to flogging in the army arose primarily from a deep personal loathing for physical cruelty. His father had hated the notion of corporal punishment, and had refused to send his children to schools that allowed it. The government's Army Discipline Bill, debated in the summer of 1879, proposed to retain flogging for some hundred offences. On 17 June Chamberlain delivered a savage attack on the Bill, denouncing flogging as 'degrading, brutal, cruel and unworthy of our civilization; injurious to every interest of the army in effect on recruiting and otherwise'. He also claimed that 'he knew that the horror of this punishment on the part of a great number of the working class was very great indeed'.[135]

His own dislike of corporal punishment had been reinforced earlier in the year by an incident concerning his elder son Austen, then fifteen years old and a pupil at Rugby school. Chamberlain naturally entertained high hopes of Austen, whom he had set upon an educational ladder (Rugby and Cambridge) that was to prove much more orthodox than his own (University College School, the Milk Street cordwaining business, and Nettlefold and Chamberlain). In April 1879 he discovered that Lee-Warner, Austen's house master, had saved his son from a flogging, and wrote a letter which, while expressing gratitude, also contained a thoroughgoing denunciation of corporal punishment, and, interestingly for one who was to attract much support from this quarter later in his career, the Jingoes:

I knew that this brutal punishment was still in vogue at our public schools, after having almost disappeared from the army and navy, and being reserved in our gaols for outrages of a particularly savage character, but it never entered my head that it would be applied for any but the worst offences, as for lying, stealing or indecency.

Accordingly, as I believed my boy would not be guilty of such things, I did not suppose that he incurred any liability to a punishment against which my blood revolts and of which . . . I cannot think without disgust and indignation.

It is this kind of treatment which destroys all sense of proportion in a boy's notion of offences, making gross immorality no worse than some slight breach of discipline; while the ready appeal to physical force is a natural preparation for the rowdy Jingoism which is the characteristic of many educated middle-class Englishmen.[136]

By his opposition in the House of Commons to the retention of flogging in the army, Chamberlain found himself allied with the Irish nationalist M.P.s against the government and a good many of the Liberal party as well. It also brought Chamberlain into a head-on collision with the Whiggish Lord Hartington, who had become the Liberal leader after Gladstone's retirement. Hartington requested Chamberlain to withdraw his motion in Committee on 7 July which, in effect, was a protest against the government's failure to concede on the flogging issue. Chamberlain refused, and eventually, as Hartington breezed in and out of the House, was provoked to say, 'It is rather inconvenient that we should have seen so little of the presence of the noble Lord lately the leader of the Opposition, but now the leader of a section only'. Hartington hastened to make peace, and on 17 July himself moved to abolish corporal punishment for military offences. The move failed, but that it took place at all is a remarkable tribute to the influence Chamberlain already wielded and to the party leadership's need to placate him.

Chamberlain's views on foreign affairs during the period 1876–1880 were also clearly expressed in Parliament. He took the opportunity to attack Disraeli's handling of the Near Eastern crisis, the Zulu War of 1879, and the invasion of Afghanistan in 1878. One of the main reasons for Chamberlain's assault on the government lay in his belief that such enterprises diverted Parliament's attention from the urgent business of reform at home by pursuing a policy 'of *continual*, petty, fruitless, unnecessary and inglorious squabbles'.

His opposition to Disraeli's foreign adventures was not, however, based upon a straightforward anti-imperialist viewpoint, nor upon the convictions of an unbridled 'Little Englander'. Chamberlain's attitude towards empire at this stage of his career was complex, and indeed John Morley was subsequently to claim that Chamberlain 'was always an Imperialist'.[137] Certainly he was not disposed to advocate the dissolution of the British Empire, any more than his friend and ally Charles Dilke whose recently published *Greater Britain* (1868) looked forward to the glories of a maturing Anglo-Saxon colonial system.

Fundamentally, Chamberlain was anxious to preserve British interests overseas, but only, he claimed, when there was justice in the pursuit and maintenance of such interests. In November 1875 he had reacted to Disraeli's *coup* in purchasing the Khedive of Egypt's shares in the Suez Canal Company by telling Morley that, 'The Tories have done a clever thing about the Suez Canal, and even *The Times* admits that it is unlikely that the Liberals would have been as wise or as plucky.'[138] At this stage, however, he was not even convinced that it was desirable, let alone just, to 'have a finger in the Egyptian pie'.[139]

As to the Afghan War, Chamberlain questioned the need for 'the scientific frontier' to Britain's Indian Empire so ardently advocated by those who favoured a forward policy. Nor was he convinced that the government's Near Eastern policy was clearly dedicated to upholding British interests, though he did try to distinguish between interests that were acceptable to him and those that were not:

> The Government said they would not interfere unless British interests were affected. He would not presume to say that this policy was a gospel of selfishness, because he did not know in what sense the words British interests were used. If they only meant a jealous fear lest our trade should be injured, then it was unworthy of us; but if, on the contrary, they meant that we had undertaken a vast responsibility in connection with our Indian Empire, whose happiness lay in the continued security of our rule, then he said that these were interests to guard, and, if necessary, to defend, even by the sword.[140]

Was the sword, then, to be put to equally firm use against the

Zulus, to promote a 'scientific frontier' for the British colony of Natal? Not that the Zulus were easy meat for British swords; in January 1879 they had annihilated their foes at the Battle of Isandhlwana, a humiliation which dealt a further blow to the credibility of Disraeli's expansionist policies. Chamberlain berated the government, and Sir Bartle Frere (Governor of Cape Colony and British High Commissioner for South Africa), for their part in launching the invasion of Zululand. Asking whether 'it was a crime for a nation to remain free and independent', and pointing out that 'there were signs that [the Bantu of Natal] now preferred to live under this intolerable tyranny of Cetewayo [the Zulu ruler] to remaining under the benificent government of the High Commissioner', Chamberlain asked the Conservative administration to consider seriously the necessary limits to imperial expansion:

We were undoubtedly the greatest colonizing nation on the face of the earth. Surely it was time for us to lay down clearly and plainly—to define accurately—the spirit and temper in which we were going to discharge the vast obligations which we had undertaken. Everywhere we held territories acquired in the first instance by aggression and conquest; everywhere, with a reputation which he was sure was not calculated to secure the love of our neighbours, we came into contact with tribes more or less savage, more or less independent, more or less powerful; and everywhere our Colonists called upon us to exert the whole force of this country in order to secure the proper subordination of those Native tribes to the handful of Englishmen who claimed the right to be supported by the whole power of the British Empire. He asked the House, where was this policy to stop? It seemed to him, if it went on as it had commenced, they would have very shortly the whole responsibility of the government of South Africa on their hands, as well as of vast areas of country in other parts of the world.[141]

This passage makes odd reading in the light of Chamberlain's subsequent bid to establish British supremacy in South Africa by force of arms and to push through elsewhere a programme of imperial consolidation. Circumstances had, of course, altered twenty years later, and the Boer War was, arguably, necessary in order to guarantee full civil rights for the thousands of British subjects who had emigrated to the Transvaal after 1886 in search of gold.

Moreover, the empire that Chamberlain subsequently wanted to consolidate consisted primarily of the English-speaking colonies and those tropical dependencies that seemed likely to repay British investment. In the late 1870s he did not consider the conquest of Zululand or Afghanistan essential to Britain's interests. Nor did India particularly attract him and in January 1876 he told Morley, in response to the latter's suggestion that one day he might aspire to be Secretary of State for India, 'I don't think I should like India. I am not cosmopolitan, and should prefer to try my hand on England.'[142]

Chamberlain gave the Commons an explanation of the circumstances which would justify Britain going to war in April 1878 when he spoke against the government calling out the army reserves three months before the Treaty of Berlin enabled Disraeli to claim that the Near Eastern crisis had resulted in 'peace with honour'. Chamberlain remarked that:

> He thought that he had said enough to show that, at all events, he was not an advocate of 'peace at any price.' He thought there were two cases in which a country was justified, and even called upon, to go into war—the one, in which, he believed, all were agreed—namely, when its interest or its security was really in danger from attack; and the other—on which there might be greater difference of opinion, for he held that great nations had duties and responsibilities like individuals, and there were times in which they were bound to fight, not for selfish British interests, but for great causes which were in danger, or great principles which were imperilled—in order to succour the oppressed, and do justice to the weak. Such a case had occurred when we had expended valuable lives in order to put down the barbarous and odious traffic in slaves. But he said that under present circumstances, neither of these conditions existed. Our interests were not seriously attacked, and our security was not endangered.[143]

While Chamberlain was making his mark in the House of Commons he still had his private life to lead. He took a variety of foreign holidays in the company of old and new friends. In 1876, shortly after entering Parliament, he was met by Jesse Collings in Cologne and then journeyed to Sweden (to investigate the 'Gothenburg system' of the municipal control of the sale of strong spirits) and on to Lapland where they 'lived on hermit's fare—milks, rusks, black bread, fish, etc., but no intoxicating drink, and no meat except some potted beef we had with us to season our frugal repasts.'[144] A year later he set out with John Morley for Salzburg; there they separated, Morley not sharing Chamberlain's taste for relentless activity and sightseeing, and the latter travelled to Innsbruck, Cortina, Venice (which was, he felt, imbued with a 'strange charm'), the Italian Lakes, Verona, Milan and Paris. In the French capital, Chamberlain called upon Louis Blanc but could not see him and had 'an interesting *quart d'heure* with Gambetta', the republican statesman then engaged in the struggle to deny President MacMahon a royalist majority in the elections to the Chamber.

At home, his young family enchanted visitors like John Bright, who early in 1880 asked him to 'Give a kind message from me to your sister and to your nice boy [Austen] and to those charming little girls who made so pleasant a picture in your house. I do not forget Charley [the dog] and his sweet temper, and whose companionship I quite envy.'[145]

The Chamberlain children, their early years so cruelly affected by the deaths of Harriet and Florence Chamberlain, were deeply dependent upon their aunts (from both sides of the family) for that consistency of love and affection that should encompass childhood. Both the Kenrick and the Chamberlain aunts, however, seem to have played the difficult role of surrogate mother with considerable success, even though Clara (Chamberlain's youngest sister) once greeted Neville Chamberlain on his return from a term at Rugby with the welcoming words 'Neville, your cap's crooked', thus causing him to vow he would never kiss her again.[146]

Chamberlain's burgeoning public career meant that he had little time for his children. Neville was to recall that 'For a good many years I respected and feared him more than I loved him.' Austen Chamberlain has also left a clear account of the enormous amount of work his father put into the composition of his speeches—often lengthy public speeches that were as essential to the task of publicising his views and policies as Baldwin's interwar radio chats, or the television exposure of modern times: 'in his early days he could only deliver one speech a month because it took him a fortnight to prepare it and a fortnight to recover from it. . . . Again and

again, I have known him shut himself up in his library from breakfast to lunch, from lunch to dinner, and again till the early hours
of the morning, and emerge at last with nothing definite accomplished. "I cannot get my line," he would say and he would admit
at times that in despair he had taken refuge in a French novel.'[147]

There was a certain coldness, a reserve, in Chamberlain's
relationship with his young children that is clearly reflected in a
sequence of letters sent to Austen, then aged twelve:

> You may as well take notice, once for all, that each of you
> [Beatrice and Austen] is to forward my letters to the other, as I
> can only write one every week.[148]
> My birthday is not till July 8th so you have been a little pre-
> mature with your good wishes. However I thank you for them
> all the same & also for the Knife & Pencil which I suppose you
> intended for me though you said nothing about it in your letter.[149]

One letter, however, reflects a wry humour, though mingled
with rebuke:

> Bye the bye you left a letter of Charlie Dixon's [George Dixon's
> son] behind you, & what do you think was in it?—'Come at once
> & we will have some brown-paper cigars. *N.B.* Don't say any-
> thing about the cigars'.
> If you are going to have secrets, I advise you not to leave your
> letters about open. As to brown paper cigars, I tried them a long
> time ago & very nasty they are. If you like them, I don't admire
> your taste.[150]

Chamberlain's attitude towards his children was partly founded
upon a natural reserve, but partly upon the fact that childbirth had
twice made him a widower. Whether consciously or not, there
seems little doubt that Chamberlain harboured resentments against
his children on that account. Austen was convinced that this was
the case, and recounted two incidents as evidence. The first
occurred after Chamberlain became engaged to Mary Endicott
who became his third wife in 1888. One evening he began to talk
to Austen about the latter's mother, prompting him to say, 'Do
you know, Sir, that this is the first time that you have ever spoken
to me about my mother?' Chamberlain replied, 'Yes, I know. Until
happiness came again into my life, I did not dare to—and even
now I can't do it without the tears coming into my eyes.'[151]

The second incident can be related in Austen Chamberlain's own words:

> It was one day in my 'teens that I spoke critically to him of a friend of his, left early a widower with an only child. 'He doesn't seem to care much for the boy,' I said, 'or to see much of him,' and my father, quick as always in a friend's defence, blurted out before he saw the implication of what he was saying, 'You must remember that his mother died when the boy was born,' and in a flash I saw for the first time, what he had so carefully concealed from me, that in my earliest years I had been to him the living embodiment of the first tragedy of his life.[152]

Chamberlain's apparent success (amazing though this may seem) in masking such powerful private feelings was in odd contrast to the voluble expression of his political views—many of which were so provocative as to earn him a considerable notoriety among the established sections of society. As the recognised spokesman of the National Liberal Federation, he whipped up enthusiasm among his audiences at public meetings with uninhibited thrusts such as ' "Peace with Honour" is really peace with humbug.' *The Times* strongly disapproved of his 'Billingsgate' turn of phrase, and other journals reviled him for his forthright views.

. As yet Ireland, with its simmering problems and discontents, had not called for Chamberlain's 'Billingsgate' talents. Home Rule and land reform were, however, issues which threatened to be markedly more prominent in Westminster's deliberations after the emergence by 1877 of Parnell as the leader of an Irish party committed to achieving their 'national right to self-government'.

John Morley was convinced, from the outset of their friendship, that Chamberlain was 'never a Home Ruler'.[153] Certainly the latter was anxious for a reforming Land Bill and ready to concede a measure of self-government to the Irish nationalists, but during his Sheffield election campaign of 1874 he had publicly repudiated the idea of a separation that would threaten the integrity of the United Kingdom.[154] In 1877, amid Irish attempts to obstruct Parliament's legislative programme, he told John Morley, 'I fear you have a half-kindness for these rascally Irishmen who are bound to give us a great deal of trouble yet, and perhaps to force on the English Parliament that 'Iron Hand' or system of clôture [the guillotine] which has been found necessary in almost every other deliberative assembly.'[155]

After he had made common cause with Irish M.P.s in his opposition to the Army Discipline Bill, Chamberlain (together with Dilke) explored the possibilities of promoting 'a more cordial understanding between English Radicals and the Irish National Party', in a meeting with Parnell and Major Nolan in February 1879. No parliamentary alliance emerged from this meeting, but Chamberlain summed up Parnell as 'less opportunist and more irreconcilable than Nolan. He insisted on the importance of the Home Rule question, and was opposed to any arrangement that would prevent or hinder the prosecution of the national movement by the Irish party.'[156] A few months later, writing anonymously in the *Birmingham Daily Post*, Chamberlain said of Parnell, 'It is impossible to exaggerate the industry of this gentleman—not to admire his unflinching determination in what he believes to be right—his courage, his coolness.'[157] This might well have been a description of the writer himself, which may explain the respect Chamberlain felt for Parnell at this time.

The Irish tempest, however, had not yet begun to blow full force when Disraeli announced on 8 March 1880 the dissolution of Parliament and a General Election. In November 1879 Chamberlain had written cheerily to Dilke, 'Things look bad for the Tories. We shall have a majority at the next election I feel confident.'[158]

He returned to Birmingham for three weeks strenuous campaigning before the election day on 31 March. The Conservatives concentrated their most ferocious attacks upon him, and he told Collings as the campaign neared its close, 'Nothing can exceed the virulence with which the Tories have attacked me. No slander has been too gross—no calumny too improbable.'[159] Despite the publication on polling day of a fictitious Conservative placard showing their candidates comfortably ahead at 12 o'clock, the Caucus made sure of a comprehensive victory and the final result was:

Muntz, P. H.	(L.)	22,969	elected
Bright, John	(L.)	20,079	
Chamberlain, J.	(L.)	19,544	
Burnaby, Major Fred.	(C.)	15,735	not elected
Calthorpe, Hon. A. C. G.	(C.)	14,308	

Chamberlain's inferior showing to Muntz and Bright may have been caused both by the Tory assault upon him and by his comparative notoriety. He was certainly galled by the result, especially after his mayoral reforms for the town, but John Bright hastened to comfort him: 'Don't give yourself a moment's annoyance about it. In this world men often suffer for their virtues as well, and as much, as from their vices.'[160]

Polling throughout the country closed on 3 April. The final result was a crushing victory for the Liberals in terms of seats won from the Conservatives—over 100—giving them an overall Commons majority of about 110 seats, or 176 if the Parnellites were counted as allies. In terms of the popular vote, the election was a much closer contest, and it has been estimated that a mere 4,054 votes lost to the Liberals would have cost them seventy-two marginal seats.

In the counties as well as the boroughs, however, the Liberals did well enough to secure their greatest majority since Victoria ascended the throne in 1837. What part had Chamberlain's National Liberal Federation played in this triumph? In the sixty constituencies where there were Liberal organisations affiliated to the Federation, the Liberals won twenty-eight of them from sitting Conservatives, though elsewhere six seats were lost despite similarly active local organisations. Chamberlain and Schnadhorst were to claim striking success for the Caucus, not only in the boroughs, but also in ten counties where it carried the day.

Other factors, however, were at work. Gladstone's impassioned Midlothian campaign undoubtedly touched some tender middle-class consciences though in his newly-chosen Scottish constituency he triumphed by 1,579 votes to 1,368, a remarkably slender majority of 211. The Eastern question, Disraeli's controversial forays into Zululand, Afghanistan and the Transvaal, the falling export trade and economic depression, allied, as always, with a host of local issues, all contributed to the defeat of the Conservatives. There is evidence, too, that the Nonconformist vote returned strongly to the Liberal cause after the confusion of 1874, a development for which Chamberlain could take some credit.

Who would lead the new Liberal government? Hartington was still the party's leader, though his standing had shrivelled in the heat of Gladstone's Midlothian resurgence. The Queen had no wish to have Gladstone as Prime Minister once more and wrote

that 'she would sooner abdicate than send for or have anything to
do with that half-mad firebrand who would soon ruin everything
and be a Dictator.' Nonetheless there seemed to be no viable
alternative to Gladstone, and a reluctant Queen summoned the
Midlothian ogre to kiss hands.

Chamberlain had made it clear to Sir William Harcourt as early
as January 1880 that 'I had no doubt the balance of advantage
would be greatly in favour of Gladstone's lead—though I did not
conceal my own personal feeling that he would be King Stork, and
that some of us frogs would have a hard time of it under him.'[161]
But would King Stork now find a position in his Cabinet for the
most persuasive and powerful of the Radical frogs?

SIX

CABINET MINISTER
1880–5

The victory which has just been won is the victory of the Radicals—
Gladstone and the Caucus have triumphed all along the line, and it
is the strong, definite, decided policy which has commended itself
and not the halting half-hearted arm-chair business.

Chamberlain to Dilke, 1880

GLADSTONE TOOK office on 23 April 1880 hoping that
his personal return to power would be merely a temporary
interlude necessary to untangle the worst results of Disraeli's excesses and in particular to reconstruct 'the whole spirit
and effect' of the nation's foreign policy. Given the Liberals' handsome overall majority, the government's path towards certain
reforms at home and a dignified and effective handling of foreign
affairs seemed, at first sight, to be straight enough.

In the event, Gladstone's second ministry provided an un-
edifying spectacle of Cabinet division, confusion over aims, and
bouts of unpopularity so severe that stones were hurled through
the windows of 10 Downing Street when the news of General
Gordon's death at Khartoum reached England. Gladstone's failure
to guide his ministers effectively resulted partly from his inability
to conduct Cabinet business efficiently and to communicate his
views with unfailing clarity, and partly from the deep ideological
schisms that characterised the ministry. Far too often Cabinet
meetings produced indecision and vacillation, and after a while the
Prime Minister decided to summon as few as possible and thereafter tried to conduct the government's business by a wearisome
process of personal contact and intervention. This in turn contributed further to ministerial schism, since Hartington and the
Whigs, on the one hand, and Chamberlain, the new Radical
representative, on the other, felt able (and indeed sometimes
obliged) to pursue independent courses.

Chamberlain's place in a Cabinet dominated by those Whig

grandees for whom Gladstone, in essence, felt so much regard was by no means certain in the aftermath of the General Election. Gladstone was quite well aware that Chamberlain had exploited the public outcry over the Bulgarian massacres chiefly for the purpose of promoting Radical solidarity; nor did he unreservedly welcome the growing power of the National Liberal Federation, though he had blessed it at its baptism; moreover, the Radical future conjured up by advanced Liberals in 1880 repelled rather than attracted him. In any case, Chamberlain had been in the House of Commons for less than four years and if expediency demanded a Cabinet place for a Radical other than the aging totem John Bright, then Dilke, with his baronetcy, his cosmopolitan sophistication and his diplomatic and foreign policy skills, was an extremely strong candidate.

As it turned out, by the end of April 1880 it was Chamberlain who had a seat in the Cabinet as President of the Board of Trade and Dilke who remained outside, though in the relatively prestigious post of Under Secretary for Foreign Affairs. Chamberlain's remarkable promotion was seen by some Radicals to be at Dilke's expense, and for years there were to be murmurs that somehow Chamberlain had contrived his own advancement by means not altogether honourable.

The events which preceded Chamberlain's appointment as President of the Board of Trade are complex and open to differing interpretations. Before examining them, it must be pointed out how strong were Chamberlain's claims for Cabinet office: his power-base in the country was extremely impressive and founded upon his evident capacity to speak nationally for Nonconformists and Radicals and, more practically, upon his authority within the National Liberal Federation—the organisation that was widely credited with the party's victory in the General Election. Any incoming Liberal Prime Minister would have been well advised to nurture Chamberlain, though this is something that Gladstone eventually failed miserably to do—to his own and his party's cost.

In a sense, Chamberlain engineered his entry into the Cabinet through his own initiative. On 4 April with the election results still coming in and pointing unmistakably to a Liberal victory, he wrote to Dilke proposing a joint policy to the question of administrative office:

My Dear Dilke,

I find the same fault with your letters that the Scotch laird found with the dictionary—'the storres are vara pretty but they are unco[mmon] short'.

The time has come when we must have a full and frank explanation.

What I should like—what I hope for with you—is a thorough offensive and defensive alliance and in this case our position will be immensely strong.

I am prepared to refuse all offices until and unless *both of us are satisfied*.

Can you accept this position with perfect satisfaction? If you think I am asking more than I can give I rely on your saying so.... I shall support your claims cordially and just as warmly as if I were personally interested.

But my own feeling is that if you are stronger than I am in the House, my influence is greater than yours out of it—and therefore, that, together, we are much more powerful than separated; and that in the short time—if not now—we may make our own terms. To join a Govt. as subordinate members—to be silenced and to have no real influence on policy—would be fatal to both of us. If we both remain outside, any Government will have to reckon with us and on the whole this would be the position which on many grounds I should prefer.

I am ready to make all allowances for the difficulties in the way of giving to both of us the only kind of place which it would be worth our while to accept. If these are insuperable, I will give a hearty support to any Government which is thoroughly liberal in its measures; but I am not going to play the part of a Radical minnow among Whig Tritons....

You will see that my proposed condition is—both of us to be satisfied.

As to what *ought* to satisfy us, if you agree to the principle, we will consult when the time comes, but my present impression is—All or Nothing.[162]

Dilke replied next day, agreeing on the desirability of continuing to work together and that each should see the other was satisfied. He declared that, 'My first enquiry when I hear anything will be— what about you?' He added, however, a cautionary note: 'The real difficulty will arise if they offer the Cabinet to one of us, and high office outside it with a promise of the first vacancy in it to the other.'[163]

Two days later Dilke left for Toulon for a fortnight's holiday. Did this decision to absent himself at such a crucial time reflect a relaxed and honourable attitude towards the imminent Cabinet-making, or the belief that the Queen would insist on either Hartington or Lord Granville as Prime Minister and in that event his own place in the Cabinet was assured? Certainly Victoria was, at this stage, twisting and turning to avoid summoning Gladstone to Windsor. Gladstone's own position was not clear, moreover, though on 18 April John Bright told Chamberlain that he thought their former leader would take the premiership if pressed.

On 16 April Chamberlain told Morley that 'I wish Dilke were at home. . . . I doubt if it is worth his while to go in alone, and if we are both outside we should be very strong. If, however, the temptation is too strong for him, I should not press him to stay outside for me, but should let him follow his own inclination.'[164]

What was Chamberlain up to? Was his own ambition so well under control that he could stand by and let Dilke 'follow his own inclination'? During the next few days there was little for him to be certain of, though at one stage it seemed as if he was likely to be offered the important junior post of Financial Secretary to the Treasury. On 24 April Dilke, having returned the previous day, told him that 'Gladstone disapproves of people being put straight into the Cabinet who've not held office'; he also invited Chamberlain to come and discuss the prospect of both of them holding important non-Cabinet office. Chamberlain refused to come down from Birmingham, and Dilke replied, somewhat piqued, 'If I were not so tired with my journey I'd come down. You see you talk of consultation but I can't consult you by telegraph, and in Gladstone's stand and deliver kind of business there is no time for exchange of letters with Birmingham.'[165]

On receiving Dilke's letter, Chamberlain relented and journeyed down to London where the two men agreed that it was essential for one of them to be in the Cabinet. But which one? A day or two later, Chamberlain told Sir William Harcourt (who was acting as a go-between for Gladstone and several leading Liberals) that 'personally I did not care a damn, and would rather be out, in which case I would endeavour to organise a "Pure Left" party in the House and the country, which should support the Government if they brought in Radical measures and oppose them everywhere if they did not. The result would be the running of Radical candidates in all borough elections.'[166]

Before this bombshell could explode in Gladstone's face, the Liberal leader called for Dilke and offered him the Under Secretaryship at the Foreign Office, at the same time intimating that Chamberlain might well be offered the post of Financial Secretary to the Treasury. Dilke declined the offer made to him, and pressed for a Cabinet place for either Chamberlain or himself.

Gladstone subsequently saw Harcourt, who spelt out Chamberlain's threat of a Radical separatist revolt, with the running of Radical candidates in borough elections. This was an extremely alarming prospect for an incoming Prime Minister constructing a Cabinet top-heavy with Whigs; it would cause a party split, and an intensification of class conflict. John Bright, who had accepted the Duchy of Lancaster, meanwhile urged Chamberlain's claims on Gladstone, and argued that the latter should be brought into the Cabinet as President of the Board of Trade.[167]

On 27 April, Gladstone once more called Dilke to him and told him the surprising news that Chamberlain had been offered by letter the Presidency of the Board of Trade with Cabinet rank. Dilke then accepted the Under-Secretaryship for Foreign Affairs and went off to the Reform Club to tell Chamberlain the news. Chamberlain, who had not received the letter, went straightway to see Gladstone, who repeated the offer. With the offer now safely made, Chamberlain was able to demur; he spoke highly of Dilke, and even talked of them both serving in minor office. Gladstone, however, still maintained his original offer, which he said owed much to Bright's urging. Chamberlain then sought time to consult Bright; this was granted, and Bright encouraged him to accept Gladstone's offer.

So Chamberlain was in the Cabinet. Less than four years previously he had been Mayor of Birmingham, and his meteoric rise was resented by many, as he himself had anticipated:

As I expected, the announcement . . . excited a good deal of discontent and ill-feeling. Dilke himself, although he must have been disappointed at not receiving the offer of a higher office, behaved admirably; but there were many other Radicals who thought that their claims were as good or better than any that I could put forward and were inclined to resent the quick promotion which I had, however, unwillingly secured.[168]

On 30 April Chamberlain took over the Board of Trade, after a lengthy discussion with his predecessor Lord Sandon. On 3 May he journeyed to Windsor, which he had never seen before, to kiss hands on his appointment to Cabinet post. This was the first meeting between the Radical, allegedly republican, spokesman for the labouring masses and the Queen-Empress, granddaughter of George III. Chamberlain wrote his sister Clara an amusing account of the occasion when 'Fawcett, Mundella and myself were introduced to Royalty—and 3 dangerous Radicals were made Ministers of the Crown.' The party that left for Windsor by special train at 12.10 p.m., included Gladstone and Lord Granville (who had already reassured the Queen that 'Chamberlain is not as strong as is supposed, but an admirable organiser with pleasing manners.')[169]

Eventually Chamberlain and the incoming ministers were taken into a little square room where they 'knelt on one knee . . . and took the oath of allegiance, and then a small, fat, red hand was thrust quickly under each of our noses and respectfully mumbled by us.' This made him a Privy Councillor. Within twenty minutes he had kissed hands again as President of the Board of Trade. 'I had hardly seen the Queen since I stood near her when she opened Aston Park some 20 years ago or more, and of course I could not see much resemblance to her former self. She looked a quiet little Lady of 60 which I suppose she is—and was dressed in black or some dark colour and a widow's cap.'[170]

As the ministers made their way back to the station, Gladstone 'expressed his astonishment and delight at the verdict of the country—and said it was the first time in our history when the English people had not been for a War Minister and a war policy. . . . In the afternoon I attended my first Cabinet Council—much like a Board of Directors only the business discussed is more important and the consequences of mistake more serious.'[171]

Chamberlain's inclusion in the Government necessitated the finding of a permanent home in London. By 16 May he had found 72 Prince's Gate in Knightsbridge where he soon moved his sister Clara and his children, and wrote to tell Jesse Collings 'I have a new butler and have ordered a new coachman and a new carriage and a new footman and a new Court suit.' These were perhaps unlikely trappings for the Radical spokesman for the urban poor, but Chamberlain wasted no time in assuming them.

In November of the same year, moreover, he changed his home in Birmingham, moving from Southbourne to a newly-constructed house at Moor Green. The new house, which he named 'Highbury' in remembrance of his family's former home in London, was built in 'the hideous roomy Victorian-Gothic style, with a vast hall of arches, stained glass and inlaid woods.'[172] 'Highbury' was a powerful symbol of Chamberlain's worldly success, if not a tribute to his good taste. It was also, with its magnificent gardens, its greenhouses, its surrounding water and woods, a place where a great man (a man, some said, one day destined to be Prime Minister) could play the host, and relax with his family. Chamberlain's children came to delight in the luxury and space that characterised 'Highbury', and relished the house's proximity to their cousins in Birmingham's Unitarian clan—including the nine children of their uncle Arthur Chamberlain, and the four of another uncle William Kenrick.

At the outset of his ministerial career, Chamberlain imagined that as the chief Radical representative in the Cabinet and as the power behind the National Liberal Federation his voice would carry considerable weight. Furthermore, he was still closely allied with Dilke and took pains to keep him informed of Cabinet proceedings; Dilke, for his part, put his own expertise in foreign and colonial matters at his colleague's disposal. Both men had, in addition, close contacts with the press, and were prepared to use such contacts. The *Birmingham Daily Post* was a loyal Chamberlainite journal, and Chamberlain had, moreover, the ear of T. H. S. Escott who wrote for the influential Conservative *Standard* (with a circulation of some 150,000). Dilke was in close contact with Frank Hill, editor of the small-selling but important *Daily News*, and both he and Chamberlain kept in confidential touch with John Morley, editor of the *Pall Mall Gazette*.

Despite these advantages Chamberlain's first attempt to shape the policy of the new government was rebuffed:

In the first discussion as to the general policy of the Government I stood alone in urging a complete reversal of the general policy of Lord Beaconsfield [Disraeli] which I maintained had been condemned by the nation. I wanted to recall at once Sir Bartle Frere [Governor of Cape Colony and High Commissioner for South Africa], to reconsider the annexation of the Transvaal [annexed in 1877] and to recall Sir Henry Elliot [British ambassador in Vienna]. For none of these proposals could I meet with any support at the time. I also urged the importance of dealing immediately with the question of the extension of the franchise, but Mr. Gladstone considered that this subject, entailing as it would a new dissolution, ought to be deferred till towards the end of the Parliament just elected. It was accordingly decided in the short session which was about to commence that certain minor, although important questions should be immediately dealt with, leaving questions of greater magnitude, and especially legislation for Ireland, to the succeeding session.[173]

Chamberlain's instincts were sound enough for the promotion of a Radical programme and also of his own interests: clear up Disraeli's mess in southern Africa, and take a tighter grip on Near Eastern affairs; next an extension of the rural franchise, together with land reform in Ireland; then an appeal to the country on the basis of these reforms (or if the House of Lords chose to block the franchise bill) and a decisive Radical victory as a result. The new electorate, therefore, would eventually be the means by which advanced Radical aims could be achieved and Chamberlain's own ambitions realised.

But even if Chamberlain's counsel had been sympathetically received by the Cabinet, the administration was preoccupied until 1883 with the eruption of the Irish troubles, and plagued by such external distractions as the Transvaal rebellion of 1880–1 and the 1882 invasion of Egypt. Before discussing the impact of these events upon Chamberlain's career, however, his work as President of the Board of Trade must be described.

Although Chamberlain had been a strikingly successful businessman and industrialist, he displayed understandable anxieties at being pitch-forked into a ministerial post that was full of mysteries, and told a friend 'If I could only have a recess before Parliament meets I should be quite *au fait* by that time. As it is, I dread having to reply to questions, and speak on subjects that I do not fully understand.'[174] In December 1880 he confessed in a speech at Birmingham that, 'I never spent a more anxious time in my life than in the few days that followed my acceptance. . . . I like the office which has been conferred upon me. I find the work congenial to me, and I find an ever-fresh interest in the many fresh subjects with which I am brought into close acquaintance. . . . When I first commenced, I found myself face to face with a hundred questions, many of them involving many technical details of which I humbly confess I was profoundly ignorant; and if I was saved from making mistakes which would have been humiliating, I owe it to the care and knowledge and intelligence of the permanent officials of my department.'[175]

Such initial anxieties as were felt by Chamberlain were soon resolved by his customary hard work and attention to detail. The Presidency of the Board of Trade, by tradition an office not much in demand among aspiring ministers, also offered considerable scope for personal initiative, since its duties and functions were not always clear-cut. There were, however, several departments within the Board: the Railway Department, the Commercial Department, the Marine Department, the Harbour Department and the Financial Department. The Commercial Department was the one to benefit most from Chamberlain's term of office, for he not only increased the amount of vital statistical work undertaken by the department, but also went far to restore many of the functions that had been transferred to the Foreign Office in 1872.

Chamberlain had two able senior civil servants to lean on in his early days at the Board: Thomas Farrer, the Permanent Secretary, and Robert Giffen, head of the statistical section. Farrer was struck, at the outset, by the new President's ignorance 'of all economic questions', but Chamberlain proved to be a fiercely loyal minister, badgering Gladstone to make Farrer a Knight Commander of the Bath rather than a more lowly Commander of the Bath, and pressing for C.B.'s to be conferred on Messrs. Gray and Trevor, Assistant-Secretaries at the Board of Trade. It is interesting, in view of the President's willingness to champion his civil servants, that both Farrer and Giffen, as staunch free traders, subsequently steadfastly opposed Chamberlain's campaign for tariff reform.

After little more than a year in office, Chamberlain proposed a radical re-ordering of his department's work when he submitted a Cabinet memorandum entitled 'Minister of Agriculture and Commerce'. This memorandum was a response to proposals put forward earlier by Sir Massey Lopes in May 1881, and which suggested that agriculture and commerce should be administered as a single department under a minister of the crown. Chamberlain argued that agriculture and commerce should not be put into the same administrative harness, but that a Ministry of Commerce should be created. The new ministry would absorb the work of the Board of Trade (which would be abolished), and would be responsible for formulating legislation and answering parliamentary questions on bankruptcy, partnership, patents, trade marks, design copyrights and all other matters affecting trade and commercial legislation.[176] Nothing came of Chamberlain's proposal for a Ministry of Commerce, and eight months later Earl Spencer, then Lord President of the Council, also rejected the idea of a separate Ministry of Agriculture.[177]

Parliamentary time between 1880 and 1883 was devoured by Ireland, Egypt, the Bradlaugh controversy and other issues, all of which left Chamberlain little opportunity to introduce a full quota of departmental legislation. In the first two sessions of Parliament, however, he introduced a Grain Cargoes Bill, for the safer stowing of these cargoes, a Seaman's Wages Bill, to secure a fairer system of payment, and an Electric Lighting Bill, which enabled municipalities to set up electricity supplies either themselves or through private companies. The latter measure provoked the criticism that its clause enabling the municipality to re-purchase private electricity undertakings at the end of a twenty-one-year period discouraged private investment in the expanding industry; in 1888 the Act was amended, and the period in dispute extended to forty-two years.

In 1883, however, Chamberlain harvested some more impressive legislative fruit. The first of these was a Bankruptcy Bill which sought, through the establishment of a Bankruptcy Department in the Board of Trade and the appointment of sixty-seven official receivers, to introduce the practice of swift and rigorous enquiry and action into failed business dealings. The Tories claimed that the Bill encouraged the spread of bureaucracy, but Chamberlain told the House of Commons during the second reading that the Bill 'does not lend itself to flights of eloquence; but it is a question which has deep interest for great masses of our people, and especially for the great body of industrious tradesmen who see, with natural indignation, that under the present system swindling is made so easy, so safe, and so profitable.'[178]

A Patents Bill was also passed in this session of Parliament and became law on the same day as the Bankruptcy Act. Chamberlain, who had become rich through the American woodscrew patent and who had dealt a great deal with the problems of patenting at Nettlefold and Chamberlain, proposed to bring the whole area under the supervision of the Board of Trade, and to encourage even the poorest inventors by drastically reducing the fees for the examination and protection of projects.

With both these Bills made law Chamberlain wrote to Gladstone on 15 August 1883 to say that the Acts 'will largely increase the importance and responsibility of the Board of Trade which will be charged in each case with a difficult and complex administration.'[179] John Morley, who had newly entered Parliament as member for Newcastle on Tyne, also wrote his congratulations: 'It has been a triumphant session for you, and therefore for your friends.'

Neither of these Acts were likely to set the electorate alight with enthusiasm. More controversial was the Merchant Shipping Bill, which Chamberlain introduced in the 1884 session of Parliament. The main object of the Bill was to ensure that shipowners should maintain their vessels in a high standard of seaworthiness and should be prevented from over-insuring their craft and hence from collecting inflated compensation when 'coffin ships' went to the bottom of the sea. In proposing this legislation, Chamberlain kept close counsel with Samuel Plimsoll, M.P. for Derby, a vehement defender of seamens' interests, and the proposer of the famous safety 'line' which bears his name. The Bill aroused the determined opposition of the shipowners (Liberal as well as Conservative) who organised a national campaign against Chamberlain's proposals. The latter was vilified in the press, at public meetings and in pamphlets. For his part Chamberlain was convinced that the Bill should become law, telling Morley in February 1884 'The more I look into the question the more I am horrified at the callous cupidity which has been fostered by a bad law and is producing untold misery.' During the Bill's second reading in May he spoke for nearly four hours, piling fact upon fact, producing a damning catalogue, naming ships that had sunk and spelling out the profits made through over-insurance. The National Liberal Federation reprinted a million copies of this speech.

Chamberlain summed up the abuses he was trying to eliminate, and the strength of the shipowners, in a letter to Gladstone on 6 March 1884:

> There has grown up a pernicious system of joint stock ship owning & the managers of these companies have spread their nets far & wide, especially in the North of England, & have secured a number of small shareholders who know nothing of shipping but are tempted by the promise of dividends of 40% with no possibility of loss if the ship goes to the bottom. The system is answerable for a great loss of life, but the existence of these widely scattered interests is the strength of the Parliamentary influence of the shipowners.
>
> I fear it is impossible to divide the Bill. The shipowners object to everything which would be of the least use in saving life, & the rest is of no pressing importance.[180]

The Bill was, however, doomed. The government was not prepared to throw its whole weight behind it, and many Liberal M.P.'s were hostile—though the 'Fourth Party', a splinter group of Tory Democrats, including Lord Randolph Churchill and Sir John Gorst, supported Chamberlain. In July 1884 the Bill was withdrawn, and, a little later, Chamberlain's Railways Regulation Bill met the same fate.

Chamberlain was also concerned, while President of the Board of Trade, with the negotiations for an Anglo-French commercial treaty, though Dilke bore much of the responsibility for the making of the treaty and kept him fully informed of developments. Chamberlain proved himself a fierce defender of British commercial interests, telling Gladstone in October 1881, when negotiations broke down, that they should not be resumed unless the French were 'prepared to give us at least the status quo, or its equivalent, in regard to cottons and woollens. . . . I am sure that we are better with no treaty at all than with one which could leave these two great industries in a worse position than at present.'[181]

Both Dilke and Chamberlain were ready to force France to bring down her protectionist tariff against British goods by threatening to give favourable treatment to wines imported from Spain, Portugal and Italy. The negotiations for the French treaty brought into focus Chamberlain's views on free trade. In August 1881 in the House of Commons, Chamberlain had vigorously denounced any alteration in the free trade system that would lead, through raising tariffs against imported food, to 'food taxes': 'If this course is ever taken, and if the depression were to continue or to recur, it would be the signal for a state of things more dangerous and more disastrous than anything which has been seen in this country since the repeal of the Corn Laws.'[182]

Though Chamberlain here recoiled from the prospect of working-class discontent (and electoral disenchantment) with higher food prices, he was by no means an unsullied Cobdenite free trader. Publicly he showed no sympathy for the M.P. for Preston, Farrer Ecroyd, and his neo-protectionist agitation against 'free imports without free trade'. Despite this coolness towards the 'Fair Trade' lobby (the National Fair Trade League had been set up in May 1881), Chamberlain, according to Dilke, was not only strongly in favour of reciprocal international commercial agreements, but also, as early as April 1882 had shown himself to be 'a Protectionist or at least a strong Reciprocitarian', and had argued that 'there was a chance that some day there would be formed a British Zollverein [customs' union], raising discriminating duties upon foreign produce as against that of the British Empire.'[183]

Even after allowances have been made for the eventual personal and political estrangement of Dilke and Chamberlain, this evidence makes it clear that the latter's approach to fiscal matters even in the early 1880s was not one of free trade orthodoxy. Chamberlain was evidently, at least in private, contemplating the merits of the free trade system and, as befitted his pragmatic and imaginative qualities, aware of the system's failings. The tariff reform campaign of Chamberlain's later years did not, therefore, materialise, fully-fashioned, out of the thin air of early Edwardian politics, as a blatant response to current economic and political needs. The ideas were germinating twenty years before.

One other preoccupation of Chamberlain's Presidency of the Board of Trade is worthy of note. A Channel Tunnel was advocated both in France, and in Britain, by a pressure group, headed by Sir Edward Watkin. Preliminary diggings had taken place at Dover, and Chamberlain inspected them. He did not, however, look kindly upon the project in either his official or his private capacity, telling Gladstone bleakly in July 1883: 'I do not think that any encouragement should be given to Sir E. Watkin. I do not believe that the French Company will be so foolish as to spend money in tunnelling

under the Channel, without any assurance that they will be allowed
to come out on English soil.'[184]

Chamberlain's tenure of office at the Board of Trade was undoubtedly marked by a sense of frustration at his failure to place
more than a modest quota of legislation upon the statute books.
For a man who had recently manipulated the well-oiled machine
of Birmingham's municipal government with such dexterity, the
feeling of frustration must have been particularly galling.

Board of Trade business was not, however, Chamberlain's sole
justification for political activity. His prodigious energies were
simultaneously engaged elsewhere—in promoting his own brand
of Radicalism, and in reacting to any number of developments,
both domestic and overseas. Indeed, if an examination is made of
his correspondence during the years of his Presidency it is clear
that his political involvement was remarkably widespread; of his
letters to the Prime Minister, for example, only a relatively small
percentage deal with matters relating to the Board of Trade. In
short, Chamberlain, as had so many others before him, viewed the
Board as a stepping-stone for higher things. In May 1882, for
instance, Chamberlain, despite subsequent disclaimers, was more
than ready to leave the Board of Trade for the Chief Secretaryship
for Ireland, following W. E. Forster's resignation from that post.
Given Chamberlain's intense concern for the Irish troubles which
had so embarrassingly emerged during the first years of the second
Gladstone administration, it seemed to many that he was the man
ideally suited to the post.

The growth of agitation in southern Ireland, led by the Land
League, for the 'three F's'—fair rents, fixity of tenure, and free
sale—reflected the grievances of the rural Catholic Irish, overwhelmingly small-holders or peasants, against the supremacy of
absentee and home-grown Anglo-Irish landlords. Chamberlain
admitted in a speech at Birmingham in October 1880, a few months
after taking office, that 'The Government came into power pledged
up to the eyes to do justice to Ireland. They were bound, if
possible, to find some means of giving to the 600,000 tenants in
Ireland some right and interest in the soil which they tilled, which
should not be in the power of absentee landlords.'[185]

Chamberlain believed that Irish agrarian crime and Fenian
outrages in England could be snuffed out by a generous Land Bill.
He was also convinced that such a settlement would, as Parnell

the Irish Nationalist leader, feared, deal a death blow to the Home Rule movement. Even in 1880 Chamberlain was opposed to Irish Home Rule, refusing to see Ireland separated from the United Kingdom, and taking the view that this would logically lead to the disintegration of the union and the Empire.

In the early months of Gladstone's government, therefore, Chamberlain resolutely opposed any further 'coercion' of Irish malcontents. In particular in November 1880 he threatened to resign rather than accept Forster's proposal to suspend habeas corpus in Ireland, arguing 'I think the proposal of Mr. Forster's so wrong in principle and so bad in policy that I could not conscientiously give it even a silent support.'[186] Although Chamberlain was to become notorious for threats of resignation (and not merely to Gladstone), this dramatic intervention from so junior a recruit to the Cabinet plainly indicates the strength of his feeling that coercion *before* the introduction of a Land Bill would provoke still more and unnecessary opposition in Ireland. Once land reforms were passed, any Irish who still agitated could be shown to be unreasonable. As Chamberlain told Gladstone in December 1880, 'if the Government Bill includes the 3 F's it will be accepted by all but the few extreme men who are not Land reformers at all, but Fenians & rebels using the Land question for their own purposes.'[187]

In 1881 a Land Act incorporating the three F's was indeed passed as Chamberlain had advocated. The Irish Nationalists, however, declared the Act a sham and began to encourage tenants to withhold rents unless they were based upon the primitive, 'prairie value' of the land.[188] As a result the Irish leaders Parnell, Dillon, Sexton and O'Kelly were arrested and placed in Kilmainham Gaol on 13 October 1881.

Chamberlain had by now become convinced that there should be no more concessions leading to separation or any meaningful form of Home Rule. He supported the gaoling of Parnell and his followers at Kilmainham, and on 25 October declared in a speech at Liverpool, 'I say to Ireland what the Liberals or Republicans of the North said to the Southern States of America, "The Union must be preserved." Within these limits there is nothing which you may not ask and hope to obtain. Equal laws, equal justice, equal opportunities, equal prosperity—these shall be freely accorded to you . . . but nature and your position have forged indissoluble links which cannot be sundered without being fraught

with consequences of misery and ruin to both our countries, and
which, therefore, we shall use all the resources of the Empire to
keep intact.'[189]

Within this firm framework, Chamberlain was prepared to work
tirelessly to reconcile the Irish leaders to the continuation of the
union. In April 1882 Chamberlain and Captain O'Shea acted as
go-betweens in negotiations which produced the so-called 'Kilmainham Treaty', an understanding by which the government
undertook to release Parnell and the other imprisoned leaders and
to legislate to help Irish tenants pay their arrears in rent, in return
for Parnell's dropping of the No Rent Manifesto and his cooperation
in making the Land Act work. Chamberlain thought this deal 'and
Mr. Parnell's new attitude could settle the Irish question.'[190]

The Irish question, alas, could not be so easily solved. Forster
resigned as Chief Secretary for Ireland rather than agree to
Parnell's release. But the new Chief Secretary, Lord Frederick
Cavendish, went to Ireland with Lord Spencer, the newly-
appointed Viceroy, to try to promote the programme of conciliation
that Chamberlain had helped to negotiate. Parnell and the other
leaders were let out of Kilmainham on 2 May, but on 6 May Lord
Cavendish, and a senior British official, were stabbed to death by
Irish terrorists in Phoenix Park.

The compromise of the 'Kilmainham treaty' was now in ruins
and Parnell's recent moderation rendered useless. Parnell, and
Justin McCarthy, indeed called upon Chamberlain at Prince's Gate
in the immediate aftermath of the Phoenix Park murders, where
Chamberlain recorded that 'Parnell was white as a sheet, agitated
and completely demoralised. . . . "They will strike at me next,"
were his words. He asked me, "What shall I do—what can I
do?" '[191]

Following Lord Cavendish's murder Chamberlain was again
passed over as Chief Secretary, though he warmly approved of the
new appointee, the Radical Sir George Otto Trevelyan. Why was
Chamberlain not appointed Chief Secretary on either opportunity
in May 1882? Chamberlain himself advocated Shaw, an Irish
M.P., in a letter to Gladstone on 2 May the day that Forster's
resignation was announced;[192] he also urged Morley to press for
Shaw's promotion. Parnell, O'Shea, Dilke and others all believed
that Chamberlain should, and would, be offered the appointment.
After Lord Frederick Cavendish's assassination there was renewed

speculation that Chamberlain would be made Chief Secretary. On 7 May Chamberlain's brother Arthur wrote 'Dear Joe, I cannot believe that W.E.G. would be so mean as to ask you to take *now* the appointment that he did not offer when it seemed your due. But if you should go over there, it is impossible that we should let you go alone . . . and if you think it your duty to accept the post, you must allow one of us to be with you—not to get in your way and follow you about, but to be handy when you have the time to talk, so that you should have one of your own family to talk with.'[193]

In fact on 8 May Gladstone offered the Chief Secretaryship to Dilke, but without a seat in the Cabinet. Dilke firmly refused the offer and promptly wrote to Chamberlain, 'but *you* (and not I) are the man because you believe in success and I don't. Still I would act or serve under you, and if it were thought I could be of any use I would join you in Dublin on the day the House was up, and spend the whole autumn and winter with you as your chief private secretary.'[194] In the end, neither Dilke nor Chamberlain became Chief Secretary.

Did Gladstone refrain from offering the post to Chamberlain because he recognised his ambition and was reluctant to place him in a position which (if success had come to him) could have greatly enhanced his prestige? In 1888 Gladstone told Morley that he 'never knew that Chamberlain desired to succeed Forster, however others did. . . . Had I known Chamberlain's wish, I should not have set it aside without consideration and counsel.'[195] It is difficult to believe that Gladstone had no inkling of Chamberlain's desire to become Chief Secretary, just as it is equally difficult to accept Chamberlain's later claim that he 'had the greatest horror of it and believed that if I had to take it, it would probably destroy me as it had done Mr. Forster.'[196]

After Trevelyan's appointment to the administration in Dublin castle, Chamberlain kept a keen interest in Irish affairs. He wrote to the Viceroy Lord Spencer protesting against the new Crimes Bill that followed hard on the heels of the Phoenix Park murders, and arguing that 'It will only further embitter the relations of the two countries, and Home Rule with all its possible dangers and consequences will be within measurable distance.'

In order further to cut the ground from under the feet of the Home Rulers, Chamberlain began to canvass the idea of giving Ireland, after the next General Election, a form of 'local government more complete, more popular, more thoroughly representative than anything which has hitherto been suggested.' Utterly convinced of the value of the reforms made possible by strong local government in Birmingham, Chamberlain hoped that Ireland could be transformed, if not overnight at least fairly promptly, into a Greater Birmingham set among the waves of the Atlantic Ocean. Chamberlain's plan for an Irish Central Board that would have legislative powers over land, education and communications was put before the Cabinet on 9 May 1885, when all the Whig peers (except Granville) rejected it. Though Gladstone declared the scheme was as 'dead as mutton', Chamberlain was to revive it in July 1885 as part of a 'National Councils' plan that included England, Scotland and Wales, if their inhabitants should so desire it.

Chamberlain's efforts to stem the Home Rule tide were primarily based upon his desire to maintain the integrity of the British Empire. His Radical public stance and his private convictions were, in this respect, sorely tried by the Transvaal War of 1880–1, the British invasion of Egypt in 1882, and the fiasco of General Gordon's death at Khartoum in 1885.

As early as June 1880 Chamberlain had told Gladstone that with regard to the recently-annexed Transvaal, with its sparse but determined Afrikaner population, 'I doubt the wisdom and permanence of the annexation. Unless some unforeseen circumstances lead to a large immigration of Englishmen into the Transvaal, I believe the Boers will, sooner or later, worry this country into granting their independence.'[197] By the end of February 1881 the Afrikaners had resoundingly defeated British forces under General Sir George Colley in a brief campaign that had culminated in the humiliation of the battle of Majuba Hill. Chamberlain apparently had few qualms about the restoration of the Transvaal's independence, though he anticipated future conflict with the Boers over the issue of British suzerainty. Nonetheless, he hoped that 'When left alone, [the Boers] would be compelled to come to terms with their [Bantu] neighbours and to treat them with ordinary fairness.'[198] His magnanimity towards the Transvaal doubtless reflected the fact that in 1881 no serious British economic or strategic interests were involved in the country. The high principles that thus prevailed in 1881–2 were, however, to be rendered less powerful by the discovery of huge gold deposits on the Witwatersrand in 1886.

But British interests were very much involved in Egypt and the Sudan. The Suez Canal was a vital commercial and strategic link between Britain and her Indian and Far Eastern interests. The Egyptian revolt against the Anglo-French system of Dual Control, spear-headed by army officers under the leadership of Colonel Arabi Pasha, seemed by 1881 to threaten the basis of European control of Egyptian affairs. In June 1882 rioting in Alexandria caused a large number of European deaths, and British patriots clamoured for military intervention. The Liberal Government eventually, and with misgivings, sanctioned an invasion of Egypt which (with the French standing aloof) resulted in the defeat of Arabi Pasha and the beginning of seventy years of British occupation and domination.

Lord Granville described Chamberlain as 'almost the greatest Jingo' when the Cabinet discussed the Egyptian problem. This was not true early in 1882 when Chamberlain argued that the Egyptian revolutionary movement 'might be the legitimate expression of discontent and of resistance to oppression. If so, it ought to be guided and not repressed.'[199] Chamberlain's 'jingoism' was provoked by the Alexandria riots of June; as a result he joined the Cabinet hawks and supported 'Hartington in pressing for active measures.' These measures included the bombardment of Alexandria, which John Bright (who resigned from the Cabinet over the use of force in Egypt) put down to Chamberlain's insistence upon strong-arm tactics.[200] While other Radicals denounced the Egyptian invasion as a war fought for the British bondholders (shareholders in the Suez Canal Company), Chamberlain was calling for Arabi's overthrow. Chamberlain was aware of his embarrassingly different posture, and tried in a Cabinet Minute of October 1882 to square the situation: 'We have in Egypt interests and duties. The interests are a fair guarantee for the peace and order of the country, and the security of the Suez Canal and our route to India. The duty cast upon us, as the Liberal Government of a free nation, is to secure to the Egyptian people the greatest possible development of representative institutions.'[201]

In the Sudan crisis of 1884–5 Chamberlain did not look kindly upon the Mahdi's occupation of Khartoum and the death of General Gordon in January 1885, believing that 'We must retake Khartoum even if we leave it again immediately.' As it happened, Gladstone's will eventually prevailed: Khartoum was not reconquered, and the Sudan was abandoned, for more than a decade, to Dervish self-rule.

Chamberlain's Radical-Imperialism (like Dilke's) was, in short, becoming plain for all to see. John Bright had reproached him for his aggressive attitude towards the Egyptian revolutionaries, and in 1884 a visiting Cape politician, Merriman, 'could scarcely credit the statement, which he heard repeated on every side, that Mr. Chamberlain had taken a vigorous initiative in insisting upon the maintenance of our Imperial obligations in Bechuanaland.'[202] It was true, just the same.

Concern for imperial consolidation and aggrandisement did not as yet bulk large in Chamberlain's political preoccupations. His political enemies denounced him for his extreme Radicalism and his overweening ambition, not for his imperialism.

On the home front, Chamberlain launched himself upon an aggressive Radical campaign in the years 1884–5. He had begun his preparations for this onslaught upon privilege and property in 1883: the Cabinet and the nation had to be convinced that whole-sale reforms (including Ireland) were necessary. Chamberlain's techniques of persuasion were fundamentally those of private contact with friends, colleagues and opponents, and public exposition through crowded meetings, lengthy speeches and press articles. Late in 1883 he used the *Fortnightly Review* (now edited by his crony T. H. S. Escott) to promote his views; anonymous articles, written by Escott, Morley, Jesse Collings, Francis Adams and Frank Harris, put forward the Chamberlain line. He contributed a significant article himself, entitled 'Labourers' and Artisans' Dwellings'.

By July 1885 the 'Radical Programme' had emerged, printed in booklet form, and the first campaign handbook in British political history. While the items of the 'Radical Programme' had surfaced gradually over two years, a major measure of franchise reform had been forced through Parliament: the Reform Act of 1884 enfranchised hundreds of thousands of agricultural labourers, in Ireland as well as the rest of the United Kingdom; in 1885 a Redistribution Act set up mainly single-member constituencies.

Franchise reform and Chamberlain's 'Radical Programme' went together hand in glove. Enfranchised rural voters must be won over for Radicalism; this in turn would strengthen Chamberlain's hand in his bid to refashion the political structure, to dispense with the Whiggish element in the Liberal alliance, and to make moderates choose between the right and left wing of the party. In the process, Chamberlain's claims for the leadership of the purified, advanced Liberals would be rendered irresistible.

Did Chamberlain want more than this? Certainly he wanted social justice—the civic gospel recast on a national scale. Was the 'Radical Programme', as it claimed, 'the death-knell of the *laissez-faire* system', an exercise in socialist confiscation and redistribution?

Despite the abuse which descended upon Chamberlain at this time, despite the strong and provocative political language that he employed to expound his views, there is little doubt that he was trying to preserve private enterprise and private property rather than destroy them. Disliking the strident and menacing tones of Marxist socialism, Chamberlain strove to make more acceptable the unacceptable face of late-Victorian capitalism.

The main planks in the 'Radical Programme' were provocative enough. Free elementary education. Land reform, including: measures to help increase the numbers of those able to own land; the taxation of sporting, uncultivated and unoccupied land; the provision of allotments and smallholdings by local authorities (who could call upon compulsory powers); the enfranchisement of leaseholds; higher rates for large landed estates, and a progressive income tax on the amount of land held. Various financial reforms to aid the poor at the expense of the rich; for example, a marked increase in the proportion of direct as opposed to indirect taxation, and the encouragement of local government housing and improvement schemes (which would involve an increase in the rates). The promotion of more efficient local government through the establishment of county councils. The creation of 'National Councils' in Dublin and Edinburgh to manage certain domestic matters. In the longer term, some items like the disestablishment of the Church of England, manhood suffrage, and the payment of M.P.s.

These were proposals calculated to infuriate Whig and Tory alike. Among his colleagues, Hartington and George Goschen were quick to criticise him, and he gave them, and others, a glorious opening when in a speech on 5 January 1885 he propounded his theory of 'ransom', asking 'what ransom will property pay for the security it enjoys?' Chamberlain provided his own answer by explaining that 'society owes a compensation to the poorer classes

of this country, that it ought to recognise that claim and pay it.'[203]
In other words, welfare and reform would provide an insurance
policy for privilege and property. These Fabian tactics hardly mark
Chamberlain out as the Robespierre of Gladstone's second
administration; indeed, he was quick to point out that he was
'putting the rights of property on the only firm and defensible
basis. . . . I believe that the danger to property lies in its abuse.'
Perhaps the storm which followed his 'ransom' speech lay partly
in the very use of the word 'ransom', and subsequently he was
careful to substitute the safe, capitalist term 'insurance', and to
stress that what he meant to achieve was equity not social revolution.

Chamberlain's talent for political mud-stirring and for hard-
edged speechmaking was also clearly demonstrated in the struggle
over the parliamentary reform bills of 1884–5. The 1884 County
Franchise Bill had Gladstone's backing, but was opposed by
Hartington and Goschen on the Liberal side, as well as by Disraeli's successor as Conservative leader, Lord Salisbury—well
placed as a member of the House of Lords to obstruct the Bill's
progress. Salisbury opposed the Bill on the grounds that it would
give the Liberals a fresh electoral advantage of forty-seven seats,
and that the measure should, in any case, be accompanied by a
redistribution of seats. These arguments had considerable weight.
Less acceptable was the notion that the House of Lords, in some
mysterious way, reflected accurately 'the true feeling of the country'
on the matter.

With his Radical rural metamorphosis at risk, Chamberlain
flayed the Tories and the peers. At a speech at Denbigh on 20
October 1884 he asked, 'Are the Lords to dictate to us, the people
of England? . . . Are you going to be governed by yourselves? Or
will you submit to an oligarchy which is a mere accident of birth?'
Earlier he had attacked Salisbury for constituting 'himself the
spokesman of a class—a class to which he himself belongs, who
toil not neither do they spin.' John Morley also pitched into the
battle with the cry of 'mend them or end them'—in other words,
reform the House of Lords or sweep them away.

As it happened, the House of Lords were not pushed over the
brink by Chamberlain and the Radicals. Salisbury and Gladstone
were prepared to do a deal over franchise reform, and the committee which worked out the wheeling and dealing was chaired by

Dilke, whose inclination to compromise momentarily estranged him from Chamberlain. Two million electors were added to the electoral roll, single member constituencies became almost universal, and the Irish counties were not excluded from the legislation. Chamberlain's comment 'Not bad for a Tory Bill', was echoed more fulsomely in a letter to Gladstone on the occasion of the latter's birthday. 'The new Reform Bills are the greatest Revolution this country has undergone—&, thanks to you, it has been accomplished peacefully and with general assent.'[204]

Radicals confidently assumed that the redistributed urban seats would fall to them in the next election, though the county seats were more doubtful. Chamberlain's rigorous presentation of the 'Radical Programme' owed much to this calculation. Similarly his desire to buy off the Home Rule agitation was increased by the realisation that the reforms would add an extra twenty or so Irish M.P.s to Parnell's supporters in the House of Commons. Of these two probabilities only the increase of Irish M.P.s occurred in the election of November 1885; the great upsurge in Radical members elected for the new urban seats did not materialise, and the London results were a bitter disappointment for Chamberlain.

This latter disaster could not, however, have been predicted earlier in 1885. Until the government's resignation in June, Chamberlain flexed his political muscles, challenging the Whigs to fight him if they dared. Goschen certainly took up cudgels, protesting in January 1885 against Chamberlain's alleged invitation to the enfranchised populace to 'celebrate its advent to power by the dethronement of Gladstonian finance', and to storm the constitution 'on the principle of an enemy storming a town, who demands a ransom for abstaining from plunder.' Class unity not class war was what the nation needed, Goschen insisted.

It is clear that Chamberlain, already practised in the art of threatening resignation, would have welcomed the chance to resign in earnest over a matter of real principle during the first few months of 1885. He could then have carried the struggle into the constituencies, where, Schnadhorst assured him, the National Liberal Federation would back him to the hilt. He wrote to Morley on 2 February 1885, 'I hope and believe that you, Dilke and I stand together in this. If we do we will utterly destroy the Whigs, and have a Radical government before many years are out.'

In fact, the resignations of both Chamberlain and Dilke (since

1882 a member of the Cabinet as President of the Local Government Board) were in Gladstone's hands when he tendered his own, and his administration's, resignation in June. The issue that had finally prompted Chamberlain's letter of resignation was Ireland: notably the Cabinet's refusal to back his National Councils plan, and Gladstone's announcement in the Commons of a Land Purchase Bill for Ireland unaccompanied by any reference to Chamberlain's comprehensive scheme of Irish local government reform. Coercion, in the form of a new Crimes Bill, was also being proposed.

Chamberlain's letter of resignation of 20 May 1885 argued that, by announcing an Irish Land Purchase Bill without reference to Irish local government reform, Gladstone had broken an agreement made with himself and Dilke. The Prime Minister demurred; Chamberlain tried to clarify his position; the days passed, and his resignation was not made public.

In the early hours of 9 June a Conservative amendment to the budget, during its second reading, was passed by a majority of twelve votes. Parnell had voted with thirty-nine of his followers against the 'coercionist' administration. The Liberal government duly resigned, and Lord Salisbury formed his first administration.

Chamberlain was now unmuzzled. As a leading member of the opposition he could take the fight to the country, confident that 'The ultimate victory is to the strong, and Providence *est toujours du côté des gros bataillons.*'[206]

SEVEN

THE LIBERAL SPLIT
1885–6

It is certain that any solution of the kind attributed to Mr. Gladstone
will lead in the long run to the absolute national independence of
Ireland, and that this cannot be conceded without serious danger
and the heaviest sacrifice on the part of Great Britain. This country
would sink to the rank of a third rate power. . . .

Joseph Chamberlain, March 1886

SALISBURY'S minority Conservative government,
formed in June 1885, could hardly look forward to a long life.
Parnell and his supporters had brought down the Liberal
administration for their Irish misdemeanours; unless the Conservatives were prepared to give real substance to their apparent
sympathy for Ireland's aspirations he would doubtless withdraw
his support from them too. On taking office, Salisbury in fact re-
paid his debt to Parnell by ending coercion and passing the Ash-
bourne Act, a piece of quasi-capitalist benevolence which put up
£5,000,000 to facilitate loans to Irish tenants wishing to purchase
land. It was, however, unthinkable that the Conservatives, still
very much the party of the landed classes and the Anglican
establishment, would seriously countenance Home Rule and the
break-up of the union.

There could be no General Election until the late autumn of
1885 when the newly reorganised constituencies and the new
electoral rolls would be ready. Dilke was confident that an election
would indeed take place then and that the Liberals would be back
in power by January.

For Chamberlain, the five months of so that stretched ahead
before the probable election contained both an opportunity and a
challenge. The opportunity lay in the chance of strengthening the
Radical cause in the country through a powerful exposition of the
'Radical Programme'. The challenge was Ireland: could a formula
be found which satisfied the Parnellites and at the same time fall
short of separation?

In July the final item of the 'Radical Programme' was put in

place. It was a re-vamping of Chamberlain's earlier solution for the
Irish problem, the Central Board Scheme. Now he argued that:

> The establishment of a National Council, elected by the Irish
> people and endowed with national authority, would enable the
> Imperial Parliament to delegate to a body of sufficient weight,
> capacity, and power duties which Parliament now endeavours to
> perform, but the performance of which necessitates the neglect
> of other and more important matters upon which the attention
> of the great legislative assembly of the Empire should be
> concentrated.[207]

The National Councils plan, despite Chamberlain's avowed
intent to include the English, Scots and Welsh in the scheme as
well as the Irish, was not likely to be a great vote-winner on either
side of the Irish Channel. Accordingly when in mid-August the
Conservative ministry asked for a dissolution of Parliament,
Chamberlain was already seeking to sell other items in the 'Radical
Programme' to the new, enlarged electorate. His full-scale electoral
campaign had effectively begun at Hull, where on 5 August he was
greeted by enthusiastic crowds and huge orange posters which proclaimed him in bold black type as 'Your coming Prime Minister'.
At Warrington on 8 September he stamped the hall-mark on his
campaign by ridiculing Lord Hartington as a political Rip van
Winkle, delivering a smashing attack on those who opposed the
'Radical Programme', and stating that:

> The great problem of our civilisation is still unsolved. We have
> to account for and to grapple with the mass of misery and
> destitution in our midst, co-existent as it is with the evidence of
> abundant wealth and teeming prosperity. It is a problem which
> some men would put aside by references to the eternal laws of
> supply and demand, to the necessity of freedom of contract, and
> to the sanctity of every private right of property. But, gentlemen,
> these phrases are the convenient cant of selfish wealth.[208]

Chamberlain went on to stump the country: inveighing, at
Inverness, against the Highland clearances as 'a black page in the
account of private ownership in land'; calling his proposals 'simple,
moderate and practical' before an overflowing meeting at the Old
Vic theatre in London, and going on to deliver the ultimatum that
he would not join a government which excluded his reforms from

its programme; at Bradford he derided the House of Lords as 'the obsequious handmaid of the Tory party'.

In mid-October he closed his campaign at Trowbridge, having been, with Jesse Collings, on a tour of inspection through one of the poorest districts of Wiltshire. At Trowbridge he spoke of the plight of rural labourers and claimed that 'The source of all the mischief lies in the system by which they have been divorced from the soil. The only remedy is to be found in the reform which will once more restore them to the land.'

Here was one of the most potent of Chamberlain's electoral appeals—the proposal to make smallholdings and allotments available, through local authority funds, to rural workers. The slogan 'Three Acres and a Cow' hit home again and again among the new county voters, and paid handsome dividends in the ensuing election. This battle-cry and two others came to dominate Chamberlain's summer and autumn campaigning, and he proceeded to concentrate his powers of persuasion upon free elementary education and a graduated tax on property as well as upon the need to provide rural smallholdings.

The effect of Chamberlain's electoral speechmaking during his advocacy of the 'Radical Programme' was electrifying. His colleagues and supporters from Morley to Dr. Dale, from Dilke to Labouchere hastened to congratulate him. The crowds flocked to hear him and Ramsay MacDonald was later to recall, 'I still remember as if it were but yesterday the thrill of pleasure that went through Radical Scotland when the first speech [at Glasgow on 15 September] was delivered. Its bold audacity struck the imagination of the country.'[209] The young Lloyd George considered Chamberlain at that time to be his ideal, and another future Liberal statesman, Augustine Birrell, said of Chamberlain's Glasgow speech that 'its power of incitement was unrivalled; it had a thrilling sort of wickedness.'

Chamberlain had, by mid-autumn, 'out-Midlothianed' Gladstone, and a Radical admirer noticed that 'if audiences cheered Gladstone's name for two minutes, they cheered Chamberlain's for five.'[210] On 20 September Lord Hartington wrote ruefully to Goschen, 'Chamberlain's last speeches are I think very able, and he has the advantage over us of greater definiteness in his programme.' Goschen, indeed, conscious of the threat that Chamberlain's success posed for the right wing of the Liberal party dubbed his proposals the 'Unauthorised Programme'—a description which stuck, and which high-lighted the extraordinary situation in which an ex-junior Cabinet Minister was advocating a comprehensive range of reforms that lacked the sanction of the party leader and the majority of his senior colleagues. In September, Gladstone did manage to publish his own, personal election manifesto in his address to the electors of Midlothian; but it was a lack-lustre, non-committal offering.

The Tory party and the Conservative press meanwhile hastened to denigrate and ridicule Chamberlain. Lord Iddesleigh called him 'Jack Cade', Lord Salisbury likened him to a 'Sicilian bandit', others denounced him as a 'Dick Turpin', a common highwayman, a communist, and an anarchist, one who would willingly destroy British society to advance his own ambitions. Whigs were hard put to be much more complimentary, and the Parnellites, quite sure that he was a towering obstacle in their path, also denounced him.

The election campaign of 1885 was one of the highwater marks of Chamberlain's career. His enemies could accuse him of base opportunism, of preaching class war, of hoping to take Gladstone's place as leader (though at this time he considered the ex-Prime Minister to be a convenient bulwark against Whig reaction), but the plain fact was that he had brilliantly seized the political initiative with a programme that was genuinely radical and at the same time within the realm of practical politics. The strength of his appeal to the electorate is clearly reflected in the campaign of invective waged against him. Nor was Chamberlain merely building reforming castles in the air, confident that he would never have to inhabit them as a Cabinet minister, for by the end of October Francis Schnadhorst's calculation that the Liberals would definitely win 366 seats and might gain a further twenty-six did not seem over-optimistic.[211]

The rising tempest of Irish nationalism could, however, blow the Liberal ship off course, and leave both Radicals and Whigs stranded. Chamberlain, in 1885, did all that he could to avert this disaster within the limitations of his determination not to counten-ance separation. This often meant saying one thing and meaning another. At the end of May, for example, the day after he had offered Gladstone his resignation, he made a speech in Islington that positively overflowed with liberal and sympathetic sentiments towards Ireland:

It is a national question as well as a parochial question, and the pacification of Ireland at the moment depends, I believe, on the concession to Ireland of the right to govern itself in the matter of its purely domestic business. What is the alternative? Are you content, after nearly eighty years of failure, to renew once more the dreary experience of repressive legislation? . . . I do not believe that the great majority of Englishmen have the slightest conception of the system under which this free nation attempts to rule the sister country. It is a system which is founded on the bayonets of 30,000 soldiers encamped permanently as in a hostile country. It is a system as completely centralised and bureaucratic as that with which Russia governs Poland. . . . An Irishman at this moment cannot move a step—he cannot lift a finger in any parochial, municipal or educational work, without being confronted with, interfered with, controlled by an English official, appointed by a foreign Government, and without a shade, or shadow of representative authority. I say the time has come to reform altogether the absurd and irritating anachronism which is known as Dublin Castle. That is the work to which the new Parliament will be called.[212]

It was plain, though, that in seeking for a remedy for Ireland's ills Chamberlain would budge no further than his National Councils scheme. Since Parnell and his followers would not be satisfied with this, all that Chamberlain could hope to do was to counteract their potentially baleful electoral impact by appealing to the English voters to support moderate reform in Ireland. Privately he was adamant that the proposed National Council for Ireland would 'be only the Metropolitan Board of Works on a larger and more important scale. Above all, it will have no power of initiating special taxation, but will be confined to rating.'[213] As the election campaign developed, Chamberlain took the decision to play down Ireland as an issue, preferring instead to concentrate on issues that would be electorally advantageous.

Lord Salisbury and Gladstone, on the other hand, were prepared to struggle with the Irish conundrum. On 1 August 1885 Lord Carnarvon, the conciliatory, newly-appointed Lord Lieutenant (or Viceroy) of Ireland, met Parnell in an empty house in Mayfair with no third parties present. Salisbury chose not to inform his Cabinet colleagues of this meeting, which resulted in Carnarvon believing

that the Irish Nationalists would not press for separation but would
be satisfied with a legislative body, and left Parnell with the
impression that the Conservatives were prepared to concede some
form of Home Rule. Such an understanding would at least enable
Parnell to continue to give support to the Tories in the coming
election.

News of the Carnarvon-Parnell meeting soon leaked out, and
Gladstone decided to make a counter-bid for Irish support. He had
become convinced that some form of Home Rule would have to be
granted, and that such a concession was both morally justifiable
and politically advantageous. If either Chamberlain or Hartington
got wind of his impending conversion, however, the left and right
wings of the party might well raise rebellion and even secede. The
construction of a viable Home Rule policy would also give Gladstone the justification and incentive to stay on as leader. Despite
his disclaimers to the contrary, he did not hasten to lay down the
burden of leadership, and after his return in September from a
Norwegian cruise, undertaken to restore his health and his voice,
was easily persuaded by Lord Granville that the party desperately
needed him to stay on as its chief.

There ensued a tangled, and not always creditable, chapter of
negotiation and intrigue. Using his son Herbert, and the gossiping,
back-biting Radical Henry Labouchere, as his intermediaries,
Gladstone opened secret negotiations with the Irish. Parnell at first
kept clear of the talks, but a group of Irish M.P.s led by Tim
Healy and Justin McCarthy began negotiations with Labouchere,
assuring him that this clique 'settle almost everything almost
always, and [Parnell] accepts it'. What exactly, Healy wanted to
know, could Gladstone give them?

Gladstone, naturally enough, would not pledge himself straightway to Home Rule and indicated that the Irish Nationalists should
apply in the first instance to the Conservatives. Parnell was drawn
more and more into the talks with Gladstone, but also refused to
commit himself, and seemed, in fact, to be indifferent as to which
party might win the General Election, believing that either way his
own cause would prevail.

On 7 October Chamberlain travelled up to Hawarden at Gladstone's invitation, to meet and to thrash out some awkward in-
consistencies between the 'Radical Programme' and the 'Midlothian Manifesto'. Chamberlain spent both the 7th and 8th of

October at Hawarden where, on the second day, he spelled out the three issues which he and other Radical leaders considered to be essential to the Liberal party's election programme: free schools, the revision of taxation in the interests of the working class, and the granting of compulsory powers to local authorities to buy land. As Chamberlain told Harcourt on 9 October:

> I explained the exact nature of our conditions as above. Mr. Gladstone tried, naturally, to reduce them, but he did not appear to think them impossible. . . . He suggested the Irish question might delay [the reform of] local government, and that London government might be taken first. . . . He spoke of his intention to retire very soon after Parliament met. I protested strongly, and told him that if he did we should alter our terms, as we were prepared to take much less from him than from anyone else. . . . He is very full of the Irish question, but I do not gather he has any plans of dealing with it. He deeply regretted the failure of our scheme for National Councils, and appears to think that more will now have to be conceded at no distant date.[214]

There are two points to note here. One is that Chamberlain and Gladstone had at least tried to sink their differences over their respective electoral programmes; with Hartington also willing to close ranks, the Liberals could now hope to go into the election without exposing the gaping differences that actually existed within the party.

The second point is more momentous, and was destined to contribute substantially to the Liberal split of 1886: quite simply, Gladstone disguised his intentions over Ireland, and gave no hint of the negotiations taking place with the Irish leadership. As the two men walked through the Hawarden woods, or sat talking in the great library, Chamberlain freely expounded his views to Gladstone, who later told Granville that '[Chamberlain] is a good man to talk to, not only from his force and clearness, but because he speaks with reflection, does not misapprehend, or (I think) suspect, or make unnecessary difficulties, or endeavour to maintain pedantically the uniformity and consistency of his argument throughout.'[215]

In return, Gladstone 'did not say a word about the negotiations then going on between him and Members of the Irish Party'.[216] A somewhat mystified Chamberlain wrote to Dilke on 9 October, 'I am not quite certain what was Mr. G's object in sending for me. I suppose he desired to minimise our conditions as far as possible. He was very pleasant and very well with no apparent trace of his hoarseness. . . . He spoke at considerable length on the Irish question. . . . But I do not gather that he has any definite plan under present circumstances.'[217]

What were Gladstone's reasons for leaving Chamberlain with a mistaken impression of his changing attitude towards Ireland? One obvious reason was that if the Irish problem could be put into virtual cold storage until the election was over, then both Chamberlain and the Radicals and Hartington and the Whigs could toe the rather hazy Gladstone party line as expressed in the 'Midlothian Manifesto'. The spectre of Home Rule would thus be exorcised until the votes were counted. A second reason may lie in Gladstone's disinclination to make an upstart Birmingham manufacturer (no matter how influential) privy to his conversion to Home Rule; in this respect it is significant that Lord Derby had visited Hawarden a few days before Chamberlain and had been told by his host that 'he had come to the conclusion that the Union was a mistake . . . he did not believe the Irish irreconcilable . . . now nothing less than a Parliament of their own would satisfy them.'[218] Lord Derby's impeccable aristocratic background apparently made such confidences in order.

Gladstone had, of course, summoned Chamberlain to Hawarden to resolve other doctrinal differences between them. He was acutely aware of the hostile reactions that the 'Radical Programme' had evoked in many quarters, and consequently sought to minimise them. Shortly after Chamberlain left Hawarden, Gladstone hastened to reassure the Queen, who had expressed anxiety over the radical mood that was stirring in her realm, that he was doing all he could to tame his wild men. Again, a clandestine spirit pervades the letter:

Mr. Chamberlain is known as the most active and efficient representative at this time of what may be termed the left wing of the Liberal Party; and Mr. Gladstone recently thought it would be well to invite him to Hawarden, with a view to personal communication, which has now been affected, he thinks with advantage. Mr. Chamberlain is wholly unaware of any communication at this juncture between your Majesty and Mr. Gladstone.[219]

Did the Hawarden meeting really resolve the differences between Gladstone and the Radicals? Chamberlain noted that Gladstone 'boggled a good deal' over the Radicals' request to speak and vote as they liked on the Free Schools proposal, but that generally 'the tone of his conversation inferred that he was seeking to work with us and had no idea of doing without us.'[220] An attempt to avoid a party quarrel just before a General Election did not however imply Gladstone's conversion to the 'Radical Programme'. George Russell, who had left Hawarden shortly before Chamberlain arrived, recalled the latter's disappointed judgement of his visit that 'politically it had been a failure. Gladstone would not budge an inch towards the "unauthorised programme"; and, said Chamberlain, "If I were to recede the very stones would cry out." '[221] This is perhaps an exaggerated view: Chamberlain recognised Gladstone's disinclination to go the whole hog towards reform, but he had also received the impression that cooperation was possible and actively desired.

Ten days after leaving Hawarden, Chamberlain was told of Gladstone's Irish negotiations by the prolix Labouchere. What could Chamberlain do? Sharp political practice was not unknown to him; his enemies, indeed, claimed that it was his stock-in-trade. In any case, Labouchere had not made it absolutely clear what Gladstone's proposals were apart from telling Chamberlain that 'The G.O.M. [Grand Old Man] says that he is disposed to grant the fullest home rule etc., but that he does not think it desirable to formulate a scheme before the elections. . . . Evidently the game of the G.O.M. is to endeavour to unite the party on Irish legislation, and to make this his *cheval de bataille*.'[222]

On 25 October Gladstone, probably realising the cat was out of Labouchere's bag, wrote to Chamberlain with the delphic conjecture of 'the likelihood that Ireland may shoulder aside everything else'; he also begged Chamberlain to cooperate in 'keeping together the Liberal party till its list of agreed subjects is exhausted'.[223]

The next day Chamberlain told Gladstone 'I cannot see my way at all about Ireland. . . . I would rather let Ireland go than accept the responsibility of a nominal Union.' He also tossed in the threat

that neither he, Dilke, Morley nor probably Lefevre 'could
honestly join any Government' that was not committed to backing
the compulsory purchase of land by local authorities.[224]

Chamberlain's suspicions were now fully aroused. He told Dilke
on 26 October that Gladstone's letter of the day before 'makes me
uneasy. I hear from another source that he is trying to get Parnell's
ideas in detail etc., etc.'[225] On 4 November, with Gladstone still
striving to avoid an open breach, he informed Dilke that Lord
Granville had visited him: 'He told me nothing about Ireland—
but I am convinced that Mr. G. is trying to make a treaty all to himself. It must fail.'[226]

On 16 November the salient points of Gladstone's offer to the
Irish was passed on to Labouchere by Herbert Gladstone. It
consisted of six points which would form the basis of discussion:

1. The maintenance of the unity and integrity of the Empire.
2. An Irish Chamber for Irish affairs.
3. Irish representatives to sit at Westminster for Imperial affairs.
4. The equitable division of Imperial charges by fixed pro-
   portions.
5. Protection of the [Protestant] minority in Ireland.
6. Suspension of the Imperial authority for all civil purposes in
   Ireland.[227]

Herbert Gladstone went on to say 'I am confident that if (a) Ireland
at the Poll declares for Home Rule and (b) the Liberal Party are
put by the election into the position to take up the question, my
Father would be for entering into early communication with those
who would represent the Irish nation.'

Relayed to Parnell, this message enabled him to advise his Irish
supporters in England to vote for the Conservatives at the election.
There were two good reasons for such advice: firstly, the Carnarvon-Parnell talks still made a Tory offer on Home Rule possible;
secondly, the Irish cause might best be served by cutting the
expected Liberal majority to the bone—after all, a Liberal Government with a huge overall majority might not see the need to make
meaningful concessions to Irish nationalism.

When the poll was declared at the end of November, it provided
Parnell with a good but potentially troublesome result. The
Liberals won 335 seats, giving them a majority of eighty-six over
the Conservatives. The Irish Nationalists, on the other hand, had

eighty-six seats: this enabled them to keep out either of the two major parties; it also gave them the capacity to put the Liberals in power, but not to provide the Tories with an overall majority.

The results of the poll were disappointing for the Liberals. Schnadhorst's prediction of 366 seats had been proved badly wrong. The Irish vote accounted for some of the Liberals' failure to win a majority of English borough seats; there were approximately 150,000 Irish Catholic voters, and, given a limited electorate and small constituency majorities, the mobilisation of this vote against the Liberals was doubtless decisive in a number of cases. But there were other factors, chief of which was anxiety over the country's economic future, and here the Tory battle cry of 'fair trade' as opposed to free trade had considerable effect. In the English counties, however, the Liberals gained a majority of seats, an appropriate reward for recent enfranchisement and Chamberlain's 'three acres and a cow'.

On 4 December 1885 Chamberlain told Lady Dorothy Nevill:

> The elections have been most interesting. They have not gone as I expected, but they are not on the whole bad for us, i.e. the Radicals. . . . The 'cow' has been very well, and would have been much better if the Whigs had not been such asses, and had not done their best to discredit this admirable cry.
>
> London is an awful disappointment to me. It deserves the fate of the cities of the plain. However, I am looking for a second Schnadhorst to organize the Metropolis properly before the next election. . . . The revolution is postponed.[228]

Events moved inexorably towards doomsday. Lord Salisbury could now gain no electoral advantage from Irish support; he smartly proceeded to ditch Parnell, proclaim against Home Rule, and to indicate that he was ready to form a coalition with Hartington and the Whigs against Gladstone. Soon estimates of the numbers of Whig and Radical M.P.s who would follow Hartington and Chamberlain if Gladstone retired were being touted in the London clubs, and Herbert Gladstone admitted on 7 December that 'As to the break-up of the Liberals on Home Rule, it is possible.'

While Gladstone was privately urging the Conservatives to stay in office and to grasp the Irish nettle with Liberal support, Chamberlain was similarly telling Harcourt that he would like 'to keep the Tories with their noses to the grindstone for a year at least, and then I think the Irish question would be in a much better position for settlement.' Though Dilke agreed with Chamberlain's thinking at this point, Morley did not, and was already moving away from the Chamberlain-Dilke Radical axis.

On 17 December the political world was rocked by the bombshell of Herbert Gladstone's press interviews the day before when he had revealed that his father was prepared to take office to carry through a Home Rule programme. The 'Hawarden Kite' was now flying boldly overhead, challenging observers to applaud its progress or to pull it down.

For a while, Chamberlain was uncertain how to react. He had first heard of the 'Hawarden Kite' late at night on 16 December while at 'Highbury'. His first reaction was to tell Dilke, 'We must temporise. Our people will not stand our support of the Tories. Besides we must not play into the hands of the Whigs. It will be better to stick to Mr. G.'[229] On the night of 17 December he had to speak at the Birmingham Reform Club's banquet at the Town Hall; in his speech he denied rumours that he was party to the negotiations that had just been disclosed, attempted to screw Gladstone to the mark as having 'said again and again that the first duty of Liberal statesmen is to maintain the integrity of the Empire and the supremacy of the Crown', and affirmed the party's 'resolution to maintain unimpaired the effective Union of the three kingdoms that owe allegiance to the British Crown'.[230]

Dilke reacted to this speech by accusing Chamberlain on 17 December of veering away from their agreed policy of 'keeping the Tories in'. Chamberlain admitted that he might have 'turned round . . . unconsciously', but pleaded that, 'The situation changes every minute. The announcement of Mr. G's plans makes it much more serious, and I altered my speech somewhat to-night to meet it. . . . Finally my view is that Mr. G's Irish scheme is death and damnation; that we must try and stop it—that we must not openly commit ourselves against it yet—that we must let the situation shape itself before we finally decide.'[231]

In the same letter, written at midnight on 17 December, Chamberlain warned Dilke that 'The Tory game is to exaggerate Mr. G's performance & to go to the country on the "integrity of the Empire" '; he also warned 'that the Whigs are our greatest enemies & that we must not join with them if we can help it. . . . & that the less we speak in public for the present the better.'[232]

Gladstone reacted promptly to Chamberlain's Birmingham speech of 17 December telling the latter 'I think we are very much in accord.' Chamberlain replied by return, declaring himself 'greatly obliged by your kind letter', and saying (through clenched teeth one imagines), 'I fear that with the expectations now raised in Ireland, it will not be possible to satisfy the Irish party with any proposals that are likely to receive the general support of English Liberals.'[233] A more accurate reflection of Chamberlain's feelings were expressed the same day in a letter to Dilke, 'What a mess Mr. G. has made of it! What will be the end of it all? Why the d— could he not have waited till Parnell quarrelled with the Tories?'[234]

Between the launching of the 'Hawarden Kite' and the opening of the new Parliament in late January 1886 Chamberlain kept a low public profile, hoping to discern the precise path that Gladstone meant to tread. Unfortunately Gladstone, too, avoided public utterances, and waited to see what the Irish would settle for. Since their leader chose not to give them a clear target to aim at, dissident Liberals were inhibited in their desire to oppose him. Chamberlain put his own frustrations clearly when he told Harcourt, 'It is really monstrous that our leader should throw every obstacle in the way of counsel and should be taking his own course under the pretence that he is standing still.'[235]

Privately, however, Chamberlain waxed prolific. On Boxing Day, for example, he wrote to Dilke who had to deliver a speech on 31 December. Reiterating that 'It is a dangerous time & I myself am inclined to lie low', Chamberlain gave an outstandingly clear analysis of the Irish situation as it appeared to him:

At present there are 2 definite ideas for settlement of Ireland before public, viz (a) National Councils (b) Separation. As to (a) the fundamental principles are supremacy of Imperial Parlt. & extension of local liberties on municipal lines. It is a feasible practical plan, but it has the fatal objection that the Nationalists will not accept it. It is worse than useless to impose on them benefits which they repudiate.

As to (b). Every one professes to reject the idea of separation. If it were adopted, I have no doubt it would lead to the adoption of the conscription in Ireland—then to the conscription in England—an increase of the navy—fresh fortifications on the

West Coast & finally a War in which Ireland would have the support of some other power—perhaps America or France.

Between these alternatives there is the hazy idea of Home Rule [expressed] in Morley's speech [on 21 December] & Gladstone's assumed intentions. It is dangerous & mischievous & was rogue language on such a subject.

Those who speak ought to say exactly what they mean.

It will be found that Home Rule includes [:]

An independent separate Irish Parlt. & that all guarantees & securities—whether for the protection of minorities or for the security of the Union are absolutely illusory.

At the same time we are to continue to receive Irish representatives at Westr. in the Imperial Parliament, & we shall not even get rid of their distractions & interference there by the concession of their independence in Ireland.

To any arrangement of this kind, unworkable as I believe it is, I prefer separation—to which indeed it is only a step.

Is there any other possible arrangement which would secure the real integrity of the Empire for Imperial purposes while allowing Irishmen to play the devil as they liked in Ireland?

Yes there is; but it involves the entire recasting of the British Constitution, & the full & complete adoption of the American system.

According to this view you might have 5 Parliaments for England, Scotland, Wales, Ulster & the three other [southern Irish] Provinces combined. Each Parliament to have its own Ministry responsible to it & dependent on its vote.

In addition an Imperial Parliament or Reichsrath with another ministry dealing with Foreign & Colonial affairs, Army, Navy, Post Office & Customs.

To carry out this arrangement a Supreme Court . . . must be established to decide on the . . . several local legislatures & the limits of their authority.

The House of Lords must go—or you must establish a separate second Chamber for each Legislature.

It is impossible to suppose that the authority of the Crown could survive these changes for long. One or other of the Local Legist. would refuse to pay the expense & as it could have some kind of local militia at its back, it is not likely that the other Legislatures would engage in Civil War for the sake of re-imposing the nominal authority of the Sovereign.

As a Radical, all these changes have no terrors for me—but is it conceivable that such a clean sweep of existing institutions could be made in order to gratify the Irish demand for Home Rule? Yet this is the only form of Federal Government which offers any prospect of permanence or union for imperial purposes.

If English Liberals once see clearly that indefinite talk about Home Rule means either Separation—or the entire recasting of the whole system of English as well as Irish Govt., they will then be in a condition to decide their policy. At the present they are being led by the Daily News & Morley & Co. to commit themselves in the dark.[236]

On 21 January the Liberal leaders assembled in London to discuss their tactics when Parliament assembled. It was decided that it was best to defeat the Conservatives on an amendment to the Queen's address that did not touch upon Ireland and thus risk immediately opening up fresh and old wounds. A Chamberlainite amendment regretting that the government proposed no measures to give effect to the 'three acres and a cow' plank of the Radical Programme was chosen, and on 26 January was moved by Jesse Collings (now a Liberal-Unionist M.P. for Birmingham). The amendment was carried by 79 votes; but though 74 Parnellites had voted for it, 18 Liberals (including Hartington and Goschen) had voted with the Conservatives—an ominous sign.

At any rate, Lord Salisbury now resigned and Gladstone set about forming his third administration. His handling of Chamberlain's claims to office was maladroit and presumably malevolent as well. At first he offered him the wholly inappropriate post of First Lord of the Admiralty. Chamberlain declined this particular poisoned chalice (which threatened political death to a Radical social reformer) with good grace. Gladstone then asked him which office he preferred. Chamberlain said 'The Colonial Office', to which Gladstone replied, dismissively 'Oh, A Secretary of State!'[237] Clearly this post was to be reserved for a gentleman of noble birth; in fact, it was earmarked for Lord Granville.

Gladstone then asked Chamberlain if he would go back to the

Board of Trade, but was told that a change was preferred. A day
later, on 2 February, the Prime Minister offered Chamberlain the
Presidency of the Local Government Board. Though a minor
office, Chamberlain's passionate belief in the virtues of local
government made the offer appropriate enough. On the other hand,
it was hardly the post for a man who might hope to be Prime
Minister in the immediate future, and this must have been uppermost in Gladstone's calculations.

Chamberlain, however, accepted the offer (which carried a seat
in the Cabinet) thus confirming Gladstone's view that he was an
insincere careerist glad to remain in power at almost any price. The
Prime Minister then proceeded to add insult to injury by proposing
that Jesse Collings, whom Chamberlain wanted as his Parliamentary
Secretary at the Local Government Board, should have his prospective salary cut from £1,500 to £1,200 a year. This was not a
piece of isolated vindictiveness, since the Parliamentary Secretary
to the Board of Trade was to be treated in the same way, but it does
illustrate most powerfully Gladstone's insensitive handling of the
man whom many believed should be treated as his principal
lieutenant. Chamberlain was enraged at the proposal to cut
Collings' salary, particularly in view of the contribution the latter
had made to the Liberals' surprisingly good electoral showing in
the counties. He blazed away at Harcourt (newly appointed as
Chancellor of the Exchequer), 'Damn! Damn!! Damn!!! . . .
Collings has got him [Gladstone] more votes than all his peers put
together and this is his reward.'[238]

Always vigorous in the defence of his subordinates, Chamberlain was hardly likely to sacrifice the interests of the man widely
regarded as Sancho Panza to his Don Quixote. He told Collings
not to reply to Gladstone's offer, and threatened resignation himself. Eventually he badgered Gladstone into surrender, though the
concession was made subject to the Chancellor's consent, and
Chamberlain wryly begged Harcourt to comply: 'Ferocious
Economist, I beseech you not to dock poor Collings of his scanty
pittance.'

Chamberlain's position in the new Cabinet was, in some
respects, an extraordinary one—not merely because of the meagre
reward for his vote-winning services. With Hartington refusing to
take office, he was an obvious successor to Gladstone within the
administration. Yet he was also more vulnerable and isolated than

in the Cabinet of 1880–5. For one thing, his ally Dilke had been denied office by his current involvement in the scandalous Crawford divorce case. For another, his erstwhile confidant Morley had accepted Gladstone's offer of that bed of thorns, the Chief Secretaryship for Ireland. Morley's prodigious leap from the back-benches to the Cabinet, though superficially approved of by Chamberlain, caused a coolness between the two men which rested on Morley's conversion to, and eventual enthusiasm for, Home Rule. At first, Morley cherished the hope that he might be useful as a buffer between Chamberlain and Gladstone but 'A few days were enough to dispel the illusion.'

What did Chamberlain hope to achieve as a member of a govern-ment lumbering, apparently irreversibly, towards Home Rule? Did he not sense that his position would soon become untenable, and that his predictable resignation could be brandished by Glad-stone as the true cause of Liberal disunity? In accepting office, Chamberlain had made plain his absolute opposition to 'the idea of an Irish Parliament' and, while acknowledging Gladstone's ap-proach as based upon an 'inquiry' into the Irish question, he reserved the right to reject any scheme that might be proposed. His own alternative schemes were, in addition, not to be excluded from a 'full consideration' by the Cabinet. He may have hoped that he could use his influence to steer the government through the dangerous shoal water of the Irish problem to land them upon a safer shore where the Union remained intact and where the 'Radical Programme' could flourish.

For a time this may have seemed possible to Chamberlain. On 13 February he was summoned to 10 Downing Street to discuss Ireland with Gladstone. At the meeting Chamberlain 'urged him to deal first with the Irish land question and then with education and municipal and county government, leaving anything more entirely for future consideration.'[239] Gladstone then asked for his views as to the proper solution of the land question. As a result, Chamberlain drew up, within two days, a memorandum that was subsequently circulated to the Cabinet.[240] It was, however, never discussed in Cabinet, nor did Gladstone subsequently refer to it, though, in Chamberlain's own words 'Herbert Gladstone—and I think Mr. Gladstone himself—afterwards alluded to its suggestions in public speeches after the dissolution [of June 1886]—a course which I have always thought to have been a serious breach of

Cabinet confidence besides excessively unfair to me, who had only produced these rough suggestions in a hurry and in deference to Mr. Gladstone's personal request.'[241]

Gladstone dropped Chamberlain's Cabinet memorandum like a stone, to lie under the muddied waters of the Irish controversy. It is easy to see why. The memorandum was merely an elaboration of Chamberlain's Central Board scheme whereby the Board would administer land to be purchased by the state [the United Kingdom], and would receive all rents in the future; Irish tenants would immediately receive a permanent reduction of twenty-eight per cent on their rents, would pay the Central Board and not the individual landlord, and would be authorised to become part-owners of the land on advantageous terms; the state would incur an additional debt of £40,000,000, though as security for the payment of interest it would retain £1,200,000 a year from funds previously set aside for the maintenance of the Irish police and would also be able to retain annual sums from the Sinking Fund (a fund set aside to pay off the government's debts).[242]

The Prime Minister had no faith in Chamberlain's insistence that land and local government reform would buy off the Home Rule agitation. Gladstone was, moreover, as Chamberlain suspected on 5 February (three days after he accepted the Presidency of the Local Government Board) 'on another tack'. This tack involved secret dealings with Parnell (using the inexperienced Morley as a go-between) and the final presentation of the Gladstonian solution to the Cabinet on 13 March.

The meeting of 13 March was the first opportunity that the Cabinet had been given to discuss Ireland. In the month between his private conversation with Gladstone on 13 February and the Cabinet of 13 March, Chamberlain had busied himself in preparing a Local Government Bill. The Bill, for which he had no instructions whatsoever, proposed a comprehensive reorganisation, establishing parish, district and county councils, and giving 'to one or other of them the powers of the magistrates as to licensing and some control over existing licences'. It also proposed to give effect to one of Chamberlain's most consistently held Radical convictions—that local authorities should be given the power to purchase land for allotments (the coming home to roost of 'three acres and a cow'). But, as Chamberlain was later ruefully to record, 'as the Bill was never submitted to the Cabinet no judgement was ever pronounced on any of its intended provisions'.²⁴³ Local government reorganisation had to wait until the Conservatives' Act of 1888.

Chamberlain's chief departmental activity was rudely curtailed by the revelation of Gladstone's Irish proposals on 13 March. A Land Purchase Bill was presented to the Cabinet, involving the advance of £120,000,000 to the new Irish authority. Chamberlain immediately wanted to know the nature of the Home Rule Bill that would accompany the Land Purchase Bill, arguing that he could not judge the latter scheme fairly while remaining ignorant of the former. After 'considerable discussion and some hesitation on Mr. Gladstone's part he stated broadly the lines of his Home Rule policy and his intention to propose a separate Parliament for Ireland with full powers to deal with all Irish affairs.'²⁴⁴

This was the moment of crisis that Chamberlain had anticipated for some time. On 8 March he had been quite certain what his reaction would be, telling his brother Arthur Chamberlain firmly that 'As regards Ireland I have quite made up my mind—indeed I have never felt the slightest hesitation. If Mr. G's scheme goes too far, as I expect it will, I shall leave him.'²⁴⁵

On 15 March, having failed to resolve his misgivings, Chamberlain wrote Gladstone a letter of resignation. The Prime Minister, as usual, tried to prevaricate, and Chamberlain agreed, though with no hope of any progress, to hold over his resignation until the next Cabinet—due to meet on 26 March. This Cabinet predictably failed to satisfy Chamberlain's disquiet, and his resignation was made public the next day. Another Radical, Trevelyan, the Secretary for Scotland, resigned with him. Chamberlain wrote to Gladstone on 27 March, saying:

> It is with the deepest regret that I have felt constrained to separate myself from you & from your government in the policy you have decided to adopt. Nothing but the conviction, which I earnestly hope may be mistaken, that great changes will result from it to the security of the Empire & to all future progress in Liberal work, would have induced me to maintain my own opinion against your judgement & experience.²⁴⁶

What were the true motives that forced Chamberlain, already a veteran at threatening resignation, to resign in earnest? Two days after he sent Gladstone his letter of resignation he hastened to explain his action to J. T. Bunce, editor of his mouthpiece the

Birmingham Daily Post. News of his resignation had already been leaked to the press and he was anxious to put the best face on the affair. The letter to Bunce is significant in that it lays great emphasis on Chamberlain's belief that Gladstone's 'land purchase scheme is so unpopular with Radicals as well as others, that it has no chance whatever of being carried, and if Mr. Gladstone sticks to it he will be beaten.'[247] This explanation is somewhat unconvincing, especially since the difference between Chamberlain's and Gladstone's separate land purchase schemes was not so great as to render compromise impossible. In fact, Chamberlain seems to have been determined not to get saddled with the responsibility for precipitating a great political crisis merely on the basis of his opposition to an Irish Parliament. That this, and its implications, were impossible for him to accept, however, he made clear in the rest of his letter to Bunce:

> It is certain that any scheme of the kind attributed to Mr. Gladstone will lead in the long run to the absolute national independence of Ireland, and that this cannot be conceded without serious danger and the heaviest sacrifices on the part of Great Britain. This country would sink to the rank of a third rate power, and its foreign policy, already sufficiently embarrassing and absorbing, would be complicated by perpetual reference to the state of feeling in Ireland.[248]

The lack of a truly cordial relationship with Gladstone based upon mutual esteem and trust, was another reason for Chamberlain's resignation. Gladstone was glad to see him gone, and rashly confided to Lord Rosebery that nothing since the government had been formed had given him greater satisfaction.[249] There is little doubt that the older man had formed the indelible impression that Chamberlain was an unscrupulous careerist, completely lacking in principle; perhaps he took Chamberlain's brash self-confidence as the outward signs of a soaring ambition—and indeed the confusion is perfectly understandable. Chamberlain's aggressive radicalism disturbed Gladstone, and he had little respect for, or comprehension of, the country-wide constituency which the former, in a sense, represented: the grimy world of factories and workshops, and back-to-back terraced houses, and red-brick chapels in urban wastelands, and illiterate farm labourers toiling for a bare living wage.

For his part, Chamberlain came into office in 1886 half-expecting

Gladstone's disdain. When the wretched controversy over Collings's salary occurred, Chamberlain wrote, almost pitifully, to Harcourt, 'If this is the way he intends to treat me, it is hopeless to think of cordial co-operation.'[250] There was also the deception practised by Gladstone before the hoisting of the 'Hawarden Kite', and the underhand way in which his proposals for Home Rule had been kept from the Cabinet until 13 March 1886. The Prime Minister's ornate verbal style and his endless capacity for (at the best) self-deception were further irritants.

Did Chamberlain hope, by his resignation, to hasten the break up of the Liberal party and its refashioning, under his leadership, into a more likely vehicle for radical reform? Certainly he was convinced that the Home Rule controversy would hang like an albatross round the party's neck, denying it the will to press ahead with necessary reforms—a view shared by Trevelyan, who resigned with him. There is also no doubt that he had become impatient for Gladstone's resignation. On the other hand, Hartington and the Whigs were also in the process of leaving the Liberal fold over Home Rule; with their departure the party would be cleansed of the group that Chamberlain had previously denounced as the true enemies of progress. By hanging on to office it was arguable that Chamberlain would be better placed to pick up the pieces after Gladstone's fall; he would, moreover, stand a much healthier chance of carrying the National Liberal Federation (the Caucus) with him if he stayed in the Cabinet.

Chamberlain later denied that he had any intention of breaking up the party. J. A. Spender, at one time editor of the *Westminster Gazette*, recalled the following dinner table conversation in 1899. Chamberlain speaking 'as was his wont, with great freedom and animation' said, 'Mr. Gladstone committed the greatest offence a statesman is capable of—he broke up his party.' One of his fellow diners quickly taxed him by saying 'that is very intolerant, and from you of all men; for if Mr. Gladstone hadn't broken up the Liberal Party you would have.' Chamberlain replied, 'Not a bit of it; that is exactly the mistake which you all made. I should not have broken up the party, I should have strengthened the party by dropping the Whigs, and I should have carried not one but two or three unauthorised programmes.'[251]

Nor was the prospect that faced Chamberlain after his resignation an attractive one, despite his taste for conflict. He wrote a

revealing analysis of his future in a letter to his brother Arthur on 8
March:

> The immediate result will be considerable unpopularity and
> temporary estrangement from the Radical Party. There is little
> backbone in politics and the great majority are prepared to
> swallow anything and to stick to the machine. In the Cabinet I
> have no support worth mentioning and the only person who will
> go with me is Trevelyan who is very weak generally but in this
> matter is pledged up to the eyes.
>
> I shall be left almost alone for a time. I cannot of course work
> with the Tories & Hartington is quite as much hostile to my
> radical views as to W.G's Irish plans.
>
> But in time the situation will clear. Either Mr. G. will
> succeed and get the Irish question out of the way or he will fail.
>
> In either case he will retire from politics and I do not suppose
> the Liberal Party will accept Childers or even John Morley as its
> permanent leader.[252]

The last sentence contains an indirect reference to Chamberlain's
ambitions for the party leadership. It amounts, in fact, to a confession of such ambitions—at least in the medium term. The only
other Radical politician who might have stood in Chamberlain's
way was, moreover, decisively out of the race by March 1886, for
Sir Charles Dilke had been cited as co-respondent in a divorce case
that was to scandalise Victorian society and ruin him as a serious
contender for major office. Crawford versus Crawford and Dilke
opened in the law courts on 12 February 1886.

As the court proceedings unfolded, Dilke was enmeshed in a
sticky web of accusation and innuendo. Mrs. Crawford, the young
and delectable wife of a middle-aged husband, confessed to an
extra-marital relationship with Dilke which included the staggering
assertion that he had introduced a third party, a serving-girl called
Fanny to her, and that they had all on several occasions shared the
same bed. Not content with alleging this three-in-a-bed sexual
activity, Mrs. Crawford told the court that Dilke 'taught me every
French vice. He used to say I knew more than most women of
thirty.'[253]

Whether true or not, these allegations were hardly likely to make
smooth Dilke's path to 10 Downing Street, especially by way of
Windsor Castle. The result of the case seemed clearly to confirm

Dilke's adulterous affair with Mrs. Crawford; the court proceedings had, moreover, painted a garish picture of a philandering and debauched career that might have been taken straight from the pages of a contemporary pornographic novel.

No sooner was Dilke brought crashing down, than stories of plots behind the Crawford scandal multiplied. One theory was that Lord and Lady Rosebery were behind the whole business, and had bribed Mrs. Crawford to confess so that Rosebery could become Foreign Secretary in Dilke's place—which he did in February 1886.

More persistent was the gossip that Chamberlain was behind Dilke's fall. Certainly Dilke was later to claim that a week before the trial broke it had been agreed among the Radical cabal that he should be the future leader.[254] A motive for Chamberlain's alleged treachery thus existed. More damning is the evidence that, on 15 July 1885, two days before her confession of adultery to her husband, Mrs. Crawford had called at Chamberlain's London house and had, according to a police observer, spent two hours there before leaving.

There is no evidence of what transpired between them, but it is true that Chamberlain subsequently failed to inform Dilke of Mrs. Crawford's visit and later, when confronted with the incident, told less than the truth about the details. Even if Chamberlain did not encourage Mrs. Crawford to make her confession, he certainly did nothing (or was able to do nothing) to deflect her from that course.

A discussion of the possible motives behind a Chamberlain plot would be absorbing, but fruitless. Dilke did not believe in a plot, and later wrote that 'though a "Red Indian" Chamberlain is loyal to his friends and incapable of such treachery.' On the other hand, Dilke was to some extent the dependent partner in the friendship, telling Chamberlain in September 1881 'it is curious that in spite of what people say about the jealousies of politicians you should be one of the two or three people in the world about whose life and death I should care enough for that care to be worth the name of affection.'[255] He was also extra-sensitive to supposed slights from his friend, and in December 1882 Chamberlain found it necessary to reassure him of his good fellowship:

There is not the *slightest* ground for your suspicion. I suppose I was taken aback at finding you in my room when I was expecting a German Jew. . . . But I was not conscious of any change of manner. . . .

The fact is that you are by nature such a reserved fellow that all *demonstration* of affection is difficult, but you may believe me when I say that I feel it—none the less. I suppose I am reserved myself. The great trouble we have both been through [the death of their wives] has had a hardening effect in my case, & since then I have never worn my heart on my sleeve.

But if I were in trouble I should come to you at once—& that is the best proof of friendship & confidence that I know of.[256]

The overall impression of Chamberlain's relationship with Dilke is one of an intimacy that was likely to be disrupted from time to time by a coldness, or a rejection—hastily denied—on Chamberlain's part. That the two were as close as their reserved private natures allowed is evident from a number of examples. For one thing, Dilke's son by his first marriage, Wentworth ('Wentie'), lived with the Chamberlains at Birmingham for two years. The young Dilke was not an easy charge, but on 12 September 1882 Chamberlain wrote to his friend, in a quasi-paternal style:

My principal object in writing is to say that for some months past Wentie has been very good—much less troublesome than at first, & we have had no further complaint to make of his truthfulness. I should touch very lightly on this to his school-mistress, as it is evidently only a childish fault, & he will get over it.

He has a decided taste for natural history . . . & I think this taste should be encouraged. I think he will do very well at School now & probably be the better for the company of other boys.[257]

Apart from sharing the upbringing of Dilke's son (whose birth, like that of Austen Chamberlain, had resulted in his mother's death) the two men used each other's rooms at Westminster and elsewhere as if they were their own, and sometimes passed each other notes of an intimate nature at Cabinet meetings during the last years of Gladstone's 1880–5 administration. On 20 February 1885, for instance, Chamberlain unburdened himself to Dilke by passing him a note that revealed a good deal of his personal philosophy:

It appears that in estimating future probabilities some . . .

attach importance to the alleged fact that *I* am a confirmed atheist but that you have 'found Jesus'!

What you say [in a previous note] is very interesting. I do not know that we differ much except that I am more impatient of the *forms* of Religious people & cannot stand Church or any other service.

I began as a devout Unitarian. The death of my first wife brought the whole thing very close to me & the doctrines which did very well before broke down under that calamity. After trying to find an explanation of the 'great mystery', I gave it up once for all, satisfied that there was quite enough to occupy me in this life without bothering about what is to come afterwards.[258]

Even if the lowest view is taken of Chamberlain's character, it is still difficult to imagine him plotting to ruin one of the few men with whom he was prepared to reveal the secret places of his personality. What is significant is that Chamberlain's deportment provoked this sort of gossip. When, four years later, in 1890, Parnell was also destroyed by the O'Shea divorce case, allegations were again made that Chamberlain had instigated Captain O'Shea to start legal proceedings against his wife and the Irish leader. Certainly O'Shea was in Chamberlain's political debt, and there was also every reason for the latter to wish for the ruin of Parnell and Parnellism. In this case, there seems to be some substance in the accusations levelled at Chamberlain, and Neville Chamberlain, discussing the controversy in 1927 with Austen, later recalled some circumstantial evidence, which is intriguing if inconclusive:

I personally remember that O'Shea came to Highbury & spent I think a night there just before the (divorce) proceedings were taken against Parnell, but of course I was not present at any conversation on the subject and I do not know what was the purpose of the visit. Evidently Father knew of the proceedings beforehand but that does not prove he instigated them.

Austen also had 'a vague recollection that O'Shea sought financial assistance from Father for his divorce proceedings and that Father, who had previously once or perhaps even twice lent him £100 without any expectation of repayment, definitely refused any contribution for such a purpose.'[259]

Chamberlain's friendship with Dilke was quite plainly not

destroyed by the Crawford divorce case, nor did the latter's fall land the party leadership in his colleague's lap. Any coolness that developed between them in 1886 sprang from the political crisis that turned party and personal loyalties upside down, and resulted in Dilke voting for the Home Rule Bill.

Despite pious hopes that a *rapprochement* would take place between Chamberlain and Gladstone, nothing of the kind happened. The sticking point was the government's eventual refusal to retain Irish M.P.s at Westminster in the provisions of the Home Rule Bill. Chamberlain and other 'unionists', of all political complexions, argued that by retaining the Irish members at Westminster the essential supremacy of the Imperial Parliament in central legislative and fiscal matters would be preserved; at the same time the southern Irish and Ulster (a thorn in the side of any Home Rule negotiations) would have separate assemblies with limited powers; such assemblies could be extended to the other parts of the United Kingdom. Here was another revamping of the Chamberlainite 'National Councils' scheme, under the heading of federal government, or home rule all round.

Chamberlain was determined to vote against the Home Rule Bill, though conscious that he 'should be singled out as the cause of its defeat and should be the mark of the most bitter animosity from that section of the party that supported him. . . . Of course I should sacrifice all hope of ever having any office, whereas as Mr. Gladstone's colleague, I had the best chance of succeeding him in the leadership of the Liberal Party. I had, therefore, every inducement to come to terms if possible.'[260]

But insufficient inducement came from the Gladstonians. On 9 April Chamberlain spoke against the Bill during its first reading. The crucial second reading was due to take place at the beginning of June. In the interim, as both Home Rulers and anti-Home Rulers went grubbing around for votes, and amid desperate attempts to reconcile Chamberlain and his estimated fifty supporters to the Bill, the Radical leader gave substance to a defensive Liberal Unionist alliance by attending a meeting on 14 May summoned by Hartington. Such a closing of the ranks of Whigs and Chamberlainites was all the more necessary in view of the fact that Schnadhorst and the National Liberal Federation had gone over to Gladstone early in May.

Despite desperate last-minute lobbying aimed at winning over the Liberal Unionist waverers, the rebels held enough of their support to defeat the second reading of the Bill by thirty votes on 8 June. Gladstone then bullied his Cabinet into going for a dissolution, relying chiefly upon Schnadhorst's confident calculation that a General Election would almost certainly result in a Liberal Home Rulers' majority—with up to half of the ninety Liberal defectors replaced by no-nonsense Radicals, and the restored Irish vote in England bringing back twenty-five seats for the Gladstonians.

The General Election was due to begin on 1 July. The results were difficult to predict, though Chamberlain had no fears in Birmingham where he and four other candidates were unopposed. What was clear, however, was that the two-party system (with the Irish Nationalists bidding to hold the balance) was, for the moment at least, destroyed. Chamberlain was not the man to loiter amid political chaos and the clash of conflicting factions, and between his resignation and the General Election he busied himself with forging alliances and creating new political organisations.

EIGHT

THE LIBERAL UNIONIST: TRIALS AND OPPORTUNITIES
1886–95

... we shall find in [Chamberlain], so long as he agrees with us, a very different kind of ally from those luke-warm and slippery Whigs whom it is so difficult to differ *from* and impossible to work *with*. What results will ultimately follow in the impending reconstruction of parties I cannot conjecture. 'In politics,' said Chamberlain on Monday . . . 'there is no use looking beyond the next fortnight.'
A. J. Balfour to Lord Salisbury, 22 March 1886

FOR GLADSTONE, Home Rule promised substantial personal and political rewards: some determined and successful legislative surgery would not only cut the Irish canker from the British body politic, but also provide him with an honourable consummation to his controversial career. At the same time, the safe deliverance of Home Rule would help to ensure that Chamberlain would never get his tainted provincial hands on the Liberal party's leadership; squalid ambition (or so it appeared to Gladstone) would thus be kept at a decent distance, and the threat of unrestrained Radicalism, preaching class warfare and confiscatory socialism, would be contained. This bid for an uncontaminated future (though ignoring the looming problem of Protestant Ulster) rested, however, upon Home Rule legislation actually being enacted. In the event, this did not come about, and Gladstone's strategy collapsed, leaving the party unable to rid itself of the Home Rule incubus until the machination and compromise of 1921–2.

For Chamberlain, Home Rule proved to be the stumbling block which kept him isolated from the Liberal party and which consequently dashed his leadership ambitions. In the immediate aftermath of his resignation from Gladstone's government, however, his long-term prospects were promising enough: Gladstone, though already exhibiting Methuselah-like qualities, could not last much longer as party leader, and his departure would allow the Liberals to ditch Home Rule and bend their energies towards reforming policies. In these circumstances, Chamberlain could emerge triumphantly to heal the party's wounds and, incidentally, to scoop up the leader's crown.

Chamberlain's immediate concern when he resigned from the Cabinet in March 1886, however, was to ensure the defeat of the impending Home Rule Bill. Quite apart from preventing defections from among his own supporters in the Commons, 'Killing the Bill' entailed cooperation with the Conservative opposition and the Hartingtonian Whigs. Such cooperation would need dextrous handling, for Chamberlain was acutely sensitive to the fact that Gladstonian Liberals and assorted Radicals would be quick to cry traitor, and to pillory him for conspiracy with their political foes.

On Monday 22 March he met A. J. Balfour, and others, at a small private dinner party and spoke candidly of his feelings, poised as he was between having offered his resignation and waiting to have it confirmed by the Cabinet meeting due on 26 March. The meeting with Balfour was particularly significant. Balfour, then aged thirty-eight, was Lord Salisbury's nephew and destined to be his political heir; any conversation with him was tantamount to a conversation with Salisbury himself. Indeed Balfour proceeded straightway to 'Boswellise' Chamberlain for Salisbury, dictating the dinner party conversation while it was still fresh in his recollection. Noting that Chamberlain had 'talked with his usual "engaging frankness"— and to do him justice, very pleasantly and without "pose",' Balfour told his uncle:

You will note that throughout all this it was openly assumed that Chamberlain was going to leave the Government. I have little or no doubt that he will, but it must be remembered that Gladstone has not, or had not then on Monday communicated his scheme to the Cabinet, but apparently only enough of it to convince Joe that he at least could not swallow it!

I have a strong suspicion that Dilke's position and W.E.G.'s refusal to have anything to do with him count for something in the decision at which Chamberlain has apparently arrived. "He means" said Fowler [the Liberal Secretary to the Treasury] to me the other day "to break up the Liberal Party."[261]

Balfour then proceeded to recount some choice 'fragments of Chamberlainana'. Among them was Chamberlain's grudgingly respectful assessment of Gladstone's strength, 'I agree with what Harcourt said—"We shall never know how strong he is until he has got rid of every one of his Colleagues" '; and also his optimistic view of a prospective election, 'Well, part of my democratic creed is that if a scheme is truly absurd (and unless we are all in a dream, this scheme is so) people can be made to understand its absurdity.' On the other hand, he was quite clear as to the tight-rope anti-Home Rule Radicals were walking 'since the mere suspicion that a Radical is going to get Tory support would of itself ensure his defeat.'

What, then, could Radicals and Tories essay together? One possible venture was an assault upon the Whigs:

> *Chamberlain.* Now, Balfour, let us make a joint attack on the Whigs. The Tory policy I understand with regard to Ireland and the Radical policy I understand. The Tories go in for coercion. I believe that if that could be carried out consistently for 5 years it would succeed. The Radicals go in for very large measures of Reform and Local Government. They are ready to allow the Irish to manage and mismanage their affairs as they please up to a certain point with a determination of coming down and crushing them if they go beyond that point. Just as the North left the South alone year after year but finally imposed their will by force. But the Whigs are too frightened of the Radicals to support the Tories and too frightened of the Tories to support the Radicals. It is no particular secret now that what destroyed the last Liberal Govt. was not the Budget but the proposal of a National Council for Ireland. The Whigs in the Cabinet would not accept it and now we see them in the shape of Spencer and Granville going in for Home Rule.[262]

Chamberlain was also quick to express his antagonism to various socialist remedies for contemporary problems:

> *A.J.B.* You do not approve, I imagine, of the absurd system of Double Ownership in land which your people introduced in Ireland and are now introducing into Scotland. Of course, I am now speaking without prejudice and across the Dinner Table.
> *Chamberlain.* Without prejudice then and across the Dinner Table, holding myself quite free in an official capacity to use opposite language—I do not approve of it. My view about land has always been to municipalise it—a barbarous word, which however, expresses my substitute for absurd schemes of Land

Nationalisation. I caused my Municipality to purchase no less than £1,400,000 worth of land and that is the system which I desire to see extended. I do not know much about Broadhurst's Bill but if it would require Corporations to sell to individuals land which they have leased to them I should certainly move for excluding Corporations from its operations. . . .

Chamberlain. I think the out look is alarming. Any important relaxation of Out-Door Relief would produce most serious consequences. State Public Works are absurd. Yet if this distress goes on for three more years we may find ourselves *"en pleine révolution"*. I may be wrong but that is my instinct.

What also emerged plainly from the conversation was Chamberlain's hankering for a strong, 'Imperial' government:

Chamberlain. I think a democratic Government should be the strongest Government, from a military and Imperial point of view, in the world for it has the people behind it. Our misfortune is that we live under a system of Government originally contrived to check the actions of Kings and Ministers and which meddles therefore far too much with the Executive of the country. The problem is to give the democracy the whole power, but to induce it to do no more in the way of using it than to decide on the general principles which it wishes to see carried out. My Radicalism, at all events, desires to see established a strong Government and an Imperial Government.[263]

Balfour concluded his Boswellian account thus:

The only two observations which it occurs to me to make on those portions of the foregoing which relate to the present crisis are (1) That Chamberlain means if possible not to let Hartington be the man to throw out Gladstone's scheme: and (2) that we shall find in him so long as he agrees with us a very different kind of ally from those lukewarm and slippery Whigs whom it is difficult to differ *from* and impossible to act *with*. What results will ultimately follow in the impending reconstruction of parties I cannot conjecture. "In politics," said Chamberlain on Monday (in words with which in Randolph's mouth I am familiar) "there is no use looking beyond the next fortnight."

Yr. Affec. nephew,
Arthur James Balfour

Having thrown a life-line from his Radical schooner to the ponderous Conservative ship-of-state, Chamberlain lost no time in forging links with 'those lukewarm and slippery Whigs'. In part, his overtures to the Whigs rested upon the arithmetical necessity of rallying sufficient anti-Home Rule Liberal support to 'Kill the Bill'. It was also important to show common cause between Whigs and Radicals, but not to the extent of making the latter the lap-dogs of the former. On the other hand, if either Hartington or Chamberlain had to lead Liberal opposition to the second reading of the Home Rule Bill, Chamberlain preferred Hartington to do it and risk burning his fingers in the resulting blaze of Gladstonian indignation.

On 14 May 1886 Chamberlain gave effect to his cautious desire to cooperate with the Whigs by attending a Liberal Unionist meeting at Devonshire House with thirty-two of his followers. He justified this open alliance with his erstwhile foes in a letter written the next day to his brother Arthur:

I went to Hartington's yesterday

1st. To show that we were a united party of opponents and not heterogeneous atoms.

2. Because Hartington has frankly come over to my view and will finally adopt my policy of Federal Local Govt. as an alternative to separation.

3. Because it strengthens our party in the House to know that we are solid—and that one section is not likely at the last moment to leave the other in the lurch.

4. Because Mr. G. has burned his boats on the question of the retention of Irish members, and does not intend to make any further attempt to conciliate me, though he may try to draw off my opposition.[264]

Out of this meeting grew the Liberal Unionist Association, established at first as a temporary defensive alliance under Hartington, but in fact destined to be a permanent feature of British political life for more than two decades.

Though Chamberlain was eventually to supplant Hartington (by then Duke of Devonshire) as Chairman of the Liberal Unionist Association in 1904, he was careful in 1886 to maintain a separate identity from the early Committee for the Maintenance of the Union (the embryonic Liberal Unionist Association).

In fact, his response to the turmoil and challenge of 1886 was profoundly characteristic—reminiscent of his activities shortly after entering Parliament when he set about establishing the National Liberal Federation, and prophetic of his launching of the Tariff Reform League in 1903: he decided to establish a new constituency organisation. It was not merely that such a new Chamberlainite organisation would provide an obedient vehicle for his views; necessity also demanded it, for the National Liberal Federation was slipping from his grasp. On 7 June, a little before the final division on the second reading of the Home Rule Bill, Schnadhorst, in an interview in the *Pall Mall Gazette*, optimistically dismissed the effects of Chamberlain's estrangement from the National Liberal Federation by claiming that 'The only change, therefore, that we know of in the Caucus is that we have lost three or four officers, and gained 24 associations. . . . I think that the feeling of the local associations is as Gladstonian as the Federation, and that the local associations accurately represent the feelings of the Liberal electorate.'[265]

Despite the enthusiastic constituency support emanating from his Birmingham fief, Chamberlain needed a nation-wide organisation distinct from Hartington and the Whigs. On 4 June he told his brother Arthur:

Up to the present time I have been able to join the Unionist Committee.

I am not at all indisposed to the idea of forming a separate Committee with a headquarters at Birmingham but I have been too busy to decide on this. The object of course would be partly electoral—that is the usual caucus work—partly educational, to promote the Federal plan which I have been advocating.[266]

Three days later he came up with a name for the new organisation —the Radical Unionist Committee. On 9 June, following the defeat of the Home Rule Bill, he wrote again to Arthur Chamberlain:

The division was excellent & my men held together like bricks·

The matter of great importance now is the new organization· The best name will be

National Radical Union.

Object: To secure the control of their own domestic business by England, Scotland, Wales & Ireland under the supreme

authority of one Parliament for the United Kingdom. . . .
The Irish seem very rabid with me. They are a nice lot of
ruffians.[267]

Chamberlain launched the National Radical Union with an
announcement in the press, an invitation to the forty-six Radical
M.P.s who had voted against the Home Rule Bill to become vice-
presidents of the new body, and a personal subscription of £1,000.
Not all Radical M.P.'s were attracted to the new organisation, and
John Bright believed that it would only add to the prevailing
political confusion.

In these early days of the National Radical Union's history,
Chamberlain was also playing for time, hoping on the one hand for
a *rapprochement* with mainstream Liberalism once Gladstone had
gone, speculating, on the other, that he might be able to found a
new national progressive party in alliance with Lord Randolph
Churchill and the Tory Democrats.[268] Neither of these prospects
were to materialise: Gladstone hung on to the Liberal leadership,
and Randolph Churchill (with whom Chamberlain agreed on a
good many proposals for domestic reform) had, within a year,
resigned from Salisbury's second administration, and then, dogged
by illness, proceeded to fizzle out as a serious political force.

In fact, there was to be no dashingly independent course for the
National Radical Union to pursue; expediency demanded close
cooperation with the Liberal Unionist Association and, after a
while, the fortunes and characters of the two rebel organisations
became intertwined and extremely difficult to tell apart.

The 1886 General Election campaign revealed the extent of the
problems facing Chamberlain and his supporters. Unable to influence the Conservatives, he was reluctant to 'be the first to attack
Liberal seats'. Whatever he did, Chamberlain, was bound to be
accused of advising electors in seats at issue between Conservative
and Home Rule Liberals to vote Tory. Oddly Hartington escaped
a similarly severe castigation, perhaps due in some measure to
Gladstone's judgement that, 'There is this difference between
Hartington and Chamberlain, that the first behaves like and is a
thorough gentleman. Of the other it is better not to speak.'

Conservative and Liberal Unionist cooperation during the
election campaign was limited to a defensive alliance—a tacit
agreement to avoid a clash between the two allies in any seat con-

tested by a Liberal Home Rule candidate. This compact was to form the basis of the future electoral relationship between the Conservative Party and the Liberal Unionist Association.

The election was fought almost exclusively on the Home Rule issue, thus justifying Chamberlain's contention that the controversy was distorting the true course of Liberalism. At Birmingham on 21 April addressing the 'Two Thousand' of the caucus he had emphasised this point, saying, 'I do not believe there was a man amongst us at that time [the 1885 General Election] who thought that in a few short weeks all these matters [of social reform] would be relegated to the dim and distant future—that we should be absorbed in this vast problem of re-constituting and remodelling the arrangements between the three Kingdoms.'[269] As to the reason for this transformation, Chamberlain was quite clear, it was 'due to the force of character, to the determination and to the courage, of one illustrious man'—Gladstone.

Chamberlain's personal campaigning at the end of June and the beginning of July 1886 was characterised by savage assaults on Fenian outrages and an unashamed appeal to patriotic emotions. British federalism and the Central Councils scheme did not set his audiences alight, an impassioned 'Radical-Imperialism' did. Just as Lord Randolph Churchill was simultaneously playing the 'Orange card' ('Ulster will fight, and Ulster will be right!'), Chamberlain played the 'British patriotic and anti-terrorist card', and with equal success:

These two islands have always played a great part in the history of the world. For again and again—outnumbered, overmatched —confronted with difficulties and dangers—they have held their own against a world in arms. . . . And if . . . now, you are going to yield to the threat of obstruction and agitation; if you tremble at the thought of responsibility . . . if the British courage and pluck are dead within your hearts; if you are going to quail before the dagger of the assassin and the threats ("Never" and protracted cheering, the audience rising in a body)—and the threats of conspirators and rebels, then I say the sceptre of dominion will have passed from our grasp, and this great Empire will perish with the loss of the qualities which have hitherto sustained it.[270]

This was good vote-winning stuff, if a trifle lurid, and there was little doubt that Chamberlain had struck an electoral goldmine as rewarding as the 'Unauthorised Programme' had been a year before. Home Rule was a vote-loser, and Liberal Unionists and Conservatives were to reap the benefit. The election of 1886 was thus a novel experience for Chamberlain; he was campaigning *against* a programme of change, delivering up an 'anti'-vote for the benefit of those Conservatives who had previously assailed him so vituperatively, and whom he expected to oppose him strenuously again when the Home Rule phantom had passed away. Negative politics were new to Chamberlain, no matter how skilfully he dressed them up.

The election results saw the Gladstonian Liberals lose forty-four seats, ending up with 191. The Liberal Unionists lost some ground, being reduced to seventy-nine M.P.s, but they were still a formidable grouping; Chamberlain, Bright and five other anti-Home Rulers were returned for Birmingham. The Conservatives gained sixty-five seats, leaping to a handsome total of 316. With Parnell's Irish support staying static there was a decisive majority of 395 Conservatives and Liberal Unionists against 275 Liberal Home Rulers and Irish Nationalists. Liberal losses were mainly in suburbia and the counties. 'Three acres and a cow' was a disastrous flop: rural voters stayed at home in droves, and even the agricultural workers' leader Joseph Arch was beaten; after all, Gladstone had seemed to care little for allotments, and neither the cow nor the acres had materialised.

Gladstone resigned on 21 July. What administration would be formed in place of the fallen Liberals? Lord Salisbury tried to persuade Hartington to lead a coalition Unionist government, but the bid failed, and Salisbury himself took office at the head of his second ministry.

The Conservative Government could only hope to survive for any length of time, however, with Liberal Unionist support. Chamberlain had foreseen this eventuality when on 13 June he had proposed an agreement to Balfour. In order to enforce Gladstone's departure, Chamberlain argued, there must be a Tory administration with Liberal Unionist backing of an informal nature. He told Balfour, 'My idea is that you [the Conservatives] should form a Government with a definite and complete understanding with Hartington, and an adequate though less complete understanding with me.'[271]

In the immediate future, however, any Chamberlainite under-standing with the Tories was bound to be limited to Ireland. Given the vehemence of Gladstonian and Parnellite attacks upon his motives and integrity, Chamberlain could not afford (even if he had so desired) to come to any deals on broader areas of policy with the Conservatives and thus risk alienating working-class radical support—his trump card in terms of electoral weight and value. The Radical parson, W. Tuckwell, saw clearly the disillusion among rural labourers that had already been provoked by Glad-stone's plunge for Home Rule: 'Working men would find that their devotion had been thrown away, their confidence abused, the promised reforms to which they gave their votes postponed indefinitely, if not altogether sacrificed to a measure of which no one amongst them had ever heard.'[272] If Chamberlain had sloughed off any part of his shiny Radical skin in the immediate aftermath of the 1886 election he would have been founder-member of a rogues' gallery of those radical statesmen accused of cheating the working classes out of their just rewards—just as Lloyd George failed after 1918 to produce 'a fit land for heroes', or Ramsay MacDonald was charged with selling his soul to the Tories in 1931. There were enough enemies to call Chamberlain 'Mephistopheles', even 'Judas', in 1886 without unnecessarily adding to their numbers.

In fact, Chamberlain's position in July 1886 was extremely precarious. Believing that 'Mr. Gladstone's action has ... destroyed the Liberal Party as a controlling force in politics for a considerable time',[273] Chamberlain lacked the power to put Humpty-Dumpty together again. His creation, the National Liberal Federation, had turned on its animator and threatened to devour him; as yet the National Radical Union was a puny offspring, barely able to hold its own in the bruising political aftermath of the Home Rule crisis. Birmingham, though still faithful, could not be taken for granted.

Cut adrift from mainstream Liberalism and the party machine, reluctant, by inclination and conviction, to give support to Toryism, Chamberlain at first pinned considerable hope upon evolving a fruitful working relationship with Lord Randolph Churchill. Here was a potential political link that Chamberlain could foster while simultaneously preserving his national reputation. What the long-term prospects of continuing harmony between personalities as forceful, self-confident and ambitious as Chamberlain and Churchill

might have been was, however, a different matter; both might have
fed, gannet-like, upon the other's strengths and ideas.

In November 1886 Churchill produced his own Tory Democratic 'Unauthorised Programme' in a speech at Dartford. His
proposals included a good deal that was common ground with
Chamberlain's own 'Radical' or 'Unauthorised Programme' of
over a year before: smallholdings for agricultural labourers, local
government reform for Ireland as well as for other parts of the
United Kingdom, the renunciation of coercion in Ireland. For the
rest, Churchill pressed for a non-aggressive foreign policy and
limitations upon defence expenditure. He also proposed a progressive alliance with the Liberal Unionists; but it was difficult to
see Hartington and the Whigs warming to his plans, and the only
meaningful alliance would have to be with Chamberlain and the
Radical anti-Home Rulers.

Recklessly believing that he had sufficient party backing, and
convinced that he held the key to a glittering electoral future for
democratised Toryism, in December 1886 Churchill offered his
resignation as Chancellor of the Exchequer and Leader of the
Commons rather than accept increased military and naval expenditure. Salisbury accepted the resignation, thus putting
Churchill's challenge to his own authority to the test; Conservatives
rallied to their leader, and Lord Randolph was left to rot in the
political wilderness.

Any hopes that Chamberlain may have entertained for a new
broad-based Radical party had thus suffered a tremendous setback
since, according to Salisbury, Churchill's 'friendship for Chamberlain . . . made him insist that we should accept that Statesman as
our guide in internal affairs'. Churchill, who had not bothered to
consult Chamberlain before taking his ill-judged lunge at Salisbury's leadership, was finished as a positive political force. His
place at the Exchequer, moreover, was taken by the right-wing
Liberal Unionist, Goschen, the trenchant critic of Chamberlain's
'Unauthorised Programme'. This tangible link between the right-
wing of Liberal Unionism and the Conservative Government was
an ominous portent for Chamberlain and drove him into the
attempt, early in 1887, to negotiate some sort of agreement over
Ireland with the Gladstonians.

The Round Table Conference, a series of sporadic meetings,
took place during January and February 1887 between Harcourt,

Morley and Herschell on the Gladstonian side and Chamberlain and Trevelyan on the other. Harcourt in particular believed that Chamberlain's suddenly increased isolation provided a suitable climate for that reconciliation which probably the bulk of the Liberal party desired. From his point of view, Chamberlain stood to gain by the talks: a genuine agreement over Ireland (wildly improbable as this may have seemed) would enable him to stake his claim to the future leadership of the party; at the very least, a serious flirtation with his former colleagues would make Salisbury and Tories more appreciative of his attractions and, as a result, might possibly keep them from embarking on a heavy-handed policy of repression in Ireland.

How serious was Chamberlain's approach to the Round Table Conference? Morley, the most committed of the Gladstonian negotiators, was not at all clear. On the one hand, he told Harcourt that 'I am utterly and incorrigibly incredulous. He [Chamberlain] has found out that his egotism, irascibility and perversity have landed him in a vile mess. . . . He has proved himself to have no wisdom and no temper. Never more let me be asked to believe in his statesmanship. *C'est fini.*'[274] On the other, he wrote to Lord Ripon on 19 January 1887 that 'C[hamberlain] is evidently conscious that he has got himself into a terrible scrape, and is anxious to come back into the fold on reasonable terms. As for G.O.M., he is very shadowy, and not substantial. I think it will come right.'[275]

Chamberlain, for his part, entertained no great hope, early in 1887, that the Round Table Conference would put things to rights, telling his twenty-three-year-old son Austen on 11 January:

> I think that matters are coming to a crisis here. Gladstonianism is becoming more sectional & more irreconcilable & I do not want to reunite with a party—or faction—controlled by Labouchere, Lawson, Conybeare.
>
> I see the possibility of a strong Central Party which may be master of the situation after Mr. Gladstone goes.
>
> Meanwhile Unionism in the country is decidedly making progress & Mr. G.'s Welsh speeches have not done him any good.[276]

A week later, however, he told Walter Wren:

> I am myself hopeful of the result of the conference but no

success would be worth purchasing if it involved humiliation on either side, or the abandonment of principle. I am not going to ruin my country in order to unite my party, and I am as much convinced as ever that the effect of such a policy as that which I have opposed would be not only ruinous to the country but absolutely destructive of all chances of further Liberal progress.[277]

In the same letter he also expressed some clear and unrepentant views as to his own leadership prospects and the future shape of party reunion:

I do not care a brass pin for my political interests nor am I in the least anxious to lead the Liberal party except on my own lines. I do not intend to purchase nominal leadership by a miserable truckling to popular clamour. I have nothing to regret in reference to my past action which if it were worthwhile I could show to be absolutely consistent with everything I have previously said & done in the matter. I am perfectly convinced that if a union is to come it must be & will be on my lines, & when this happens it is possible that some of the gentlemen who are now abusing & insulting me will regret that they did not support me throughout in which case there would have been no division of the party with all its disastrous results.

Mr. Gladstone's Home Rule Bill was drawn hastily & on wrong lines. It cannot be amended so as to make a satisfactory measure. Fortunately it is now dead & out of the way & there is some chance of building up on a fresh foundation.[278]

Despite the misgivings felt on both sides, the Round Table Conference had made some progress by the middle of February. An Irish Land scheme had been agreed in principle, and Harcourt had promised to draw up a Home Rule scheme based on the Canadian federal constitution, though reserving points of disagreement. Chamberlain was by now expressing considerable admiration for the Canadian federation as a practical example of what his 'Home Rule all round' plan might entail, though John Bright (who thought the conference 'a piece of impudence') gloomily confessed 'I cannot get up any enthusiasm for schemes based on systems of federation or on the example of the Canadian constitution.'[279]

These preliminary agreements of the Round Table Conference proved, however, to be false omens. Gladstone was inflexibly opposed to a real compromise, though reluctant to be the first to break off negotiations. It was Harcourt, in fact, who ended the talks by repeatedly evading Chamberlain's attempts to clarify certain points—notably the Gladstonian contention that acceptance of the two abortive bills of 1886 (the Home Rule Bill and the Land Purchase Bill) provided the basis for the new discussions.

On 9 March Chamberlain (who had earlier proclaimed in a letter to the *Baptist* newspaper that 'The issue of the Round Table Conference will decide much more than the Irish Question. It will decide the immediate future of the Liberal party, and whether or no all Liberal reform is to be indefinitely adjourned.') acknowledged to his ally Trevelyan that the Conference had ended as far as he was concerned. He added:

I have met with a series of excuses, the validity of which I entirely contest, and am forced to the conclusion that having ascertained our views, Harcourt and his friends now shrink from committing themselves to any opinion on them. . . .

Lastly (and I think this is the true reason for their conduct) Harcourt says that time is working on their side. . . . He therefore declines to fix any time for the resumption of our discussion, and seems to think that he can keep us waiting in the antechamber until his present mood of exultancy gives place to the next fit of depression. I do not think his conduct loyal or wise, and I shall now act independently and without further reference to the Conference.[280]

Time certainly did appear to be on the side of the Gladstonians: the Conservative Government's recent lurch into coercion, Irish disturbances, the intransigence of the Irish Nationalist M.P.s at Westminster all seemed to prove that the nation had no real alternative but to accept Home Rule and thus rid itself of an increasingly onerous, and potentially crippling, burden.

Though Harcourt was somewhat reluctant to have to let the Round Table Conference wither away, and was still clutching at Chamberlainite straws in the middle of March, the plain fact was that the failure of the discussions marked the end of the only quasi-formal attempt to bring the Radical anti-Home Rulers (and maybe

after them the Whigs) back into the Liberal fold. On the Gladstonian side there was perhaps no real inclination, and no real brief,
to make the talks succeed. John Morley, in particular, took a
cynical view of the proceedings, gloating to Ripon on 7 February
of the embarrassing position Chamberlain had got himself into:

> But it seems to me we are justified to a great extent in going into
> the Conference by fact of the distrust and suspicion about J.C.
> wh. has now entered the minds of his allies. . . . The differences
> between what he [Chamberlain] has committed himself to, and
> what is said by Hartington . . . were too patent to escape notice.
> I don't think we shd. have screwed him up to this point, without
> the temptation of the Round Table. He will carry off not one
> single scrap of substance from us.[281]

With old friends like this, Chamberlain had no need of enemies.
He was, however, as apparently full of confidence and vigour as
ever. Lady Stanley recorded her impressions of him at a dinner
party in London while the Round Table Conference was still in
progress:

> If there is no humility about Mr. Chamberlain, there is no
> arrogant assumption. . . . If I feel that a becoming diffidence is
> rather *wanting*, this is made up for by what seems calm prescience
> and consequent decision, marking him as a man who *must* win in
> the long run.

According to Lady Stanley, Chamberlain also said on this occasion:

> Of course, I shall be Premier there is nothing more certain. I
> will rebuild the fortress. . . . We shall not have Home Rule. We
> shall have improved government in Ireland . . . great reforms
> throughout Great Britain and Ireland, but it shall never come to
> granting Home Rule.[282]

In July 1887, with the passions evoked by Ireland still blazing
and the Conservatives (for whom Balfour as the new Chief
Secretary was about to apply the old remedies of coercion alter-
nating with a little kindness) proving difficult over reducing judicial
rents in an Irish Land Bill, Chamberlain was in a more depressed
mood, telling the Birmingham divine Dr. Dale, 'Politics continue
odious to me, and I fear the condition of things cannot be expected
to improve at present.'[283]

Chamberlain was, in fact, in an uncomfortable political limbo: Gladstone was proving as durable and intractable as ever; he could not contemplate taking office in a Conservative administration; the national government, headed by Hartington, and for which he and Lord Randolph Churchill still hankered had not materialised; there was, moreover, the real possibility that Liberal Unionism would wilt and die, starved of air and light by the towering growths of Gladstonian Liberalism and the Conservative party on either side.

Suddenly, at the end of August 1887, Lord Salisbury went some way towards lightening Chamberlain's political preoccupations by inviting him to lead the British delegation in a Joint Commission set up to solve the long-standing feud between the self-governing colonies of Canada and the United States over fishing rights off the coast of north-eastern Canada and New England. This fish war had recently been characterised by the seizure of American vessels and the firing of blank shots across their bows.

Chamberlain accepted Salisbury's invitation promptly and with a sense of relief. Ten days earlier he had written to Morley, during a dull stay at Hunstanton, 'I am seriously thinking of a long retirement later on, and of a visit to India or perhaps even to Australia.'[284] Now he was bound for the great English-speaking republic for which he had often professed admiration, conscious of the fact, conveyed to him by Salisbury, that the Queen approved 'very highly' of his appointment.

The American mission gave Chamberlain a new lease of life. His letters to friends and relatives at home positively bubble with enthusiasm and self-satisfaction. This was not merely because the negotiations went well, resulting in the signing of a treaty on 16 February 1888—though this was later rejected by the United States' Senate; it was also due to receiving widespread and distinguished support for his conflict with Gladstone, and to the new experiences and sights which flooded round him.

Affirmation of his political worth was particularly gratifying to Chamberlain at this point in his career, and he received it in full measure, both in the United States and in Canada. For example, the American Secretary of State, Bayard (he told his daughter Beatrice in a letter of 2 December 1887) had said that Gladstone had 'left the realm of law for that of passion'. Chamberlain added, 'Almost all the leading Americans here are Liberal-Unionists in regard to this question.'[285] In the middle of December, the President, Grover Cleveland, met Chamberlain. The two men discussed Gladstone's Irish policy 'of which he [Cleveland] evidently does not approve at all. In fact if he only knew it, Mr. G. has hardly a single supporter for his actual scheme outside the Irish and he has many severe critics of his methods of controversy and his recent utterances.'[286] At the end of the month Chamberlain journeyed to Ottawa where he met the Tory Prime Minister of Canada, Sir John Macdonald, who:

> spoke much of the Irish question in which he has no sympathy with Mr. Gladstone. . . . I have just received a deputation from the Sons of England who have presented an address in a strongly Unionist sense congratulating me on my firm stand for the integrity of the Empire. It is an association of Englishmen here & in the U.S. who have been moved by recent events to organise themselves in opposition to the Irish vote.[287]

Though wryly anticipating that British reaction to his diplomatic success would consist of a declaration by 'the prophet of evil . . . that I have sacrificed British interests to satisfy my personal ambition and vanity',[288] Chamberlain received a number of heart-warming contacts with Birmingham emigrants:

> On going away [from Toronto] a working man said he was a Brum and added—"You've not changed at all Sir—You're still the same old Joey". I shook hands with him and went off in high spirits.[289]

He also told Beatrice Chamberlain on 24 February 1888 that he had received a very pleasing letter from a Birmingham working man in Philadelphia, and . . .

> the other day walking in Washington I met and was accosted by another who spoke warmly of the Town and my part in its public life. It is pleasant to have these greetings all over the world and they are some reward for all the annoyance of political controversy.[290]

Apart from chance meetings of this nature, Chamberlain's North American mission included a whirl of official banquets, parties, afternoon teas, private dinners, sight-seeing excursions, interviews and calls. He walked perilously under the Niagara Falls on New Year's Day 1888, and two days later told Beatrice:

Life at Ottawa must be awfully dull in the ordinary way—the place is so small and there are no amusements except skating and tobogganing. . . .

I reached Toronto and 9 pm having dressed in the [railway] car and found a large dinner party "of the prettiest women in Toronto" waiting for me. This I am informed in the Papers was because I am well known as a connoisseur of female beauty.[291]

In fact, Chamberlain was on the look out for a wife. Fifty-one years old, slim, handsome, and with more than enough energy to revel in the killing pace of his American visit and still to sit up into the early hours talking animatedly over innumerable cigars, he was extraordinarily conscious of the appeal of American women. His letters to Beatrice clearly reflect his impressionable state:

A young lady asked which was the Chief Commissioner [Chamberlain]. On that distinguished individual being pointed out, she said: "Wal, I think he's lovely". . . .

I am compelled to admit that as far as I have seen the average of American female beauty is higher than ours. You see a very large number of nice looking girls in the streets and the proportion of good figures and of well dressed women is very large.[292]

I never saw so many bright and pretty women. . . . I have taken to dancing and revived my waltzing and polking. . . . All anxious they say to have my secret of perpetual youth. I give them my receipt freely, "No exercise and smoke all day".[293]

On 26 November at a lavish reception in his honour given at the British Legation in Washington, Chamberlain first met Mary Endicott, the daughter of the American Secretary of State for War. Chamberlain was immediately attracted to this good-looking girl of twenty-four, descended from Massachusetts Puritan stock, and told Beatrice on 9 December that she was 'one of the brightest and most intelligent girls I have yet met'.[294] By the time he left America, early in March 1888, Chamberlain had wooed and won a girl younger than his two eldest children Beatrice and Austen; he sailed from New York in the Cunarder *Umbria* with Mary

Endicott's portrait in his dispatch case, and plans to return in November to marry her.

During the seven months that separated him from his third marriage, Chamberlain plunged with new zest into his familiar English surroundings. He deluged Mary Endicott with letters, writing several times in each week, and sometimes every day. The letters are tantamount to a diary, and not only do they illustrate Chamberlain's extraordinarily wide-ranging interests and enthusiasms, but they also indicate a relaxation in the defences he had built round his innermost feelings.

He wrote about all manner of subjects: books, plays, astronomy, flowers, shopping, speech-making, Mr. Gladstone's style of oratory, Randolph Churchill, the Local Government Bill, Birmingham politics, the death of Matthew Arnold, his feelings upon his birthday, and a multitude of other topics.

18 April 1888: Above all I hope you will be pleased with your new home when you come to take possession of it. It has quite a new interest for me now that I constantly connect it with you and see you in imagination in every room.

20 April: I never saw the child yet that I could not get on with, and I think I must have it from my father who was especially tender with children and touched by their hopes and sorrows.

22 April: After dinner I got down one of the farces I wrote a long time ago and read it to the family, who proved a most indulgent audience. Then Neville played to us a *lied* of Mendelssohn's and part of a sonata by Beethoven.

1 June: Did I tell you that I have arranged a rosehouse for you at Highbury?

28 June: Take my advice and never marry a politician, but you may marry a horticulturist—a grower of orchids for instance. . . .

21 July: I went out to get a little fresh air. On my way I turned into a shop and bought a little blue china, etc., for the decoration of Highbury. I am just like a woman in this; it is a relief to my mind to buy something.

11 August: Went to the theatre to see—what do you think? *Joseph's Sweetheart*. I am sorry to say it was very stupid and we left after the third act. The piece is based on a novel of Fielding's, *Joseph Andrews*.[295]

Chamberlain's letters also reveal how his love for Mary Endicott,

and the joy that it brought him, enabled him to put his past un-
happiness into more realistic perspective:

> *8 July 1888*: This is my birthday, and it is natural that I should
> go back to last year and dwell on the changes made in my life. ...
> How much I owe you. Then I was much harder, striving to steel
> myself and play the game of life till the cards fell from my hands
> and caring little how soon that time came. Now, all this artificial
> insensibility is broken down: my youth comes back to me. ...
> *22 July*: I also want to go to Camberwell where I was born, to
> Highbury where my boyhood was passed, and to Highgate and
> Hampstead where I have reminiscences. I have never visited
> these places because I have been either too much occupied, or
> else, when I have had spare time, all the happiness of my life has
> been behind me, and I have decided not to risk recalling it to
> memory after the reality has passed, whereas now I can confront
> the past without fear.[296]

On 15 November Chamberlain married Mary Endicott in St.
John's Church, Washington, in an episcopalian service quite
appropriate for a lapsed Unitarian, though the bride's New
England Puritan tradition was upheld by the presence of the
Reverend Mr. Franks from Grace Church, Salem. Mary Endicott
wore a grey travelling dress, and, at her request, Chamberlain
sported white violets, not his traditional orchid, in the lapel of his
black coat. At the wedding reception at the Endicotts' house,
President Cleveland proposed the toast to the bride and groom. By
Christmas Eve, Chamberlain had brought his new wife back to
'Highbury' by way of Paris, the French Riviera and San Remo.

Mary Endicott Chamberlain became a fixed part of Chamberlain's life the very time when he most needed domestic stability
amid his shifting political fortunes. For two years before he met his
future bride, Chamberlain had conducted an awkward courtship
of Beatrice Potter (later to become the Mrs. Sidney Webb of early
Fabianism). The attachment had foundered on Chamberlain's
almost total failure to make allowances for Beatrice Potter's blue-
stockinged independence of mind; for her part, Beatrice's somewhat glib judgement that his 'intense sensitiveness to his own
wrongs was not tempered by a corresponding sensitiveness to
the feelings and rights of others', reflected her conviction that

Chamberlain wanted a submissive partner for a wife, a cypher to his own personality, and a passive supporter of his own ambitions.

Chamberlain's heavy-handed wooing of Beatrice Potter led her to discover in him the qualities of an 'enthusiast and a despot', one who could crush opposition without qualms. This view was doubtless due in part to an exchange Beatrice recorded in her diary:

> *Chamberlain*: I have only one domestic trouble, my sister and daughter are bitten with the women's right mania. I don't allow any action on the subject.
> *Beatrice*: You don't allow division of opinion in your household, Mr. Chamberlain?
> *Chamberlain*: I can't help people *thinking* differently from me.
> *Beatrice*: But you don't allow the expression of the difference?
> *Chamberlain*: No.[297]

In fact, Chamberlain's persuasive and diplomatic powers were as essential a part of his political armoury as his forcefulness and desire to dominate. Beatrice Potter in fact recognized these subtler qualities when she went in 1884 to visit Chamberlain in his Birmingham stronghold. She recorded the magnetic control that Chamberlain exerted over his audience at a public meeting; he was greeted with wild enthusiasm, but 'At the first sound of his voice they became as one man. Into the tones of his voice he threw the warmth and feeling which was lacking in his words, and every thought, every feeling, the slightest intonation of irony and contempt was reflected in the face of the crowd.'[298]

Beatrice also offered an accurate enough, but critical, analysis of Chamberlain's mastery over Birmingham:

> . . . the submission of the whole town to his autocratic rule arises from his power of dealing with different types of men: of enforcing submission by high-handed arbitrariness, attracting devotion by the mesmeric quality of his passion, and manipulating the remainder through a wise presentation of their interests, and consideration for their petty weaknesses.
>
> It is to this power that Chamberlain owes all the happiness of his life, and it is the reaction of this power which intensifies his sympathies and also his egotism.[299]

But her Birmingham visit also showed Beatrice that within 'Highbury' (where 'there is very *much taste*, and all very bad.') the

Chamberlain women were kept in their proper place, 'From the great man they get conversation but little sympathy, possibly they don't give it. He comes and goes, asks his friends and entertains them, and sees little of his womenfolk. In Birmingham they make kindly homely hostesses, and are useful to him; in London they are glum, and sit silently between the distinguished men who dine with the future "Prime Minister".'[300]

Nor was the assembled Chamberlain-Kenrick clan altogether to her taste, 'The Men look earnest and honest, the great man's brothers perhaps have a bit of the cad in dress and manner; the women are plain and unpretentious, essentially ungraceful, might be labelled "for use and not for ornament", and are treated accordingly.' Beatrice also noticed that at dinner a guest from Liverpool 'fawns upon and flatters Chamberlain until I feel inclined to shriek with nervous irritation'.[301]

Despite her misgivings and the subsequent failure of Chamberlain's courtship of her, Beatrice had fallen passionately, if fitfully, in love. Between two such masterful personalities, however, a one-sided passion was too humiliating and heavy a burden to allow of consummation through marriage. Beatrice became engaged to Sidney Webb in 1891, remarking resignedly 'On the face of it it seems an extraordinary end for the once brilliant Beatrice Potter . . . to marry an ugly little man with no social position and less means. . . . And I am not "in love", not as I was.' There may, however, have been some comfort in the fact that she found Sidney Webb, with 'His tiny tadpole body, unhealthy skin, lack of manner, cockney pronunciation', fairly easy to dominate.

Mary Endicott Chamberlain, on the other hand, had no urge to dominate; she was content to become a good platform wife, a loyal supporter of her husband's political ambitions, and a devoted nurse and helpmate after his crippling stroke in 1906. Because she had no desire to challenge his cherished beliefs, Chamberlain found it easy to take great pains to please her in details, to act the fond and magnanimous husband. He had made no such concessions to Beatrice Potter; but, then, nor had she to him, remarking tactlessly when he showed her his spectacular orchid house at 'Highbury' that she loved only wild flowers, and noting that 'he seemed curiously piqued'.

In short, Mary Endicott exactly satisfied Chamberlain's preconception of what a good wife should be. London society took to

her with ease, Lady Dorothy Nevill announcing that 'No-one ever
had a more perfect wife than he. . . . She is the most charming
woman imaginable'. Queen Victoria also noted, five months after
Chamberlain's marriage, 'Mrs. Chamberlain is very pretty and
young looking and is very ladylike with a nice frank open manner.'[302]

The new Mrs. Chamberlain also helped to improve Chamberlain's relations with his children. Hitherto truthfulness, discipline
and obedience had been demanded of them; now, Chamberlain
felt able to give more in return, and to unbend as never before; he
was also able to acknowledge the cause that 'She [Mary Endicott]
brought my children nearer to me'.[303]

The Chamberlain children were by now adults or in their late
teens. Beatrice, until her father's remarriage, had been responsible
for household affairs at 'Highbury'; she was also something of a
confidante, and fiercely involved in his political activities. Austen,
described by Beatrice Potter as 'a big fair-haired youth of handsome feature and open countenance, and sunny, sympathetic
temperament', had Parliamentary ambitions; in July 1887 there
was the chance of his being adopted as Liberal Unionist candidate
for the Border Burghs constituency and Chamberlain told his son
plainly, 'Don't prosecute your jingo inclinations. It is no use being
jingo without an Army and we must in the future adopt a much
stricter policy of non-intervention than in the past.'[304] Before the
next General Election, however, Austen withdrew his candidacy
from the Border Burghs and stood at a by-election for East
Worcestershire in March 1892. Although he was eventually returned unopposed for East Worcestershire, the constituency,
despite its proximity to Birmingham did not prove to be easily
malleable Chamberlainite material; some Tories in East Worcestershire resented a Liberal Unionist candidate, causing Chamberlain
to write angrily to Viscount Wolmer (later second Earl of Selborne)
that there was an attempt 'to prevent Austen from standing in order
to increase the chance of an alternative Conservative candidate.
For this purpose the disestablishment cry has been raised . . . and
may interfere with hearty and unanimous Conservative support . . .
we will on *no* account allow a Conservative to have the seat.'[305]

Neville Chamberlain's prospective career, on the other hand,
was not likely to provide embarrassing evidence of disharmony
between the Liberal Unionists and their Conservative allies.
Nearly twenty years old when his father re-married, Neville was

destined for a business career and attended Mason College (later to be subsumed into the newly-founded Birmingham University) where he studied commerce, metallurgy and engineering design. Somewhat solitary, deeply dependent upon his family and, to the outside world, extremely reserved and aloof, Neville appears to have established fairly quickly a warm attachment to his stepmother. There were, in addition, the three daughters of Chamberlain's second marriage: Ida, Hilda and Ethel, all in early womanhood and all able to benefit from the closer family feeling that Mary Endicott brought to her new home.

If Chamberlain's private life had been so beneficially re-ordered by 1888, his public career was beset by contradiction and un-certainty. The mission to America had been as successful as he could make it, and Chamberlain had written jokingly to Beatrice, 'Would you like to be the daughter of a G.C.B. or do you prefer a peerage? If I succeed I shall consider myself entitled to ask for anything, and I need hardly add that I shall take nothing.'[306] Lord Salisbury received him warmly on his return and at the Queen's request offered him the Grand Cross of the Bath. Chamberlain refused this honour (though insisting that his colleagues and assistants on the mission should be suitably rewarded), and instead asked for a signed portrait of Victoria. Such a token of official esteem was, however, an inadequate talisman amid political perils.

Though Birmingham made him a freeman of the town at the end of March (the first honour of that kind it had ever bestowed) the local Liberal Association was no longer a loyal instrument. Chamberlain lost no time in hustling his supporters out of the old organisation and in creating his own Birmingham Liberal Unionist Association, affiliated to the National Radical Union. By 23 April 1888 he was able to tell Mary Endicott, 'My new organ-isation is going like wildfire. I will give my opponents a taste of my quality and teach them not to tread on my tails again. . . . I will see if I cannot kick every single Gladstonian out of the [Town] Council and replace them with good Unionists.'[307]

Chamberlain's purge of Birmingham's political machine was carried out with his customary flair and ruthless efficiency, and the 1892 General Election results amply confirmed his re-asserted supremacy, causing Arthur Balfour to write admiringly, 'You *do* know how to manage things in Birmingham. I never saw such smashing results.' In 1892, though the number of contested seats

)se, Chamberlainite Unionists swept the board; Chamberlain
_imself had a majority of over 4,000 in the west division constitu-
ency, and heavy inroads were made into Gladstonian support in
the neighbouring areas of Walsall, Wednesbury and Wolver-
hampton.

The importance to Chamberlain of his rock-solid Birmingham
base cannot be exaggerated. Liberal Unionism could not be
guaranteed a long and healthy life, but Birmingham itself would
not wither away. He therefore took care to pet and pamper
Birmingham with consistent skill. He continued to promote civic
improvements, of which the most spectacular was the founding of
Birmingham University between the years 1896 and 1900. He gave
£2,000 himself towards the endowment fund, and was instru-
mental in prising a donation of £50,000 out of Andrew Carnegie,
the millionaire American steel magnate, and a further £50,000 out
of an anonymous benefactor. Not surprisingly Chamberlain was
the new University's first Chancellor.

Chamberlain's need to cosset his political base was, however, not
merely expressed in the form of tangible improvements. His tariff
reform campaign of 1903–6, though garnished with lofty Imperial
sentiments, was, more practically, an attempt to assuage the
anxieties of West Midlands' manufacturers and workers feeling
the pinch of foreign competition, even in home markets. 'Tariff
reform means work for all' was not an empty slogan in Birmingham's board-rooms and factories.

But even if Chamberlain could once more rely upon Birmingham's loyalty in the period from 1888–92, his political future was
cloudy. Gladstone was still going strong, and Home Rulers and
Irish Nationalists had little desire to see him back in the Liberal
fold. An alliance with the Conservatives, though an increasingly
more likely prospect, was riddled with problems.

On his return from America, Chamberlain had written to Wolmer, 'As far as I can judge things are going well with the Unionist
party, & I shall be glad to be able once more to take my part
amongst you. . . . I think we ought at once to start a new Labourers'
League and put Collings at the head of it.'[308] This brisk letter
neatly illustrates Chamberlain's need to make his cooperation with
the Conservatives (and Whig Unionists) respectable through per-
suading the Salisbury Government to accept certain reforms; such
reforms would enable Chamberlain to maintain his Radical

reputation—at least in part—and thus to continue to hold the Gladstonians at bay in Birmingham.

By 1891 the Tories had carried enough reforms (with Liberal Unionist support) to satisfy Chamberlain that not only was the alliance delivering sufficient goods to Radicalism but that it would be possible for him to take office in a Conservative-Unionist Cabinet. The reforms delivered up in the period included the establishment of a democratic system of County Councils in England, Wales and Scotland between 1888 and 1889; the extension of free elementary education to the whole country, by 1891; and a number of measures for providing allotments and smallholdings. On 1 May 1891, Chamberlain wrote, perhaps ruefully, to Dr. Dale that:

> I have in the last five years seen more progress made with the practical application of my political programme than in all my previous life. I owe this result entirely to my former opponents, and all the opposition has come from my former friends. I am bound to bear this in mind in my future speeches.[309]

More practically, Chamberlain was becoming increasingly dependent upon the smooth working of the electoral 'compact' over Parliamentary seats. His own band of Liberal Unionists was reduced to forty-seven at the 1892 election, despite the electoral compact, and despite a robust Chamberlainite showing in the West Midlands. With dwindling personal support, the temptation to work even more closely and harmoniously with the Tories was exceedingly powerful. In 1892, in fact, Chamberlain took over the leadership of the Liberal Unionists in the Commons from Hartington (now elevated to the upper house as Duke of Devonshire); this amounted to an official announcement of continuing close cooperation with the Conservatives. The mechanics of cooperation were to be rendered more agreeable by Chamberlain's harmonious personal relationship with Balfour, leader of the Tory party in the Commons, and by the need of both Liberal Unionists and Conservatives to wage a coordinated campaign against the Second Home Rule Bill.

But if Chamberlain increasingly came to depend upon his alliance with the Tories, they also needed him. By absorbing some of Chamberlain's Radicalism (even putting it into legislative form) and by a close association with his charismatic qualities, Conservatism could emerge from the desolate past of minority electoral status and become a national party once more—perhaps even become the natural party of Government, just what the Liberals had seemed to be before the split of 1886. With Randolph Churchill in decline, Chamberlain could supply a substitute form of Tory Democracy and swing enough of the working-class vote away from the Liberals.

How difficult would it be for Chamberlain, with his Nonconformist, republican-Radical background, to work with the House of Cecil and the aristocrats and gentry of the Conservative leadership? Admittedly the bookshop magnate W. H. Smith had risen to the dizzy heights of Secretary of State for War in Lord Salisbury's first and second administrations, but Chamberlain's political reputation was another thing altogether.

In fact, it is arguable that Chamberlain had already undergone a personal and social metamorphosis. Never stinted of material comfort in his Unitarian childhood, Chamberlain had developed a marked taste for luxury and splendour by the time he was Gladstone's President of the Board of Trade. Early in 1887 he had said at a private London dinner party, 'I think the only expensive taste that I would like more lavishly to indulge in is orchids, but as for fine houses, carriages etc., I do not care for or desire any of these things. . . . I find so little pleasure in mere money-making and in what wealth affords that business offered me but little inducement to continue in it';[310] there were many indications to the contrary.

Frank Harris, for example, has left an account in his racy *My Life and Loves* of a conversation with Chamberlain at his London home in 1885:

> One day I waited for him in his dining room, where there were several Leighton pictures [Leighton was a "society" painter], and he introduced them to me pompously as "All by Leighton, the President, you know of our Academy." I nodded and Chamberlain went on, "I gave 2,000 pounds for that one."
> "Really?" I gasped.
> "Yes," he replied, "what do you think it's worth?" I could not help it; I replied, "I don't know the value of the frame."[311]

In July 1887 Edward Hamilton recorded in his diary his impressions of Chamberlain at a party given by the Duchess of Manchester, where the Birmingham Radical, wearing eyeglass and orchid, was indulging in a game of baccarat, played for high stakes, with the Prince of Wales, Lord Randolph Churchill and assorted aristocratic youths.[312] The blandishments of high society living were as seductive for Chamberlain a year later when he wrote to Mary Endicott from Lord Rothschild's country seat at Waddesdon:

> There are terraces and fountains . . . the most beautiful furniture, a priceless selection of exquisite china and some splendid pictures. There is a great deal of liberty at these big parties. . . . I had a delightful talk with Arthur Balfour—about Froude— literature—Voltaire—the art of writing—history—Burke—the French Revolution etc., etc., and now I am alone in my room trying . . . to give you some impression of this luxurious society which though certainly not the end of things, is full of a certain charm and not altogether unprofitable. Every man and woman here is in some way gifted above the average, and though for the main part they do not go very deep, they make life for the time [being] very ornamental and recreative.[313]

If Chamberlain was already clearly at ease in the most exalted social circles, there remained the problem of going into political harness with the party which Lord Salisbury himself described as 'a party shackled by tradition; all the cautious people, all the timid, all the unimaginative belong to it.'[314] By no stretch of the imagination could Chamberlain be called traditionalist, or timid, or unimaginative. There were, however, causes which seemed to him to transcend the day-to-day inconveniences of cooperation with the Tories and to justify the course he was about to undertake: one cause was, naturally enough, Home Rule, but two others were the need to combat collectivist socialism and to consolidate Britain's imperial assets.

Home Rule was thrust once more to the centre of political controversy in the aftermath of the 1892 General Election which gave Gladstonians, Irish Nationalists, and one independent Labour M.P. (Keir Hardie), a combined majority of forty over their Unionist opponents. The Liberal government, once more obliged to produce a Home Rule Bill at Gladstone's insistence, and to maintain its parliamentary majority, put the proposed legislation (which had been much amended in Committee) before the Commons for its third reading in 1893.

Chamberlain had opposed the Bill with all his habitual skill and verve, provoking shouts of 'Judas' and an unseemly fist fight on the final night of the committee stage when he castigated the Gladstonians in scornful terms: 'The Prime Minister calls "black" and they say "it is good", the Prime Minister calls "white", and they say "it is better". . . . It is always the voice of a god. Never since the time of Herod has there been such slavish adulation.'[315]

The House of Lords eventually threw the Bill out by a huge majority, and Gladstone, bracing himself for an anti-Lords dissolution, was prised out of the premiership by his colleagues. Lord Rosebery, a Liberal-Imperialist, race-horse owner and society swell, succeeded him.

Chamberlain delivered a mainly inaccurate judgement on the new situation to his son Neville on 11 March 1894:

> Rosebery is a dark horse—many people are willing to give him a chance. Weak kneed Unionists are glad of any excuse for saying that H. Rule is no longer a danger. Yet myself I believe that Rosebery must follow Mr. G's policy & is not big enough to break away from it. Therefore we have the same fight before us without the personal influence of Mr. G's age & character. This must tell in our favour when people have had time to recognise that Rosebery's accession has not changed the issue.[316]

Rosebery, in fact, put Home Rule firmly in the lumber-room of the Liberal party's policies, whence it was to re-emerge only in 1910 when, once more, a Liberal Government was dependent upon Irish parliamentary support.

The Home Rule crisis of 1893-4 did more than remove Gladstone—whom Chamberlain and his wife visited cordially at Dollis Hill on 28 June 1894, and who said to his former rebel minister 'with apparent feeling, "You have often been very kind to me" '[317] —it also provoked Chamberlain, the scourge of the peers in 1884, to defend the House of Lords. He argued that the Lords were a necessary defence against the 'despotism' of a Government forcing its legislation through the House of Commons by use of the guillotine. In November 1894 he told the Duke of Devonshire (formerly Lord Hartington):

Personally, the House of Lords seems to me to fulfil excellently the necessary duties of a second chamber. It is able to secure delay and reconsideration where there is no strong popular feeling, while it is powerless to oppose permanently the clearly expressed will of the nation. The only question is whether it . . . could resist, even for a time, the decision of a large majority of the House of Commons.[318]

His support for the House of Lords' powers of delay and veto was not necessarily a piece of shallow opportunism. Chamberlain based his case on the logical position that in 1884 it had been the Lords who had opposed 'the will of the people', but that in 1894 it was the Commons who were guilty of the same offence and the Lords who were reflecting popular opinion. He was, however, willing to consider a drastic reform of the upper house, and examined Leonard Courtney's plan for an elected assembly of life peers. In addition, he believed that the introduction of the principle of holding a referendum upon controversial issues would have helped the political crisis of 1893–4, and went so far as to advise the Lords to pass the Home Rule Bill but with the proviso that the Bill should be put to the nation for their verdict in a referendum.

Even amid the political and constitutional uproar unleashed by the second Home Rule Bill, Chamberlain was conscious that 'the electors are much more interested at the present time in social questions and the problems connected with the agitation of the [Independent] Labour Party than they are with either the House of Lords or any other constitutional subject. . . . The resolutions of the Trade Union Congress [in 1893 and 1894] . . . amount to universal confiscation in order to create a Collectivist State.'[319]

Here, in Chamberlain's eyes, was a menace of greater danger to national domestic harmony than Home Rule. Marxist socialism, which seemed to be seeping into the trade unions and inspiring their leaders, was anathema to Chamberlain. His earlier, much abused, doctrine of 'Ransom' had been designed to provoke the 'Haves' into a more responsible attitude towards their own wealth and property, and towards society's 'Have-nots'. 'Jack Cade' Chamberlain had been, in fact, a very moderate quasi-Fabian capitalist, striving to avoid class warfare and to render a *laissez-faire* economy more equitable.

In 1894 it was not merely the trade unions and the Independent

Labour party that disturbed Chamberlain. Across the river from
Parliament, at County Hall, the London County Council was in the
hands of the Progressives led (ironically enough) by Beatrice and
Sidney Webb and pushing towards a full-blooded programme of
metropolitan municipal socialism. Worse still, working-class
demagogues and middle-class Fabians seemed to be driving men
of property out of the Liberal ranks into the arms of the Tories,
thus leaving the Liberal party dangerously susceptible to socialist
pressure and infiltration.

In 1895 Chamberlain wrote a play entitled *The Game of Politics*
in which he caricatured the demands of the new radicals as expressed in the manifesto of the 'New Party':

> . . . we demand the immediate abolition of the invidious dis-
> tinctions and odious principles by which the toilers of the earth
> are dispossessed of their rights, and a luxurious oligarchy battens
> on their labour.
>
> We regard the House of Lords as a nest of hereditary mis-
> creants, and we require in the name of an outraged democracy
> its instant destruction. . . .
>
> Wealth wrongfully acquired must be redistributed, and the
> unholy gains of the greedy capitalist must be utilized for the
> benefit of those whom he has worsted in the struggle for
> existence.[320]

Even if allowances are made for an amateur dramatist's licence,
Chamberlain presented here an ugly impression of destructive
class conflict.

The spectre of militant socialism and collectivism was, on the
one hand, bound to tie Chamberlain closer to his Conservative
allies and, on the other, to intensify his attempts to inject some
policies of meaningful social reform into the Unionist programme.
In 1891 he first publicly proposed an old age pensions scheme, and
later advocated that local authorities should make loans available
to members of the working class who wished to purchase houses.
He also pressed a number of other reforms upon the Conservative
leadership, including an amendment of the Artisans' Dwellings
Act to encourage street and public improvements, the setting up of
arbitration courts to settle industrial disputes, compensation for
industrial injuries and accidents, labour exchanges, cheap train
travel for workers, the control of foreign immigrants by an Aliens'

Immigration Bill (directed against East European Jewish refugees, and a sop to working-class fears of unemployment), an eight-hour day for miners, reduced hours for shop assistants, and an end to private profit on sales of alcohol (a resurrection of the 'Gothenburg' proposals of a decade and a half before).

Presented to Lord Salisbury in October 1894 in the form of a 'Memorandum of a Programme for Social Reform', these proposals were not merely proof that the old 'Radical Joe' was still alive and kicking (and fundamentally unaltered), but also showed the means by which the Conservative and Unionist alliance could cut the ground from under the feet of socialists and the Liberal supporters of the radical 'Newcastle programme' alike.

Never a man to pull his punches, Chamberlain asked Salisbury, via Wolmer, if 'some of the most important social questions' might be dealt with immediately by being introduced by the House of Lords, thus spoiling 'the game of the Gladstonians':

> In order to do this effectively the House of Lords must be prepared for something in the nature of the reforms suggested in my speech last night. I believe that in principle Lord Salisbury is not opposed to any of them; and I suggest as especially worthy of attention the House Purchase Bill, the extension of the Citizens' Dwellings Act, the establishments of Courts of Arbitration, Compensation of Injuries & Accidents, and Alien immigration.
>
> If the House of Lords sent down a batch of Bills liberally conceived and dealing with these subjects the Government would be in a difficult position. If they refused to consider them and put them aside for Welsh Disestablishment and other Constitutional reforms, I think we should have them in a trap. If, on the other hand, they attempted to deal with them, they would have no time for Irish or Welsh measures and there would be a revolt of their supporters.[321]

Salisbury replied guardedly to these proposals on 25 October 1894, using Wolmer as the go-between. Yes, he was generally sympathetic to Chamberlain's tactics, subject to a discussion of the details involved; yes, he could see his way to introducing an Aliens' Immigration Bill and an Arbitration Bill into the Lords, but might not the financial aspects of the purchase of working mens' dwellings infringe House of Commons' privileges? Salisbury also expressed sympathy for the proposed Employers' Liability Bill, but saw several difficulties—one regarding domestic servants, and the other arising from employers' resentment that the proposals had come from the party while in opposition. Furthermore, who in the Lords was the right man to handle these delicate and important social questions? For himself, Lord Salisbury would be prepared to father the Aliens' Immigration Bill.[322]

In effect, and anticipating the imminent fall of the Rosebery Government, Chamberlain was opening negotations with the next Prime Minister; boldly stating his terms for full cooperation as a Cabinet minister.

Apart from the need to provide ameliorative social reform, Chamberlain also concentrated upon a theme much more seductive to the rank and file of Conservatism—the consolidation and development of the Empire. There was nothing new in Chamberlain's regard for Britain's imperial possessions or in his desire to foster cooperation between English-speaking peoples. Speaking at a dinner in Toronto at the end of December 1887, while on his American diplomatic mission, he said:

> I am an Englishman. I am proud of the old country from which I came. I am not unmindful of the glorious traditions attached to it, of those institutions moulded by slow centuries of noble endeavour; but I should think our patriotism was warped and stunted indeed if it did not embrace the Greater Britain beyond the seas—the young and vigorous nations carrying everywhere a knowledge of the English tongue and English love of liberty and law. With these feelings I refuse to speak or to think of the United States as a foreign nation. They are our flesh and blood. . . . It may be that the federation of Canada may be the lamp lighting our path to the federation of the British Empire. If it is a dream—it may be only the imagination of an enthusiast—it is a grand idea. . . . Let us do all in our power to promote it and enlarge the relations and goodwill which ought always to exist between sons of England throughout the world and the old folks at home.[323]

British tutelage over non-Europeans also won praise from Chamberlain. In December 1889 he visited Egypt which, though not technically part of the Empire, was in effect a protected state. From Kalabesh on the Upper Nile he told Austen Chamberlain:

I have no doubt as to the future of Egypt—if we come away before our work is firmly established the country will go back again in a few years to the old conditions of corrupt and arbitrary administration.

My conclusion is therefore that I hope we shall stay, in spite of Mr. Gladstone and the French who have equally strong opinions in favour of evacuation.[324]

Believing that social reform and progress in Britain could be subsidised by the commercial development and, if necessary, the expansion of the Empire, Chamberlain was clear, in the final days of the Rosebery administration, that the Cabinet post he must have was that of Colonial Secretary. The Colonial Secretaryship would provide him with the opportunity to compound his patriotism and his radicalism; it would also, no matter the size of the Conservative majority at the impending election, enable him to keep his brand of Liberal Unionism sweet with his senior partners in the new government.

As the election drew nearer, Chamberlain, though not doubting its result, was acutely aware of the need to preserve a separate Liberal Unionist identity—a need heightened by a current squabble with local Tories over whether the seat at Leamington Spa (previously the Speaker's) should go to a Liberal Unionist. On 7 April 1895, he wrote to his son Neville:

Still, whenever the election does come I think the Unionists will have a large majority. But après? I do not like the prospect. The baser sort of Tories would like to keep all the spoils for themselves & throw away the Liberal-Unionist "crutch" on which they have depended. It is a short-sighted view, not shared by the leaders but it may work mischief.[325]

After the election, Chamberlain stoutly resisted suggestions that the respective organisations of the Conservatives and Liberal Unionists should be amalgamated. He stuck firmly to his Birmingham base; a wise decision in view of the outcome of the next decade.

More immediate still, however, was the question of Chamberlain's place in the next Government. On 25 April he again told Neville he expected 'a great majority', but 'then I suppose there will be a Coalition Government & I shall have to take office once more—Sufficient unto the day is the evil thereof.'[326]

On 21 June the Government was defeated by a majority of seven on a motion criticising the Secretary of State for War, Campbell-Bannerman. Two days later, Lord Rosebery resigned the premiership, and was succeeded by Lord Salisbury on 24 June. Salisbury decided to form a government, with Chamberlain as Colonial Secretary, and to ask for a dissolution. Polling began in the boroughs in mid-July after a short campaign. The first results started to come in on 13 July; they indicated a Unionist landslide. A Liberal débâcle ensued; Harcourt lost his seat at Derby, and Morley his at Newcastle. In all, the Gladstonian Liberals lost over ninety seats, and managed to hold only 112 in England—where they were reduced to enclaves in the West Riding and the Pennines, the north-east, the south-west, nine seats in London, and a few along the east coast. Keir Hardie's seat was also lost in the rout. The Conservatives had 293 seats and the Liberal Unionists fifty— a Unionist majority of 152, and an overall Tory majority of twelve. After an interlude of nine years, Chamberlain was safely confirmed in Cabinet office once more.

NINE

COLONIAL SECRETARY:
THE FIRST PHASE
1895–99

> That empire . . . hangs together by a thread so slender that it may
> well seem that even a breath would sever it. . . . I remember on one
> occasion having been shown a slender, a frail wire, which a blow
> might break, and I was told that it was capable of transmitting an
> electrical energy that would set powerful machinery in motion. May
> it not be the same in the relation that exists between our Colonies
> and ourselves?
>
> Chamberlain, 1895

O N 24 JUNE 1895 Lord Salisbury, with Balfour, had met
Chamberlain and the Duke of Devonshire to hand out the
spoils of victory to the leading Liberal Unionists. Salisbury
made it plain that he anticipated no difficulty over both Conservatives and Liberal-Unionists pursuing an agreed set of policies, as
outlined in recent speeches, though disestablishment and the
'Church would be as in past times an open question'. He then
offered four Cabinet posts to the Liberal Unionists, while stressing
that his nephew Balfour would be First Lord of the Treasury and
Leader of the House of Commons. Chamberlain left an account of
the ensuing conversation:

Lord S. asked what my wishes were.

J.C.: I had desired to take the Colonies, but if it were thought
that under present circumstances I would be more useful at the
War Office, I would take that.

Lord S. asked if I would take the Home Office.

J.C.: I said I had never thought of it and did not think I should
like it.

Balfour: He hoped I understood that the whole field was open
to me. If I preferred the Chancellorship of the Exchequer there
was no reason why I should not have it.

J.C.: I said I had told Goschen I should not put forward my
claims to that office, and again said I should prefer the Colonies

—in the hope of furthering closer union between them and the United Kingdom.[327]

The next day Chamberlain was confirmed as Secretary of State for the Colonies, an office he was to hold for over eight years—a staggeringly lengthy tenure of this generally uncoveted post. Of the other Liberal Unionists, Devonshire declined the Foreign Office and became Lord President of the Council with nominal responsibility for the Education Department; Lord Lansdowne went to the War Office and Sir Henry James grudgingly accepted the Duchy of Lancaster and a seat in the Cabinet. Another Liberal Unionist, Viscount Wolmer, (Salisbury's son-in-law, and later to become the Earl of Selborne) was appointed as Chamberlain's Under Secretary at the Colonial Office.

Chamberlain's immediate following also scooped up adminis-trative prizes: Austen Chamberlain was appointed Civil Lord of the Admiralty, and the Birmingham loyalists, Collings and Powell Williams, received minor office. Some Tories argued that 'the Birmingham gang' had got more than they deserved, and such criticism was yet further evidence of the misgivings felt in certain sections of the Conservative party at working closely with 'Radical Joe'—misgivings earlier expressed in the undignified squabbles over the Liberal Unionist parliamentary candidatures at East Worcestershire and Leamington. In recognition of some of the perils of dependence upon Tory goodwill, Chamberlain refused, in the aftermath of the General Election, to countenance a fusion of the Conservative and Liberal Unionist organisations arguing that these groupings should be seen as 'the two wings of the Unionist party'.

Still, Chamberlain had nothing to complain of in Salisbury's treatment of him. Whereas Gladstone in 1886 had frostily rebuffed his request for the Colonial Office with the words 'Oh. A Secretary of State', Lord Salisbury, through whose veins coursed the bluest of blue blood, had offered him his pick of the senior Cabinet offices. Chamberlain's family were 'in wild excitement' over his appoint-ment, and from Andros in the Bahamas, where he was struggling to establish a successful sisal plantation, Neville Chamberlain told Austen of a local reaction:

John was rather amusing on the subject of Father's appointment. "Oh yes, Sir, I year de ole mahn got all o' we to do wid now."

And then after a reflective pause, "Well, w'en he moo fum dere, Sir, he got to be king. Yessir dye kyarnt kyar him no way higher ceppin he be a king. Yessir."[328]

Why did Chamberlain request the Colonial Office in 1895? The Exchequer or the Home Office would have placed him much closer to the heart of the Whitehall administrative machine, and also in one of the three great departments of state. The Home Office he turned down flat; it would, after all, have given him no opportunity to refashion Britain's world role. The Exchequer would probably have destroyed his remaining Radical reputation, placing him in the unenviable position of keeper of the public purse subject to a Conservative majority in the Commons.

The Colonial Office, on the other hand, would provide him with an unrivalled chance to promote the material well-being of Britain through a business-like re-ordering of imperial trade and the proper use of imperial resources; perhaps also new territory would have to be acquired for the Empire. Chamberlain, always a superb propagandist, could use the Colonial Office as a platform worthy of world-wide attention. At the same time, the financing of imperial improvements, and, if they arose, campaigns of conquest, would need the approval of the Exchequer and Parliament. Chamberlain, essentially an outsider amid a Conservative majority administration, and in an outsider's ministry, would ultimately depend upon resolute support from the Salisbury-Balfour axis and the tolerance, at the very least, of the Conservative rank and file. In this latter respect, however, the choice of the Colonial Office was positively advantageous; Tory sentiment for Queen and Empire would help to make smooth Chamberlain's chosen path.

This path proved, however, to be a difficult one to tread: at times it seemed transformed into a great highway linking imperial vantage points; at others it became a perilous track, teetering through quagmires, and sometimes fading out altogether. Whatever its character, Chamberlain trod the imperial pathway confidently and with zest, though the bustle and noise of his progress could sometimes not conceal the barren results of much of his work.

Chamberlain took formal charge of the Colonial Office, only the second major office of his career, on 1 July, shortly before his fifty-ninth birthday. Despite his youthful appearance, therefore, he was about to enter his sixtieth year, a circumstance which, in conjunction with his natural drive, may have accounted for his urgent assault upon imperial problems. Chamberlain was, however, not yet 'an old man in a hurry'; indeed Balfour, who was twelve years his junior, said wryly, 'The difference between Joe and me is the difference between youth and age: I am age.'

The Colonial Office itself was the first object of Chamberlain's attentions. Flora Shaw, later Lady Lugard, colonial correspondent for *The Times* wrote:

> The change at the Colonial Office was marvellous; it was a total transformation; the sleeping city awakened by a touch. Everyone in the department felt it, and presently everyone in the Colonial Service felt it to the furthest corners and loneliest outposts of the Queen's Dominions. Before it had been a leisurely and sleepy place—such a thing as a Colonial Minister standing up to a Prime Minister or to a whole Cabinet in the interests of his Department never had been known. One little detail shows the difference. Good Lord Knutsford had been irreverently called by his subordinates 'Peter Woggy', but they called this successor 'the master'.[329]

Chamberlain refurbished his department, throwing out old furniture and carpets, repainting, ordering new maps, getting electric lighting installed instead of candles. Sitting at his desk, with a large globe showing the countries of the Empire on his right side, he worked steadily through the red dispatch boxes, ringing a bell when he had finished, and saying in his cool peremptory voice, 'The machine is ready to take some more.' Capable of getting through an immense amount of work in a short time, Chamberlain rose late and dictated to his secretaries at Prince's Gardens before arriving at the Colonial Office at about half-past eleven in the morning. At one-thirty he left to take lunch at the Athenaeum or the Devonshire; he rarely returned to the Colonial Office after that, but went to the Commons and there often worked late in his private room. He preferred to dine either at home in Prince's Gardens or in the House; afterwards, if the pressure of business allowed, he enjoyed going out to a play, or to talk; then he often spent more time at his papers and correspondence, going to bed at about two o'clock in the morning.

He was a good listener, particularly when any information relevant to his department could be gleaned. Sir Frederick Lugard (later Lord Lugard) has left an account of how Chamberlain used to quiz him on the subject of West Africa:

> When he screwed his eye-glass you feit as if you were going to be sifted to the marrow. If you were carried away by enthusiasm and betrayed yourself as the talk travelled into seeming or real inconsistency . . . he would take you up at once quick as a flash and show how closely he had been following you:
> "How does that follow?"
> "Then how do you reconcile that with what you said before?"
> You were pulled up sharp and had to cast back and either correct yourself or explain better. He brought you to absolute clearness. [330]

The Empire which Joseph Chamberlain surveyed in 1895 was a motley collection of territories. The Indian Empire was the responsibility of the Secretary of State for India and thus outside Chamberlain's province; this was just as well since he had never shown much interest in the subcontinent, something referred to by Lord Curzon (Indian Viceroy from 1898–1905) when he later called Chamberlain 'colony-mad'. Otherwise, the Colonial Office portfolio covered eleven self-governing colonies of white settlement with a European population of some eleven million, and a jumble of crown colonies, protectorates, and chartered territories, having a population of a little under forty million.

When Chamberlain went to the Colonial Office, the Empire had become respectable, compared with sixty years earlier, and imperialism was a perfectly acceptable, arguably a progressive, creed. Even the Liberal party had tried to come to terms with these new enthusiasms, and a substantial section, led by such promising younger spirits as Rosebery, Asquith, Grey and Haldane, became known as the Liberal-Imperialists. Gladstonian Liberals, Radicals, and Labour men might scorn such attitudes, but the 'Lib-Imps.' (or 'Limps') seemed likely to inherit the party's future.

The imperialism of the 1890s had provoked sufficient clamour and strident sentiment to convince both critics and supporters of Empire that unprecedented forces were at work. It became fashionable to discern a 'New Imperialism', and to define its salient characteristics. The jingoism of the music halls, and the literary and journalistic excesses of imperial devotees, grew as a variety of poorly-armed, non-European foes went down before the maxim guns. The competition for colonies in Africa and the deepening crisis in the Transvaal lent an unusual excitement to routine diplomatic and political manoeuvring. After 1896 the development of a cheap popular press, that could present great events for the digestion of the barely literate reader, fed countless starved imaginations.

Herded into factories and workshops, subjected to industrial regulation, and denied full political freedom, it was hardly surprising that many Victorian working men should rejoice at the far-flung exploits of red-coated infantry, or at the steel shield that the Royal Navy flung across the oceans. Perhaps in this sense, imperialist sentiment was merely an inflated patriotism. It is also tempting to see symptoms of national insecurity intermingled with jingoistic exultation. In the 1890s Great Britain, for all her territorial pomp and splendour, was without allies and openly disliked by many in Europe and the United States. 'Splendid Isolation' was in fact uncomfortable and costly; a rationalisation of a predicament, not a calculated policy. The rapturous public reactions to the triumph at Omdurman or the relief of Mafeking can thus be seen as the responses of an uncertain people.

Belief in Britain's imperial mission included the assumption that the Anglo-Saxon race embodied virtues denied to less fortunate members of mankind. Britain and her settlement colonies, therefore, belonged to an English-speaking confederacy devoted not only to self-interest but to the loftier ideals of personal freedom and stable political institutions. Despite the embarrassing activities of the Irish Fenians, the United States was considered part of this international free-masonry; Imperial Germany was an immature but successful cousin. The subject peoples of the Empire were thus being ruled for their own good by benevolent overseers.

Towards the end of the century the economic justifications for Empire were enthusiastically reinterpreted. Talk of surplus capital, over-production, trade following the flag, endorsed the new territorial acquisitions in Africa. Partly this was a restatement of the conviction that successful commerce was Britain's truest interest; partly it was a reaction to the post-1870 economic depressions and to fiercer competition from abroad. At any rate, Rhodes in Africa, and Chamberlain at home, were able to advocate expansion on the grounds of trade advantages. Chamberlain in particular set about painting an attractive prospect of the profitable use of underdeveloped imperial estates; his undoubted appeal to the working classes came to rely heavily upon the questionable equation between imperial possession and domestic prosperity, and after 1903 the tariff reform campaign took the calculation one stage further.

From the 1880s there had been talk of the reorganisation of the white-settled Empire. Imperial federation, a more unified imperial defence system, preferential tariffs within the Empire, were seen as practical possibilities. Colonial Conferences discussed these proposals, and Chamberlain came to advocate each of them to a greater or lesser degree. By the first years of the twentieth century, however, little had been achieved. The self-governing colonies were jealous of their status and wary of subordination in grand-sounding schemes of imperial cooperation. They clearly preferred voluntary and informal support for the Mother Country to rigid prior commitments.

Within the United Kingdom the ideal of Empire was by no means universally acceptable. The masses must have had a hazy picture of the finer points of imperial responsibility and endeavour. There were, moreover, many dogged and well-informed critics of the 'New Imperialism'. The obvious capitalist drive behind many annexations, the activities of organisations like Rhodes's British South Africa Company (accused by the *Investors' Review* in 1894 of swindling its shareholders), the braggart militarism, the manifestations of racial arrogance, were all the subject of bitter attack in Parliament and in the country at large. Set beside the urgent need for social reform in Britain, extravagant imperial attitudes could seem at best irrelevant and at worst callous and indifferent.

The embarrassingly divisive and disastrously prosecuted Boer War of 1899–1902 was to provide the critics of Empire with a superabundance of ammunition. Events in South Africa also pricked the grossly inflated imperial bubble, and restored a certain sobriety and perspective to the pursuit of imperial policy. In the election of 1906 the Liberals were swept to their last great victory and annihilated the party that had presided over the excesses of *fin de siècle* imperialism. The 'New Imperialism' was shown to be hollow and largely meaningless. Although it had not lacked brilliant propagandists, it was essentially a brash cover for an altered set of national priorities. In Africa it is even arguable that the 'New

Imperialism' was chiefly the means of defending the old Empire in
India and Australasia.

During Chamberlain's Colonial Secretaryship the Empire was,
nevertheless, at its zenith. One in every four members of mankind
lived beneath the Union Jack, more than a quarter of the globe was
coloured red. The Empire encompassed every climate, and an
astounding variety of peoples lived within its borders. Although it
was the *British* Empire, in some ways it was anything but British.
Scarcely twelve per cent of its citizens were European, let alone
British and its most commonly practised religions were Hinduism
and Islam, not Christianity. British administration had hardly
penetrated the hinterlands of recently acquired colonies in Africa
or the Pacific. Many of its resources remained untapped by
British entrepreneurial and technological expertise.

Within a few months of taking office, Chamberlain was developing the themes that were to become characteristic of his Colonial
Secretaryship. On 15 July in a speech at Walsall he expounded his
'underdeveloped estates of the realm' thesis:

> Great Britain, the little centre of a vaster Empire than the world
> has ever seen, owns great possessions in every part of the globe,
> and many of these possessions are still almost unexplored,
> entirely underdeveloped. What would a great landlord do in a
> similar case with a great estate? If he had the money he would
> expend some of it at any rate in improving the property, in
> making communications, in making outlets for the products of
> his land.[331]

'Joseph Africanus', as the newspapers already called him, was
not merely advocating investment in tropical Africa, the West
Indies, and other far-flung, economically backward possessions;
towards the end of 1895 Chamberlain pushed through the invasion and conquest of the Ashanti kingdom in the Gold Coast.
Kumasi fell without a shot being fired and King Prempeh, surrounded by the grisly remains of human sacrifice, prostrated himself at his conquerors' feet. Chamberlain abruptly dismissed some
British protests at the campaign, telling his Permanent Under-
Secretary, Sir Robert Meade, 'The attempt to excite English
sympathy for the King of Ashanti is a fraud on the British public.
He is a barbarous chief who has broken the Treaty, permitted

human sacrifices, attacked friendly chiefs, obstructed trade, and failed to pay the fine inflicted on him after the war.'[332]

The need to increase the amount of trade between Britain and the Empire was another theme quickly seized upon by Chamberlain. Trade statistics showed quite clearly that the United Kingdom's exports to foreign countries rose in volume between 1883 and 1892 from £215,000,000 to £291,000,000, while during the same period exports to the Empire decreased from £90,000,000 to £81,000,000. During the same timespan, Britain's imports from foreign countries rose from £328,000,000 to £423,000,000 while imports from the Empire actually fell in value, from £98,000,000 to £97,000,000. Inter-imperial trade, therefore, accounted for a dwindling proportion of Britain's imports and exports: less than a quarter of the whole. By 1900 the proportion had risen slightly to almost exactly a quarter; on the other hand foreign imports to the self-governing colonies was increasing, totalling almost £50,000,000 by 1902.

These were disturbing facts for a Colonial Secretary so firmly committed to strengthening inter-imperial links and with a sensitive ear for the complaints of businessmen and industrialists. In November 1895 Chamberlain took action by publishing, after consultation with colonial representatives, a dispatch addressed to the 'Governors of Colonies on the Question of Trade with the United Kingdom'. In the dispatch he wrote:

> I am impressed with the extreme importance of securing as large a share as possible of the mutual trade of the United Kingdom and the Colonies for British producers and manufacturers, whether located in the Colonies or in the United Kingdom. . . . I wish to investigate thoroughly the extent to which, in each of the Colonies, foreign imports of any kind have displaced, or are displacing, similar British goods, and the causes of such displacement.[333]

Applying the marketing techniques he had used nearly four decades before at Nettlefold and Chamberlain, he went on to ask for accurate descriptions and, if possible, specimens of the goods that were ousting their British counterparts (shades of the blue packets for screws for the French market). The results of Chamberlain's early initiative to promote inter-imperial trade were not particularly promising, and within eight years he had latched on to

tariff reform as a palatable enough antidote to this imperial malaise.
The dispatch of November 1895 was, however, seen by some
contemporaries as the opening shot of a campaign 'to bring about
that federation which, at the beginning of his career as Colonial
Minister, Mr. Chamberlain described as one of those dreams
which tend to fulfil themselves.'[334]

Chamberlain had already defined the problems, and the potential,
of the imperial connection in November in a speech delivered at
the Natal dinner in celebration of the completion of the Durban to
Johannesburg railway link:

> That empire . . . hangs together by a thread so slender that it
> may well seem that even a breath would sever it. . . . I remember
> on one occasion having been shown a slender, a frail wire, which
> a blow might break, and I was told that it was capable of trans-
> mitting an electrical energy that would set powerful machinery
> in motion. May it not be the same in the relation that exists
> between our Colonies and ourselves? And may not that thread
> be capable of carrying a force of sentiment and of sympathy that
> will yet be a potent factor in the history of the world?[335]

These were brave days for Chamberlain. He was enjoying a
political honeymoon with the press, and revelling in his departmental work. In November 1895, Mary Endicott Chamberlain
told her family in America that the widespread praise in the press
was a welcome stimulant:

> He feels the encouragement, and it helps his interest and energy.
> He says a "smash" must come—they cannot go on in this way,
> for friend and foe have been at one, and some day something will
> have to be done which will bring a howl instead. Meanwhile it is
> pleasant while it lasts. . . . It is quite a new sensation for him. He
> is very well, busy as the day is long, and in excellent spirits—
> many fewer headaches. He sleeps like a child and finds getting
> up in the morning an awful struggle.[336]

The howls of Chamberlain's enemies could indeed not be
silenced for long, and early in the New Year the reverberations of
the Jameson Raid plunged him into a controversy that destroyed
his integrity in the eyes of many contemporaries and which today
still taints his reputation even after the passage of more than eighty
years.

The Jameson Raid, which began on 31 December 1895, arose out of the conflict of British and Afrikaner interests in South Africa. During Chamberlain's Presidency of the Board of Trade the Liberal Government had restored the Transvaal's independence after the brief war of 1880-1; however, the republic was still subject (arguably) to British suzerainty. Federation between the British colonies of the Cape and Natal and the Boer republics was apparently further away than ever, despite the fact that the Orange Free State had close reciprocal commercial and customs links with the Cape and Natal. The most constructive view of Anglo-Afrikaner relations in the early 1880s, therefore, had rested on the assumption that commercial self-interest and the need for British military protection against the Bantu would gradually draw the Afrikaner republics into the Imperial sphere of influence. The Transvaal War of 1880-1 had admittedly aroused deep-seated suspicions and antagonisms—but at least the Afrikaners had won the war and regained their independence.

But in 1886 the discovery of enormous gold deposits in the Transvaal destroyed the chances of a leisurely absorption of the two republics into the Imperial system. The gold strike on the Witwatersrand transformed the sleepy dorp of Johannesburg, within a decade, into a modern, bustling city of 50,000 European inhabitants. A great gold-mining industry sprang up on the Rand, in almost absurd contrast to the slow, pastoral economy of the rest of the Transvaal.

The burgeoning industrial complex based on Johannesburg brought untold riches, and unprecedented problems, to the Transvaal. The gold boom boosted the Transvaal's revenue from £196,000 in 1886 to more than £4,000,000 in 1896. Yet the gold-mining industry had been financed chiefly by British capital, and British technological skills had been needed to dig the precious ore out of the ground. British citizens had thus flooded into Johannesburg and the mining areas, and it was soon reckoned (though wrongfully) that these foreign immigrants actually outnumbered the Transvaalers.

Here was the genesis of the 'Uitlander problem' and, indirectly, of the Jameson Raid. Paul Kruger, the resolute, pious and shrewd President of the Transvaal (formally known as the South African Republic) was determined to keep political power out of the hands of the 'Uitlanders', or 'foreigners'. He thus steadfastly refused to

accord them full civil rights, including the franchise. Though some
Uitlanders were indeed enfranchised, and a few sat in the Volksraad,
the Transvaal's Parliament, the vast majority remained unable to
vote.

It is not difficult to see why Kruger took his stand on the
Uitlander question. Given full enfranchisement, and their apparent
majority, the Uitlanders might well vote in an English-speaking
government, and achieve the bloodless *coup* of a revolution through
the ballot box. Such a triumph would make a mockery of sixty
years of Afrikaner determination to avoid British domination; the
heroic endeavours of the Great Trek, the establishment of the new
republics, the smashing victories of the Transvaal War of 1880–1,
would all have been in vain. Kruger put his feelings plainly when
he said of the Uitlanders on one occasion, 'Their rights! Yes, they'll
get them over my dead body.' And on another, 'I will not hand my
country over to strangers.'

Kruger's denial of full civil rights to the Uitlanders presented
the British Government with the moral justification for pushing
the Transvaal to the brink of hostilities. Chamberlain and some of
his Cabinet colleagues proved particularly susceptible to the
Uitlander predicament. There was, of course, an important
principle involved—that of the protection of British citizens overseas. But more than that, Chamberlain came to believe that it was
essential to extend British influence throughout southern Africa,
from the Cape to the Zambezi and beyond.

Chamberlain's ultimate view of the South African problem was
essentially business-like. The Transvaal with its expanding
economy was a choice and tempting plum. Furthermore, it became
increasingly likely that, as it grew in wealth and standing, the
Transvaal would come to dominate South Africa; any future
federation might well be under the republic's *vierkleur* rather than
under the Union Jack.

Inside South Africa itself, Cecil Rhodes had become convinced
by 1895 that the Transvaal Government must be overthrown—by
force if necessary. Rhodes was the Empire's standard-bearer
against Kruger. Nicknamed 'the Colossus', Rhodes was an essentially curious figure, squeaky-voiced, assertive, and abnormally
fearful of women. Yet he had built up substantial interests in the
Rand gold industry, had founded his own colonies in North and
Southern Rhodesia, north of the Limpopo river, and had become

Prime Minister of the self-governing Cape Colony in 1890. He put his millions to work in the cause of both the British Empire and his own grandiose fantasies. His own company, the British South Africa Company, had opened up the Rhodesias; his private army, the police force of the British South Africa Company, had crushed the Mashona and Matabele; his armed paddle-steamers plied the Zambezi. 'What, Mr. Rhodes,' Queen Victoria once asked, 'have you been doing since last we met?' Rhodes allegedly replied, 'Merely adding two provinces to your majesty's dominions.'

On 31 December 1895 Rhodes attempted to overthrow Kruger's republic by an armed raid launched from the Pitsani strip, newly acquired from the Bechuanaland Protectorate. The invasion of the Transvaal was undertaken, almost impetuously, by Rhodes's friend and lieutenant from his Kimberley mining days, Dr. Leander Starr Jameson. But the Jameson Raid was a disaster. The Uitlanders of Johannesburg were meant to rise in rebellion and link up with Jameson's troopers, drawn from the Rhodesian-based British South African police force. The British High Commissioner for South Africa and Governor of the Cape, Sir Hercules Robinson, (who was incidentally a shareholder in Rhodes' British South Africa Company) would then have stepped in as mediator.

None of this worked out. The Uitlander uprising was a half-hearted affair, confirming some British statesmen in their view that Mammon not Queen Victoria was the true idol of Johannesburg. Jameson's invasion force was routed, quickly rounded up by Afrikaner commandos, and handed over to the British authorities for trial. The raid ruined Rhodes's standing in Cape politics, and he was obliged to resign his premiership. Kruger's reputation, however, was boosted by the humiliating failure of the raid, and the German Kaiser Wilhelm II sent him a telegram of strident congratulation. Apart from the Kaiser, Afrikaners throughout South Africa rallied to Kruger: moderate, anti-Krugerite opinion in the Transvaal was temporarily silenced; the Orange Free State looked more benignly upon its northern sister republic; in the Cape, the Afrikaners, who accounted for two-thirds of the white population, felt more strongly than ever their ties of kinship with the Afrikaners of the republics—and Jan Hofmeyr's Afrikaner Bond party brought down Rhodes's premiership by withdrawing its support in the Cape parliament.

How far was Chamberlain implicated in the Raid? Certainly he had sufficient motive for conspiring with Rhodes. For one thing, he wanted Kruger's overthrow and believed the latter's position to be weak. For another, a swift, perhaps almost bloodless, *coup* by Rhodes would relieve him of overt responsibility for the subordination of the Transvaal to the Imperial interest—something he desired but thought of as a long-term objective involving a campaign of diplomatic attrition.

The issue of Chamberlain's guilt or innocence hangs upon several specific points. Firstly, why did Chamberlain allow the cession of the Pitsani strip to Rhodes (even though it was supposed merely to provide a 'railway corridor' between Rhodesia and the Cape) when he knew that an Uitlander uprising in Johannesburg was extremely likely and that Rhodes could be expected to assist such an insurrection? Chamberlain subsequently claimed that though he knew (in common with countless others) about the Uitlander uprising he had no prior knowledge of the raid. Yet it is clear from evidence cited in Jean van der Poel's *The Jameson Raid* that Robinson and his Secretary Sir Graham Bower believed Chamberlain to be in collusion with Rhodes. Robinson said to Bower after a conversation with Rhodes, 'The less you and I have to do with these damned conspiracies of Rhodes and Chamberlain the better'; but he then ordered Bower to allow troops to be moved down to Pitsani—the jumping-off place for the raid. Furthermore, on 2 October, Chamberlain wrote to Robinson asking for his opinions on the prospective rising in Johannesburg, 'with or without assistance from outside'.

In view of both Robinson's and Bower's fore-knowledge of the raid, and their belief that Chamberlain also knew, it is interesting to read an indignant letter that Chamberlain wrote to H. W. Massingham, editor of the *Daily Chronicle*, on 29 March 1897 when the Select Commons Committee of Inquiry into the Raid was sitting:

I read in the Daily Chronicle this morning that three high Imperial authorities were privy to the Jameson Raid.

This is so entirely contrary to the fact that I am convinced it must be the result of some unwitting mistake on the part of the writer, & I trust that you will take an opportunity of correcting it, as such a statement in your paper may have the worst results in affecting the minds of President Kruger and his advisers.

I assume that the writer refers to the High Commissioner [Sir Hercules Robinson], Sir Graham Bower, and Mr. Newton. If so, the High Commissioner has in the most categorical & explicit terms absolutely denied all privity to the raid and all knowledge of Mr. Rhodes' ulterior intentions in putting troops upon the border.

Sir Graham Bower has undoubtedly admitted that he received the confidence of Mr. Rhodes, but he has positively stated that he did not communicate his knowledge to the High Commissioner.

Mr. Newton cannot be considered as a "high Imperial authority", as he only had a limited power at Mafeking.

The important point, however, to which I desire to call your attention is the implied accusation against the High Commissioner, for which I am convinced there is not the slightest foundation, & which you would be the last to make without reason against a sick & absent man.[337]

On 4 November 1895 Fairfield, assistant Under Secretary at the Colonial Office, had told Chamberlain:

You will see that events are moving rapidly in South Africa. Rhodes, having accepted the responsibilities imposed upon him, is naturally very keen to get the Protectorate question settled and has been telegraphing all day to this end. . . . Rhodes wants you . . . to authorise the Bechuanaland Border police to enlist with the [British South Africa] Company. This they would be delighted to do, as we are strict masters. . . . Rhodes, very naturally, wants to get our people off the scene as this ugly row is pending with the Transvaal. That I think is also our interest. . . .[338]

Rhodes got what he wanted: the Pitsani strip, plus the disbandment of the Bechuanaland Border police and their voluntary re-enlistment under the British South Africa Company. It is impossible to believe that Chamberlain was unaware of the extraordinary significance of these concessions.

A second major point concerning Chamberlain's complicity is connected with the famous 'missing telegrams' sent to Rhodes by his agent Harris from London and supposedly revealing collusion.

These telegrams were not produced at the subsequent Committee of Inquiry, and Chamberlain claimed that their full content would be misinterpreted abroad. Balfour, at least, was aware of the significance of the 'missing telegrams', and later admitted to his uncle Salisbury that if they were laid before the Committee of Inquiry the Afrikaners would be encouraged to fear the worst.[339] These telegrams do not, in fact, provide conclusive proof of a Chamberlain-Rhodes conspiracy, though they are open to that interpretation. Chamberlain indeed claimed that they were black-mail, 'a deliberate plot to commit the Colonial Office involuntarily and by partial confidence to a general approval of Rhodes's plans, and then use this afterwards as a screen for the whole conspiracy.'[340] An extract from one of these telegrams, sent on 21 August, illustrates the problem of confident interpretation: 'You are aware Chamberlain states Dr. Jameson's plan must not be mentioned to him.'[341] This message could be an attempt to implicate Chamberlain in the event of the raid's failure. On the other hand, it could well reflect his desire to remain in 'official' ignorance of the conspiracy no matter what the outcome.

A third point at issue concerns Chamberlain's evident desire to hurry up the prospective *coup* against Kruger's republic during December. Fairfield told Bower that the Colonial Secretary wanted more speed, and Rhodes (according to Bower) also believed that Chamberlain was putting pressure upon him for a quick end to the affair.[342] In defence of Chamberlain it could be argued that he was indeed trying to hurry things up—but, since he allegedly knew nothing of the raids, it was the Johannesburg Uitlander rising that was the object of his concern. There was certainly at least one good reason to get the uprising over with quickly The United States Government, led by President Grover Cleveland, had recently adopted a positively bellicose attitude towards Britain in connection with the long-standing border dispute between Venezuela and British Guiana. Faced with American sabre-rattling in defence of the Monroe Doctrine, Britain, stuck in one of the most cheerless phases of her 'splendid isolation', hardly wanted to cope with two international crises simultaneously—though in the event this is what occurred.

There is one further factor to consider. It relates to no specific piece of evidence, but is a general assessment of probabilities. Quite simply, it is beyond belief that Chamberlain, a newly-appointed minister with an outstandingly incisive and enquiring mind, with the need to dominate and control events, and with years of experience of political duplicity and sharp practice, could have remained perfectly unaware of the plans for the raid. If he knew of the plans and failed to squash them he as good as authorised Jameson's invasion of the Transvaal.

The raid and its embarrassing aftermath led to an inquiry conducted by a Select Committee of the House of Commons during the first half of 1897. Chamberlain's early reaction to an inquiry was expressed in defiant terms to Balfour on 2 February 1896. The Colonial Secretary expected 'no good . . . only a raking of the mud. . . . But how can we resist it without raising a suspicion that there is something behind it. . . . I do not believe that there is much to be discovered; and if the worst that is alleged was proved, I do not think it would make much difference to the course which ought to be pursued.'[343]

The Committee of Inquiry cleared Chamberlain of complicity and treated an unrepentant Rhodes with restraint. It is now easy to see why, and what made Chamberlain so confident in February 1896 that the inquiry would not 'do any harm'. For one thing, Rhodes refused to produce the 'missing telegrams', and the Committee of Inquiry was content with Chamberlain's quotations, from memory, of their contents. Rhodes's refusal to cooperate fully with the inquiry was not simply the result of his truculence. In the aftermath of the raid it seemed very likely that the British Government would take away the British South Africa Company's charter—its official sanction for its administrative activities in the Rhodesias. Chamberlain certainly advocated that, at the very least, the Company's teeth should be drawn by placing its armed forces under the control of the Crown.[344] If anyone was being blackmailed, therefore, it was Rhodes not Chamberlain. Rhodes's non-cooperation over the 'missing telegrams' was the price he paid for the continuation of his mastery over his private empire.

Another explanation as to why the inquiry failed to dig up all the facts lies in the reluctance of the Liberal representatives on the committee to press their investigations to the utmost. At first sight this seems strange, given the political capital to be made out of the Unionists' discomfiture. The most convincing reason for the Liberals pulling their punches is quite simple: Rosebery, who had been Prime Minister until June 1895 (six months before the raid), and Harcourt, who, as Leader of the Opposition in the Commons, was one of the leading Liberals on the Committee of Inquiry, were both alleged to have been involved in plots with Rhodes before they fell from office.

It is difficult to believe in Harcourt's earlier complicity in the planning of the Jameson Raid despite the allegations to this effect that appeared in the *Western Morning News* in December 1896.[345] In the middle of December, Chamberlain wrote a letter to Selborne which had a clandestine flavour about it, but which also seems to demonstrate Harcourt's determination to pursue the truth:

> Your letter re. [missing] Telegrams was not marked private out-side and was therefore opened by my Secretary. It does not matter in this case but please note that he opens every letter except those marked private or with the frank of any of my colleagues in the corner. . . .
>
> Apparently H[arcourt] has asked for all the telegrams for 1895. I do not know that this matters as probably it is in the earlier telegrams that the allusions to Rosebery are to be found. He agrees that we must give the Committee whatever they ask for and they will certainly support any request by the leader of the Opposition, who will evidently establish himself as Public Prosecutor.[346]

Chamberlain conducted a vigorous investigation into the allegations against the two leading Liberals. By 6 January 1897 his Birmingham henchman Powell Williams had made thorough inquiries among journalists and pressmen, and Chamberlain told Selborne that 'the affair is a mare's nest. I think we had better drop all further enquiries in this direction.'[347] Clearly Chamberlain stood to gain in several ways if the allegations could be substantiated, and in a letter to Selborne on 30 December 1896 spelled out one potential benefit:

> I do not believe that either Rosebery—and still less—Harcourt—knew—but if I can show that these Conspirators professed that they did, it will be a pretty good indication of the readiness with which they accepted stories of the complicity of prominent Statesmen and will of course discredit any attempt on their part to involve me.[348]

He went on to emphasise the difficulties that could face the Liberals on the Committee of Inquiry:

If they [Rhodes and his agents] have any—even the slightest *prima facie* evidence that Rosebery—and in this case especially Harcourt—was precognisant of their proceedings they may be able to secure better treatment from Harcourt or the Committee than would otherwise be the case. [349]

Harcourt's apparent zeal to dig out the 'missing telegrams' of 1895 may simply have reflected his desire to uncover the facts—especially if his own conscience was clear. If Rosebery's name was sullied in the process this would help to confirm Harcourt in the leadership of the Liberal party in the Commons and perhaps open up his way to the leadership of the party as a whole. Nonetheless the telegrams in question were not produced, and the Commons Committee had little choice but to whitewash Chamberlain, who would hardly have received such benevolent treatment if all the evidence that has subsequently surfaced had been put before the inquiry. Indeed J. L. Garvin's confident judgement that 'He had not a shadow of complicity with the Raid' has a hollow ring today. Chamberlain's own fighting words are a more accurate indication of the realities of a struggle to avoid political ruin: 'I don't care a twopenny damn for the whole lot of them; but if they put me with my back to the wall, they'll see some splinters.' [350] Rhodes did not put Chamberlain's back against the wall, and though some splinters still flew, the wounds, though uncomfortable, were not fatal.

The Raid did, however, wreck immediate hopes of any solution to the Uitlander problem that would satisfy British interests. Chamberlain was thus faced with the daunting task of reconstructing Imperial policy towards southern Africa only six months after taking over the Colonial Office.

Southern Africa was, of course, only one of Chamberlain's departmental and personal preoccupations. He believed that Britain's commercial and territorial interests should be pursued in a spirit that was openly aggressive—in marked contrast to the discreet shufflings of traditional diplomacy. Unfortunately the Colonial Office lacked the personnel and the resources to proceed independently of the other great departments of state, especially the Treasury. Chamberlain also needed the goodwill and the whole-hearted support of his Cabinet colleagues. This was something that he never consistently achieved: Balfour was a man singularly lacking in the passion that would have provided fuel for the fiery chariot of Chamberlain's Imperial ambitions; Salisbury was above all inclined to avoid trouble; Sir Michael Hicks Beach, the Chancellor of the Exchequer, was coldly unreceptive to schemes of aggrandisement; the Duke of Devonshire more-or-less slumbered as Lord President of the Council.

Despite these disadvantages, Chamberlain generally felt no inhibitions in pressing his views upon his colleagues. One of the first great international confrontations of his Colonial Secretaryship, however, required delicate handling. The Venezuela border dispute, which brought Britain into a head-on collision with the United States, was an acute embarrassment for Chamberlain with his American wife and his frequently professed admiration for American institutions. Above all, the friction was an unpleasant reminder that Anglo-Saxon harmony could not be automatically guaranteed. Chamberlain was an unashamed race-patriot, a believer in Anglo-Saxon virtues, and could say, 'I have been called the apostle of the Anglo-Saxon race, and I am proud of that title . . . I think the Anglo-Saxon race is as fine as any on earth.'

On 20 December 1895 he tried to explain American hostility in a discursive letter to Selborne:

. . . I am afraid that a large number, and probably a majority, of Americans would look forward without horror to a war with this country. This is so different from the feeling prevailing here that it needs explanation. . . . At bottom, I believe, it is due to the extreme sensitiveness and vanity of the Americans as a nation. They are jealous of this country, and suspect us always of an assumption of superiority of which we are not conscious ourselves; but they are convinced nevertheless that we look down upon them, and they would not be sorry to prove that they are bigger & stronger & better than we are. . . . Cleveland is a coarse-grained man, with, I think, a good deal of the bully in his composition. He has yielded to the Jingoes, but not altogether without sympathy with their views. . . . The Americans believe in the Monroe Doctrine as some people believe in the Bible—without knowing much of its contents, but accepting it as of divine inspiration. . . . The Monroe Doctrine knows nothing of arbitration.[351]

Chamberlain proceeded to move with caution, doubting whether it would be wise to exasperate the United States further by moving troops to protect the border of British Guiana. On the other hand, he agreed with Selborne that 'the Americans are not people to run away from; in fact I do not know any nation from whom we can afford to accept a kicking.'[352] Nine months later, with the British Government trying to relax tension and favouring arbitration, Lord Salisbury told Chamberlain, via Selborne, that he hoped the Colonial Office would not insist on sending instructions to the troops in British Guiana to repel a Venezuelan surveying party.[353] Chamberlain replied pacifically on 21 September 1896 that he agreed it was best to avoid conflict.[354]

Though a British dispute with Venezuela was to flare up six years later, almost producing an Anglo-German blockade of the country that had offended the interests of both powers, the border crisis of 1895–6 provided the opportunity to promote a *détente* with the United States. In the autumn of 1896 Chamberlain himself went to the United States to negotiate with Richard Olney, the Secretary of State, and these conversations went far towards putting Anglo-American relations upon a friendlier footing. Among Chamberlain's colleagues, Balfour was a consistent advocate of the 'special relationship' between Britain and America (even composing a paper in 1909 entitled 'The Possibility of an Anglo-Saxon Confederation'). The discomfitures of 'splendid isolation', and the growth of American naval strength, also made *détente* an attractive proposition. The flourishing friendship between the two countries was further boosted by Chamberlain's warm support for the United States in the war of 1898 against Spain.

In other spheres of interest, Chamberlain was much less circumspect. He was determined to uphold British colonial interests in West Africa where there were clashes with the French. He was prepared to fight for these ends, telling Selborne in September 1897, 'We ought—even at the cost of war—to keep the hinterland for the Gold Coast, Lagos and Niger territories.' He also firmly supported the military action of Sir George Goldie in north-west Nigeria, asking Selborne, 'What alternative has [Goldie] to the extreme one of turning the French out of Boussa by force? If the policy of occupation of a number of small posts is good for the French why shd. it be bad for us?'[355] Chamberlain complained three months later of Lord Salisbury's conciliatory attitude in West Africa: 'I thought he was entirely with us and now he is prepared to give away everything and get nothing. I am more than sorry to differ from him, but I cannot stand it. I would rather give up office than allow French methods to triumph in this way. We shall pay for it sooner or later and I cannot be party to such a surrender.'[356] In fact, by 1898 a combination of diplomacy and force had resulted in the final partition of West Africa between Britain, France and Germany.

Chamberlain's hostility towards the French in West Africa was also, perhaps, an indication of his strong desire to establish an Anglo-German alliance. Salisbury, indeed, wondered in April 1898 whether Chamberlain actually wanted a war with France in order 'to push' the alliance with Germany.[357] Though the German Government, according to Balfour, 'did not at all like Joe's methods of procedure in Africa',[358] Chamberlain 'went very far in the expression of his own personal leaning towards a German alliance.'[359] The Anglo-German negotiations early in 1898 did not, however, result in an alliance. That Chamberlain returned to the project on several occasions between 1898 and 1902 is a clear reflection of his belief that an alliance with Germany would harmonise with Anglo-Saxon global influence.

In China where British, Russian, French, German, Italian, American, Portuguese and Japanese interests in trade and territory coincided, Chamberlain was for as strong action as in West Africa. In this sphere of influence, however, he saw Russian ambitions and Chinese unreliability as the chief hazards. In February 1898, he hectored Balfour with failing to clamp down on Russian activities, saying, 'If matters remain as they are our prestige will be gone and our trade will follow. I would not give a year's life to the Government under such conditions.'[360] Six months later he accused Balfour of 'letting the Chinese off very easily after their treatment of us in the Pekin-Hankow contract . . . I thought you meant to mark your displeasure.'[361]

In his drive to develop the underdeveloped estates of the realm, however, Chamberlain had less need to cajole and bully his colleagues; the colonial empire was, after all, his departmental responsibility. Nonetheless any departure from the accepted principle, that crown colonies should generate their own wealth to reinvest in local development, was fraught with difficulty. Whitehall and Westminster took the view that Government subsidies to dependent colonial territories breached the long-standing tradition of colonial self-help. Chamberlain wanted to change this attitude, as well as to encourage private capitalist investment in the colonies.

Chamberlain had himself pointed the way when he sent his son Neville to establish a sisal-growing business on Andros in the Bahamas. Neville began setting up the plantation in April 1891, and remained in charge of the Andros Fibre Company for the next six years. Austen Chamberlain had accompanied his brother on an early fact-finding mission and had written enthusiastically to his father on 3 January 1891 that the improved economy in the Bahamas 'is mainly due to the establishment of the hemp industry [hemp is made from sisal] . . . there is one at least of our West Indian possessions on whose condition we can dwell with satisfaction.'[362] Neville's subsequent struggle to make the Andros venture succeed prompted a suggestion from his father in January 1892 that he might require additional European help, but Chamberlain concluded 'Probably a native might be better if you could depend on his honesty & energy but they are sans qualities in some of our colonies.'[363]

But the Chamberlains' Andros venture crashed; the price of sisal tumbled and there were crop failures on the plantation. Joseph Chamberlain lost £50,000 in the process. None of this provided a compelling advertisement for his campaign to encourage more investment in tropical crown colonies. In November 1899 he pressed Balfour to spend a £22,000,000 dividend from Britain's Suez Canal shares upon the crown colonies. Balfour demurred, pointing out that only those colonies likely to remain permanently dependent should receive such bounty, and also proposing that a third of the money should go towards necessary public works in Britain—light railways in the Scottish Highlands and Ireland for example. However Balfour was prepared to acknowledge that 'Whereas *your* Colonial enterprises would, if properly managed, be probably remunerative, the kind of public work which I contemplate would bring in a small return if any.'[364]

Four years later Chamberlain was urging Richard Cadbury to invest in West Indian development:

Have you ever contemplated the possibility of securing an estate in the West Indies on which you might grow the Cocoa which you require in your industry? I have reason to believe that some of your competitors have in view such an enterprise, and if you desire to consider it this is a good time. There are large areas of Crown Land which may be bought or leased at very reasonable rates, & I firmly believe that all that is wanting to success is energy & capital, both of which have been lamentably lacking in the West Indies for many years past.[365]

Chamberlain's greatest service to the development of the tropical Crown colonies was, however, the appointment of the Royal Commission on the West Indies under Sir Henry Norman in 1896. In December of that year Chamberlain gave his Under-Secretary, Selborne, some guidance as to the appropriate references he could make to the West Indian Commission and colonial trade in general in a speech the latter was due to deliver:

. . . please emphasise the necessity of getting at the real facts, and do not indicate any kind of prejudgment of the issue. It is quite likely that the report of the Commission may show that the crisis is not what the West Indian Committee have reported it to be. All we have to justify at present is the enquiry.

You might, if you thought well, dwell on the growing desire on the part of the English people that their Government take a more active line in regard to promoting British Trade and say that while after all the best security for our commercial prosperity is to be found in the individual energy and enterprise of our manufacturers and the skill of our workpeople, we recognise that the Government is in a position to assist by developing the resources of the countries over which we exercise authority. At the present moment we are actively engaged in promoting railway enterprise in many parts of the world, and we have reason to believe that in our possessions on the West Coast of Africa, in British Guiana, and British Honduras, and in some of the West Indian Islands, we have underdeveloped resources which may be speedily utilised to the advantage of British Trade as well as for the benefit of the Colonies themselves.[366]

The Royal Commission reported in 1897. Its report was insistent that industries (such as fruit growing) should be encouraged as alternatives to the prevailing hazardous reliance upon sugar. It was also recommended that nearly £600,000 should be loaned and granted to the West Indies. Despite the misgivings of some of his Cabinet colleagues on this score, Chamberlain announced in 1898 a five-year plan for West Indian reconstruction.

Not only was the financial assistance recommended by the Norman Commission used to alleviate local distress and improve island communications, but some was set aside to encourage new industries. In addition, Chamberlain established the Department of Tropical Agriculture, as well as Schools of Tropical Medicine in London and Liverpool. In this way the Government gave its backing to necessary research work, and to improving farming methods in the West Indian islands. In 1902 Chamberlain succeeded in his objective of dismantling the system whereby certain European nations subsidised, through bounties, the production of West Indian sugar. The Brussels agreement of that year ended the bounty system and gave some relief to the British West Indies where sugar went unsubsidised.

These measures did not transform the West Indian economies overnight. The blight of neglect and mismanagement could not be so easily exorcised, and unemployment and low incomes proved endemic. But a start had been made, and some improvement was soon evident. To have put similar programmes into operation throughout the Empire, however, would have required a freer purse than Westminster's and a succession of Colonial Secretaries as dynamic as Chamberlain. This did not, unfortunately, happen.

But what of Chamberlain's expressed desire on taking the Colonial Secretaryship of furthering closer union between the self-governing colonies and Britain? Despite the other distractions of his office Chamberlain proceeded to channel his efforts for greater unity into schemes for improving cooperation in the field of defence and for restructuring imperial trade. He also entertained hopes that through the establishment of bodies such as Imperial Councils, or Parliaments, the Governments of Britain and the self-governing colonies would be able to consult each other regularly and at the highest level. For much of the time it was not quite clear which of these schemes were central to Chamberlain's main purpose, and which were ancillary. Perhaps Chamberlain himself did not know until he had explored fully the various possibilities.

Imperial defence seemed to offer a fertile area for experiment. The issues involved were practical and, to a certain extent, urgent. By the early 1870s local defence had been placed in the hands of the self-governing colonies, although in an emergency British help might be essential. The Second Maori War had demonstrated this, and events in South Africa were to provide even clearer proof. It seemed appropriate, in the circumstances, to organise some degree of inter-imperial defence planning and cooperation for the land forces of the Empire.

Unfortunately there were some serious obstacles to these aspirations. Firstly, the British army and the Royal Navy were by no means willing partners; their senior staff tended to view their opposite numbers with suspicion, even occasionally with hostility. Incredible though it may seem, before the end of the nineteenth century neither service was willing to let the other know details of its strategic planning. Secondly, the colonies were extremely reluctant to commit themselves to any military arrangement that might prove burdensome and inappropriate.

The naval defence of the Empire was another matter. The maintenance of squadrons of the Royal Navy in Australasian and South African waters was a costly business. The British Government was therefore justified in asking for some contribution to the maintenance of the navy. In 1887, as a result of discussions during the Golden Jubilee celebrations, the Australian colonies and New Zealand agreed to make annual payments for the upkeep of the Royal Navy. In the first year, £850,000 was appropriated—no small amount for the colonies involved.

This innovation, however, owed more to self-interest than to imperial patriotism. The Australasian colonies were isolated settlements on the fringe of the Asian land mass. The surging power of Japan, and the menacing, if demonstrably inefficient, presence of Russia in the East, heightened this isolation. The colonies were thus buying a measure of security. By 1897 the Cape also contributed to the navy's upkeep. Once more, the gesture was timely in view of the growing crisis in South Africa. In 1902 Natal also joined the subscribers. But Canada, secure under the mighty wing of the United States, did not pay out one penny, and even spoke of establishing a navy of her own.

One further way of improving defence cooperation lay in establishing appropriate committees. Failing this, the final responsibility for defence planning was borne by the Cabinet, a body frequently lacking the personnel to give precise consideration to such matters. A Colonial Defence Committee had been created in 1878 in response to the Russian war scare. But it was a feeble body and expired within a year. The Salisbury Government of 1885 revived it, however, and it continued to collect and circulate information. In 1890 a Joint Naval and Military Defence Committee was established, but it was bedevilled by inter-service disputes, and its work lacked clarity or distinction.

The Unionist election victory of 1895 brought a further innovation. This was the establishment of the Cabinet Defence Committee, (which superseded the Advisory Defence Council that had been set up during Rosebery's brief premiership) largely due to a powerful service lobby in the House of Commons, and to the advocacy of Arthur Balfour. The Defence Committee, however, lacked real authority, and was conspicuous for the absence from its deliberations of the Prime Minister, the Foreign and Colonial Secretaries, and even of the professional heads of the armed services. No minutes were kept, and the Committee's work was generally ill-defined and ineffective. By 1904, however, Balfour (who succeeded Salisbury as Prime Minister in 1902) had reconstituted the Committee and had transformed it into the much more effective—though advisory—Committee of Imperial Defence.

Inter-imperial trade seemed to be another promising medium for improved cooperation. The principles of free trade, however, dominated British economic theory. This meant, among other things, that if Britain had already signed a commercial treaty with Germany and subsequently concluded a further agreement with (say) New Zealand, then Germany too could expect similar preferential terms with New Zealand. In these circumstances, imperial loyalties were less significant than fiscal realities. In general terms, Britain and her self-governing colonies made plain their wish to buy in the cheapest market and to sell in the dearest.

In view of Britain's commercial success in the years following the abandonment of protection it seemed improbable that Britain would lightly abandon the advantage of free trade. But from 1870 onwards the mid-Victorian boom had begun to fade. British exports suffered alarming fluctuations, and there were severe bouts of commercial depression and unemployment. Other nations,

notably Germany and the United States, were expanding their
industries on a scale which threatened eventually to overtake
Britain's early lead. By the 1890s most of the major manufacturing
countries had adopted some measure of protection. Britain alone
clung to free trade. Chamberlain was to advocate the remedy of an
imperial *zollverein* (an imperial common market) in the early years
of his Colonial Secretaryship.

Imperial federation was another tempting will-o'-the-wisp for
Chamberlain to pursue. But, although there were enthusiastic
advocates of federation in Britain and the self-governing colonies,
the practical difficulties were enormous. What subjects were to be
reserved for the proposed Imperial Assembly? How was it possible
to avoid clashes over sovereignty between the central legislature
and local parliaments? Above all, how was the Imperial Federal
Parliament to be composed? If delegates were elected on the basis
of proportional representation, then the British members would
swamp those from the self-governing colonies. Having recently
attained the substance of domestic autonomy, the self-governing
colonies were unlikely to surrender their independence in this
fashion.

Chamberlain set off in pursuit of the holy grail of imperial
cooperation with his customary enthusiasm and drive. As events
unfolded, however, it was not always clear whether he was in fact
the most dashing of Imperial knights errant or merely a latter-day
Don Quixote tilting ludicrously at the windmills of conventional
political wisdom.

The Colonial Conference of 1897 provided a formal testing
ground for Chamberlain's ambitions. The precedent of consultation with the assembled colonial leaders that had been established
at Queen Victoria's Golden Jubilee in 1887 was repeated at the
Diamond Jubilee ten years later. In this way, Her Majesty by
attaining a ripe old age made her most valuable practical contribution to the better organisation of her empire.

The Diamond Jubilee coincided with, and helped to promote,
an upsurge in imperial sentiment. The naval review at Portsmouth,
the illuminations in the streets, the searchlights playing upon St.
Paul's, the glittering processions of troops drawn from every
quarter of the empire, all provided a glamorous and seductive
appeal—and an appeal not merely to the senses but also to duty
and honour and a global responsibility. In the *Daily Mail*, G. W.

Steevens interpreted the Queen's procession stirringly for the common man:

> Up they came, more and more, new types, new realms at every couple of yards, an anthropological museum—a living gazeteer of the British Empire. With them came their English officers, whom they obey and follow like children. And you began to understand, as never before, what the Empire amounts to. Not only that we possess all these remote outlandish places . . . but also that all these people are working, not simply under us, but with us—that we send out a boy here and a boy there, and the boy takes hold of the savages of the part he comes to, and teaches them to march and shoot as he tells them, to obey him and believe in him and die for him and the Queen. A plain, stupid, uninspired people, they call us, and yet we are doing this with every kind of savage man there is. And each one of us—you and I, and that man in his shirt-sleeves at the corner—is a working part of this world-shaping force. How small you must feel in face of the stupendous whole, and yet how great to be a unit in it![367]

Chamberlain's official dealings with the Prime Ministers and ministers of the self-governing colonies, however, were not bathed in a hazy atmosphere of patriotic emotion. The colonial statesmen were hard-headed and down-to-earth when discussing schemes to promote greater imperial unity. Chamberlain appealed to his audience with clarity, force and a little special pleading. He spoke of 'the future of our race as well as our own people'; he dangled federation temptingly before the colonial statesmen's noses; he professed his desire to bolster imperial sentiment with closer commercial links; he argued the case for improved defence cooperation by claiming, somewhat speciously, that 'during the present reign, you will find that every war, great or small, in which we have been engaged, has had at bottom a colonial interest. . . .'[368]

These appeals fell upon generally stony ground. Chamberlain explained the position candidly to the Duke of Devonshire on 4 July 1897:

> All of [the Colonial Premiers] are personally favourable to closer union. Mr. Reid [Premier of New South Wales], the cleverest of them all, is genuinely patriotic and ready to risk

something for the idea. The others are Premiers first and patriots second—and they have a natural fear that if they commit themselves too far, they may be reproached when they get home with having sacrificed colonial interests to the flesh-pots of Egypt.[369]

Chamberlain had summarised his own problems in a nutshell. Only if there was something in it for them would the self-governing colonies barter away any portion of their domestic independence in the cause of greater imperial unity. In one sphere only could Chamberlain discern any real hope of progress. Though the 'imperial *zollverein*' idea had apparently died the death of indifference at the conference, the new Canadian Liberal Government had, in April 1897, reduced its tariffs by twelve and a half per cent against British goods with the promise of a further reduction to twenty-five per cent in 1898. This was no mean concession, though Canada clearly hoped for a reciprocal British response to benefit their exports (particularly wheat) to the United Kingdom. As yet, however, the British Government could not offer fiscal reciprocity to Canada. One of the vital germs of Chamberlain's tariff reform campaign had nonetheless been sown by the Canadian offer; an alternative to 'Imperial Free Trade' now existed.

A more obvious benefit of the 1897 Colonial Conference was the decision to hold such meetings at regular five-yearly intervals. This was, at the very least, a pragmatic by-product of the campaign for greater imperial unity: like many compromises, the result was to prove uncontroversial, reasonable, economical, and not particularly efficient—but at least it was there.

As the Conference disbanded, Chamberlain could briefly draw breath. By the end of July he was almost free of the toils of the Jameson Raid Inquiry; he had kept some part of his Radical reputation by helping to steer the Workmens' Compensation Bill through the Commons; his hold upon his department was as firm as ever; if his initial hopes for the Colonial Conference had been dashed, the idea of reciprocal imperial tariff concessions was very much alive and already eliciting an interested response from self-governing colonies other than Canada.

The Uitlander problem, however, would not go away by itself. If diplomatic pressure (exceedingly difficult to apply in the embarrassing aftermath of the Jameson Raid) did not resolve the

South African impasse, then, apart from inertia, war was the only acceptable alternative.

In the autumn of 1896 Chamberlain and Selborne had debated the realities and prospects of Britain's role in South Africa. On 6 October Selborne argued that Britain's policy towards South Africa should include, at all costs, the securing of the Delagoa Bay harbour and railway under British control (thus cutting off the South African Republic's railway link to the outside world), and the permanent fixing of the Cape garrison at the highest expedient point. Selborne also thought that Chamberlain should visit South Africa to show the Afrikaners how easily they could work with the British, and to show British and Afrikaners how 'in its internal affairs a self-governing Colony is as absolutely independent as a republic'.[370]

Chamberlain replied on 14 October in a letter which revealed that he was at that stage unsure whether a victorious war with the Transvaal would necessarily serve British interests in South Africa:

It has often been pointed out that the expulsion of the French from North America was one of the causes of the American Revolution—or at least that if they had remained the Colonists would not have been so ready to quarrel with the Mother Country.

In the same way there would have been no Transvaal Republic and no talk of eliminating the Imperial Factor in S. Africa if we had not destroyed the power of the Zulus.

.... May it not be therefore that a war with the Boers and their defeat would be the signal for that United States of S. Africa which would be the worst possible result for us?

As long as the Transvaal threatens the Cape and Natal they will remain loyal however they may bluster.

It is difficult to predict the future, and I am not sufficiently certain of it to push matters to an issue with the Boers if it can be avoided. Like the Liberal Party at this moment we must let things shape themselves.[371]

On 18 October Selborne replied with a clear-sighted and virtually unanswerable analysis of the problem. It amounted, in fact, to a crisp justification for Britain's absorption of the

Transvaal—a justification which was soon to be touted by Chamberlain as well:

> In a generation the S[outh] A[frican] R[epublic] will by its wealth and population dominate S. Africa. S. African politics must revolve around the Transvaal, which will be the only possible market for the agricultural produce or the manufactures of Cape Colony and Natal. The Commercial attraction of the Transvaal will be so great that a Union of the S. African states with it will be absolutely necessary for their prosperous existence. The only question in my opinion is whether that Union will be inside or outside the British Empire.[372]

Having weathered the diplomatic squalls whipped up by the Jameson Raid, Chamberlain attempted early in 1897 to regain the initiative. In April he asked the Cabinet to increase the British garrison in South Africa by 3,000 or 4,000 men, causing Balfour to remark to Salisbury:

> [Chamberlain's] favourite method of dealing with the South African sore is by the free application of irritants; and although it does not easily commend itself to me, this method may possibly be the best. In any case, however, I cannot think it wise to allow him to goad on the Boers by his speeches, and to refuse him the means of repelling Boer attack, when as a responsible minister, he earnestly and persistently presses for them.[373]

Chamberlain set about isolating the Transvaal by a series of diplomatic manoeuvres, of which the most spectacular was the Anglo-German agreement of 1898. This agreement, pressed on Salisbury by Chamberlain and Balfour, which concerned a share-out of Portugal's colonies of Mozambique and Angola in the event of the almost bankrupt Portuguese Government having to mortgage them, involved Germany's diplomatic abandonment of the Transvaal. The German ambassador in London, Hatzfeldt, said plainly that the arrangement 'would be a public advertisement to the Transvaal Government that they had nothing more to hope for from Germany, or indeed from any European power.'

In order to prosecute Britain's case in South Africa with the utmost effectiveness, the Government had furthermore appointed a new High Commissioner and Governor of the Cape in August 1897. This was Sir Alfred Milner, ex-scholar of Balliol, ex-

Treasury Civil Servant, arch-administrator and confirmed race-patriot. Though not at the outset averse to mediation between British and Afrikaner interests, within a year Milner had come to the conclusion that war with the Transvaal was highly likely, if not inevitable.

Chamberlain and Milner now proceeded to conduct a well-orchestrated exercise in late nineteenth-century brinkmanship. The Uitlanders were presented to the British public, and world opinion, as a worthy and unjustly persecuted group—though Balfour, among other Cabinet 'wobblers' failed to appreciate this analysis. Petitions to Queen Victoria were sent from Johannesburg, and Milner officially referred to the Uitlanders as 'helots'—the slaves of Ancient Greece. In May 1899, Milner and Kruger met at Bloemfontein to try and negotiate a settlement of the Uitlander problem. Predictably, the conference failed: Kruger made concessions which the British side considered inadequate, and the meeting broke up, having created the impression in the United Kingdom that Kruger was not inclined to make reasonable sacrifices.

British public opinion was thus prepared for a war to 'free' the Uitlanders. In the Sudan, Kitchener's brilliant campaign of conquest was drawing to a successful conclusion, thus making possible a full-scale military concentration upon South Africa. As early as June 1899 Chamberlain and Milner had discussed the question of troop reinforcements; in August there were further warlike preparations; by the beginning of October there were nearly 20,000 Imperial troops in the Cape and Natal, and when fighting actually broke out on 12 October there were 70,000 British soldiers either in South Africa or on the high seas.

To cap their diplomatic campaign, the British Government actually manoeuvred the Transvaal into issuing a bellicose ultimatum on 9 October. The ultimatum demanded the withdrawal of all British troops on the Transvaal's frontiers and for those on their way to South Africa to be sent back. On 3 October the first of the British reinforcements had landed at Durban. The Spring grass was up—vital forage for the horses of the Boer commandos. The British Government rejected the Transvaal's ultimatum, the Orange Free State rallied to Kruger's side, and the great Boer War of 1899–1902 began on 12 October.

TEN

'CHAMBERLAIN'S WAR', AND OTHER DIVERSIONS
1899–1903

I come then in a spirit of conciliation, in a spirit of firmness also. The losses we have suffered, the sacrifices we have made, they must not be thrown away. . . . Yes, gentlemen, federation is now a thing to which we look forward with the most favourable anticipation.

Chamberlain in South Africa, 1902

AT FIRST sight, the opposing sides in the Boer War were ludicrously unequal. The British Empire, within whose borders dwelt almost a quarter of the human race, was at war with two sparsely populated republics in South Africa. Britain was still, arguably, the greatest power in the world, her navy apparently invincible and ubiquitous, her overseas trade colossal, her global influence immense. She controlled the Cape, Natal, the Rhodesias and Bechuanaland, all pressing upon the Boer Republics' frontiers; the Uitlanders were a fifth column within the Transvaal, and by no means all Afrikaners were spoiling for a fight.

In the end, Britain put 448,000 troops into the field; the Boers could at no time call upon more than 70,000 men, and probably never had more than 40,000 in active service—moreover, the Afrikaner forces were almost exclusively composed of civilians under arms.

If ever a war looked as if it would be over by Christmas it was this one. In Britain the mood was initially one of exhilaration as the khaki-clad infantry marched to the troopships, as the Admiralty hastily mustered 600,000 tons of shipping for men, horses and guns of the Army Corps dispatched to South Africa, as General Sir Redvers Buller, V.C., left Waterloo Station for embarkation at Southampton and the command of Her Majesty's forces in the campaign. The Imperial bard, Rudyard Kipling, wrote forcefully:

When you've shouted "Rule Britannia," when you've sung "God Save the Queen,"

When you've finished killing Kruger with your mouth,
Will you kindly drop a shilling in my little tambourine
  For a gentleman in Khaki ordered South?
He's an absent-minded beggar, and his weaknesses are great—
  But we and Paul must take him as we find him—
He is out on active service, wiping something off a slate—
  And he's left a lot of little things behind him!
Duke's son—cook's son—son of a hundred kings—
  (Fifty thousand horse and foot going to Table Bay!)
Each of 'em doing his country's work
  (and who's to look after their things?)
Pass the hat for your credit's sake,
  and pay—pay—pay!

But the dispatch of any army corps of 50,000 revealed serious inadequacies in the British military establishment. For one thing, home defences had to be pared to the bone; so serious was the depletion of forces stationed in Britain that the War Office immediately pressed the Cabinet to approve a policy of 'replacement', which involved the embodiment of a number of militia battalions and the issuing of contracts for new uniforms and supplies. George Wyndham, Under Secretary at the War Office, told Arthur Balfour, the First Lord of the Treasury, in October 1899, that unless 'replacement' was speedily effected the home army would be left without 'personnel and material' for adequate action or for training recruits, there would only be eight cavalry regiments left in the United Kingdom (not enough for home defence or for supplying the Indian army in the coming year), and that 'we are left with nothing but four gun batteries'.[374]

Despite their numerical advantage in South Africa, the British forces had hardly profited from their humiliations during the brief war of 1880–1. The average infantryman was still expected to obey rigid instructions to the last syllable, to keep splendid order, and to let his superiors do the thinking for him, whereas each Afrikaner was his own general. The British army possessed no General Staff to plan and coordinate tactics and strategy, and a paltry £11,000 was spent per annum on maintaining the Intelligence Division. The 'ideal British battle' was still one like the engagement at Omdurman in 1898, when the spear-waving Dervishes of the Sudan ran in their thousands against their opponents' maxim guns and rifles and were annihilated; Kitchener, the victor of Omdurman, was later to complain in South Africa that the Boers would not 'stand up to a fair fight'.

Nor had the British army properly understood the importance of mounted infantry. Admittedly ten per cent of the Imperial troops were mounted, but these were mainly cavalry who, although they carried the new-fangled carbines as well as sabres and lances, remained cavalrymen, not mounted infantry. The authorities were soon scouring the Empire for mounted men. Happily the self-governing colonies were able to fill an important gap or two: 1,000 expert horsemen were raised in Canada, the New South Wales Lancers played a conspicuous part in the war, and from southern Africa itself came the Imperial Light Horse (mostly recruited from the Uitlanders of Johannesburg), the Natal Mounted Volunteers, the Cape Police, the Kimberley Light Horse, and several other units.

These valuable contributions were only part of the generous colonial response to the war, and eventually 55,000 men, mostly from the self-governing parts of the Empire, served in South Africa—nearly double the number of the British expeditionary force sent to the Crimea in 1854. Even so, the bulk of the colonial troops did not arrive until the war was well under way, and it was not until the beginning of 1901 that Lord Kitchener managed to assemble sufficiently large numbers of mounted men to try to cope with Boer mobility.

The early months of the war were little short of disastrous for Britain. Boer commandos struck with telling effect in north Natal and into the northern Cape where some 10,000 Afrikaner 'rebels' joined the forces of the two republics. The strategically important towns of Mafeking, Ladysmith and Kimberley were besieged and, early in December, British armies were sent to three humiliating defeats at Stormberg, Magersfontein and Colenso during one 'black week'.

These early catastrophes were the result both of military blunders and of inadequate training and equipment. Boer mobility and their skilful use of the terrain were additional hazards, as were their superb marksmanship and the superior quality of much of their artillery—prudently bought from France and Germany in the years before the war.

Far from the war being over by Christmas, it dragged on until

May 1902—by which time Britain's victory was a tainted, almost embarrassing, anti-climax. The early humiliations of the war were relieved by the sacking in January 1900 of the fumbling Buller as Commander-in-Chief in South Africa and his replacement by the popular Lord Roberts of Kandahar and the coldly ruthless Kitchener of Khartoum. 'Bobs' and 'K' reversed the trend of the war, defeated Cronje at Paardeberg in February, marched on Bloemfontein, Pretoria and Johannesburg, and raised the sieges of Kimberley, Ladysmith and Mafeking—the latter to an outburst of hysterical and misplaced public celebration in Britain.

By the autumn of 1900 the strategic advantage was firmly in British hands; Kruger had fled to Europe and exile, and a peace seemed inevitable. Afrikaner commandos, however, fought on, led by generals as able as Louis Botha, Jan Smuts, J. B. Hertzog, Koos de la Rey and Christiaan de Wet. When Roberts laid down his command in December 1900 and returned to honour and glory in Britain, the war still had a year and a half to run. This period of 'guerilla' warfare was characterised by some of the most unpleasant episodes of the conflict. Desperate to hunt down the remaining Boer forces (some 20,000 strong) the huge British army resorted to a scorched-earth policy hoping to starve the commandos into submission. Farm-burning created another problem. The British authorities were faced with hordes of homeless and hungry Afrikaner refugees. These they herded into 'concentration camps', where early deficiencies in diet and sanitation caused the death of approximately 20,000 inmates by the time the war ended.

All of this was hardly the kind of war that Chamberlain and Milner wanted. Having manoeuvred the two Boer republics into placing their heads upon the block, the subsequent discovery that John Bull's axe was a blunt and rusty instrument was a source of deep disquiet.

Privately Chamberlain was bitterly critical of military muddle, and impatient of excuses. When the outbreak of war was imminent he had demanded that more troops should be dispatched to South Africa, but had been overruled by the War Office.[375] When a little later the Boers opened up on Ladysmith with their 'Long Toms' (their Creusot 94 pounder siege guns), Chamberlain remarked irritably that Lord Lansdowne, the Secretary of State for War, had told him 'that modern guns require elaborate platforms and mountings which took a year to consolidate. The Boers apparently find no difficulty in working their "Long Toms" without these elaborate precautions. On the whole I am terribly afraid that our War Office is as inefficient as usual.'

In public Chamberlain was able to drum up some appropriate platitudes. Speaking spontaneously before a crowd of loyalist undergraduates at Trinity College Dublin on 18 December, in the shadow of 'black week', he said:

We have had bad news, but our country has never been greatly moved by evil fortune. (Loud cheers.) In past times, we have again and again made head against adversity and we will do it now. (Prolonged cheers.) I am old enough to remember still darker days, the days of the Crimean War and the early days of the Indian Mutiny—and I hope that now as then the darkest hour will be found to precede the dawn.[376]

Amid the gloom and recrimination of the first months of the war, Chamberlain could draw some satisfaction from the rallying of colonial support for the mother country. Even Laurier, Prime Minister of Canada, overcame his anxiety not to provoke the hostility of Quebec (with its French-speaking, largely anti-imperial population) and sanctioned the dispatch of a battalion of over a thousand regular infantry to South Africa. Chamberlain wrote delightedly to Lord Minto, the Governor-General of Canada, 'I am sure that the action of Canada and of the other Colonies will leave a lasting impression in the country and will tend more than anything else to draw the Empire closer together.'[377]

This judgement proved to be merely a Chamberlainite exercise in wishful thinking. The support of the self-governing colonies did not presage imperial federation or anything like it; indeed, Laurier's offer of Canadian troops had caused a Cabinet split. If the other colonies had rallied to the Empire's cause there were good reasons, apart from unabashed imperial sentiment, why they should have done so: for one thing, the colonies relied upon a strong Britain for their ultimate defence; for another, they could ill afford to stand by and watch the privileges and rights involved in British citizenship denied by the Transvaal Boers—in this sense the Uitlanders' cause was also theirs. The Colonial Conference of 1902, held a few weeks after the end of the Boer War, was to show with unambiguous clarity that while the self-governing colonies could respond generously to an international crisis they thought first of their own interests once that crisis had disappeared. Imperial cooperation, in other words, could not be taken for granted; the bonds of Empire were only as strong as the colonies chose to make them.

Chamberlain, in fact, showed a good deal of sensitivity towards colonial susceptibilities during the war. The Bill bringing about the federation of the Australian colonies was being piloted through Parliament in 1900, and Chamberlain hoped that the new Commonwealth of Australia would adopt a fruitful attitude towards fiscal reform and imperial trade. Partly to keep the confidence of the self-governing colonies, and partly because he hoped for an eventual reconciliation between Afrikaners and British in that colony, Chamberlain steadfastly resisted Milner's desire to establish autocratic rule in the Cape. The Cape assembly was in fact prorogued in September 1900 since the effective management of Parliamentary business proved impossible in view of the hostility between Afrikaner Bond members and English-speaking Progressive members. In June 1902, with the war at last won, Milner pressed Chamberlain to agree to the suspension of the Cape constitution, something advocated by the local Progressive party, which also demanded a redistribution of seats to reduce the representation of the Cape Dutch.

The suspension of the Cape constitution held great attractions for Milner. His tidy, if somewhat narrow, mind was already feasting on the possibilities of forcibly federating South Africa: the Transvaal and the Free State had been conquered and were at Britain's disposal; Natal with its patriotic English-speaking population would probably support such a scheme; the only stumbling-block was the Cape, a self-governing colony with an Afrikaner majority among its white population. Chamberlain's democratic instincts, though conveniently submerged for the purpose of destroying the Boer republics' independence, baulked at the suspension of the Cape constitution, and the colony maintained its self-governing character. The desire to encourage future cooperation between Afrikaner and British South Africans also accounted for Chamberlain's allegedly 'soft' attitude towards an amnesty for Cape Dutch rebels. Chamberlain's attitude towards the Cape suspension crisis was summed up in a letter he wrote to Balfour on 9 September

1902 saying that he was trying 'to keep out of the conflict as much as possible leaving responsibility where it belongs—to the Government of an autonomous Colony.'[378]

Such constitutional niceties were not characteristic of Chamberlain's overall approach to the war. He wanted the republics conquered and Boer resistance crushed as soon as possible so that the great task of reconstruction could begin, especially the establishment of that 'Greater South Africa', unified and tranquil, within the British Empire. In this sense, Chamberlain was as much a 'bitter ender' as de Wet and the Boer commandos that continued the war into 1902.

The war and its ugly qualities made Chamberlain the object of a campaign of vilification in Britain and in many other countries. Some British radicals claimed from the outset that the war was being fought for Cecil Rhodes, international capitalism, and the faceless financiers of 'Jewburg'. As farm-burning increased and the concentration camps filled up, a huge outcry was raised against the war. Sir Henry Campbell-Bannerman, who had become leader of the Liberal party in 1898, felt moved to ask 'When is a war not a war? When it is carried on by methods of barbarism in South Africa.' 'Methods of barbarism' was a phrase which high-lighted a memorable controversy. But the actual improvement in conditions in the camps owed much to the persistent agitation of Emily Hobhouse, Secretary of the Women's branch of the South Africa Conciliation Committee, ('that bloody woman' as Kitchener described her). As a result, conditions were drastically improved, and by the end of the war the death-rate was down to sixty-nine per thousand. Chamberlain was later to claim that the Afrikaner mortality rate in the last six months of fighting had been lower than in peacetime.[379]

In January 1900 the Government faced a vote of censure in the Commons on their handling of the war. On 5 February, Chamberlain, looking drawn and pale as he often did under stress, rose to reply to the Opposition's case. He spoke for an hour, hardly referring to his notes, and with a restraint, a sort of confidentiality that disarmed at least some of his critics. With a breathtaking audacity he said, 'You may blame us, and perhaps rightly, that throughout this business we have been too anxious for peace. But no impartial man, no man who knows the facts, can truly and properly blame us for having been too eager for war. Our efforts were fruitless. Our objects were reasonable. . . .' He ended by asserting that the South African war was a useful stepping-stone on the way towards imperial federation, 'Meanwhile, we are finding out the weak spots in our armour and trying to remedy them; we are finding out the infinite potential resources of the Empire; and we are advancing steadily, if slowly, to the realisation of that great federation of our race, which will inevitably make for peace and liberty and justice.'[380] The vote of censure was defeated by a majority of 213 votes.

Chamberlain wrote a ruminative letter upon the reaction to this speech to his son Neville on 10 February:

My dear Neville,
    Many thanks for your letter. The speech was a remarkable success & I am now once more at the top of the hill. How long will it last? I do not value much what I call newspaper & club opinion for it is as inconsistent as the wind. Fortunately the people are more consistent & although they form their judgement more slowly are less apt to desert a leader the first time he fails to give satisfaction.
    In the last 12 months we have seen Salisbury Balfour & myself alternatively praised & abused by the "influential cliques" but I expect that the real opinion of the nation has remained pretty steady all the time.
    So I am not too much puffed up although considering the indecent joy with which my enemies flooded over my approaching downfall it gives me a cynical satisfaction to know that they are most grievously disappointed.[381]

Apart from such fillips to his self-esteem, and the optimistic, though ill-founded, speculation that the cause of imperial federation was being served by the subjugation of the Boer republics, Chamberlain was able to snatch one colossal advantage from the war: this was the victorious General Election of October 1900.

The 'Khaki' election was fought to capitalise upon the apparent victory in South Africa following the advent of Roberts and Kitchener. The contest aroused violent feelings and brought down a torrent of abuse and slander upon Chamberlain's head. 'Chamberlain's war', his enemies said, was now to be disfigured further by 'Chamberlain's election' resulting, very probably, in 'Chamberlain's victory'. Where, critics asked, had Chamberlain's much vaunted enthusiasm for social reform gone? Chamberlain defended himself against this charge in East Birmingham on 29 September, saying defiantly, but somewhat unconvincingly, 'We have not done with old-age pensions. I am not dead yet. . . . It was not a practical question until we took it up here in Birmingham and took it up in a practical spirit.'[382]

Basically, however, the country was simply asked to judge Chamberlain and the Government's South African policy. Although Unionists could not fail to respond to what amounted to a patriotic appeal, the Liberal party's attitude was ambiguous. By October 1900, the Liberals were split into three factions over the war. The Liberal Imperialists Asquith, Grey, Haldane and Rosebery supported the war though reserving the right to criticise the methods employed. The Liberal leader Campbell-Bannerman wanted above all to minimise the split within his party, but had said in June 1899 that nothing in the South African situation could justify war. On the left-wing of the party were the pro-Boers led by Harcourt, Morley, John Burns and the up-and-coming David Lloyd George. These men were unqualified in their condemnation of the war, even though in Lloyd George's case it endangered life and limb when he spoke in Chamberlain's stronghold of Birmingham. In the Commons, the Irish Nationalists unhesitatingly supported the Boers, with whom they could identify themselves as an oppressed nation.

Chamberlain weathered the abuse and innuendo that had marked the campaign. When it was over, he thanked Balfour for 'the kind things you said in my defence.' Chamberlain complained of attacks of a private character which all the Liberal leaders, save Grey, had failed to repudiate, 'allowing the insinuations to be distributed by the Radical Association at 5/- per thousand.'[383] Salisbury, too, congratulated Balfour on his opportune campaigning, 'for the political world was running the danger of being divided into pro-Boer and pro-Joe; which I think is not an exhaustive statement of the sentiments of Her Majesty's subjects.'[384]

The 'Khaki' election returned the Unionists with a slightly enlarged majority. Among the new Conservative M.P.s was Winston Churchill, then twenty-six years old and already famous for his Boer War escape, and for his work as a war correspondent for the *Morning Post*. Partly in memory of his dead friend Lord

Randolph Churchill, Chamberlain went up to Oldham to speak on the young man's behalf. Churchill left a vivid account of this visit and of the highly-charged electioneering atmosphere in Oldham during this campaign:

> Mr. Chamberlain himself came to speak for me. There was more enthusiasm over him at this moment than after the Great War for Mr. Lloyd George and Sir Douglas Haig combined. There was at the same time a tremendous opposition; but antagonism had not wholly excluded admiration from their breasts. We drove to our great meeting together in an open carriage. Our friends had filled the theatre; our opponents thronged its approaches. At the door of the theatre our carriage was jammed tight for some minutes in an immense hostile crowd, all groaning and booing at the tops of their voices, and grinning with the excitement of seeing a famous fellow-citizen whom it was their right and duty to oppose. I watched my honoured guest with close attention. He loved the roar of the multitude, and with my father could always say "I have never feared the English democracy." The blood mantled in his cheek, and his eye as it caught mine twinkled with pure enjoyment. I must explain that in those days we had a real political democracy led by a hierarchy of statesmen, and not a fluid mass distracted by newspapers. There was a structure in which statesmen, electors and the Press all played their part. Inside the meeting we were all surprised at Mr. Chamberlain's restraint. His soft purring voice and reasoned incisive sentences, for most of which he had a careful note, made a remarkable impression. He spoke for over an hour; but what pleased the audience most was that, having made a mistake in some fact or figure to the prejudice of his opponents, he went back and corrected it, observing that he must not be unfair.[385]

While the Unionists' election victory could be interpreted as a mandate for pushing the war through to the bitter end, it did not escape notice that for every eight votes cast for the Government seven were cast against it. In the new House of Commons, Chamberlain faced renewed attacks. He denied ever using the slogan 'A seat lost to the Government is a seat sold to the Boers', claiming instead that he had merely passed on by telegram a

statement from the Mayor of Kimberley which ran, 'A seat lost to
the Government is a seat *gained* by the Boers'. Due to the negli-
gence of the Post Office official, Chamberlain insisted, the vital
word *gained* had been altered to *sold*. This was a thin explanation,
but Balfour dismissed the accusation against Chamberlain as an
absurd story.[386]

Four days later on 10 December, Balfour again came to the
rescue of the beleaguered Colonial Secretary. Chamberlain had
been accused of profiteering from the war by failing to sever his
connections with several companies holding Government contracts; companies such as the Birmingham Small Arms Company,
and Kynochs. Balfour poured scorn on the accusers, asking who
would satisfy them as fit to hold office, 'Wanted, a man to serve
Her Majesty, with no money, no relations, and inspiring no general
confidence.'[387] Perhaps the vigour of the assault on Chamberlain
was an attempt by the Liberals to hide their divisions, and Balfour
was not slow to point out that the electorate had preferred a united
party to one hopelessly split by faction.

The Khaki election victory was essentially a freak result. The
Unionists had hardly justified a vote of confidence by their handling
of either domestic or external affairs. By marching to Pretoria,
Lord Roberts had carried the Unionists to an electoral triumph
that would have been unthinkable a year later. Chamberlain had
bought himself another lease of time at the Colonial Office.
Enough, perhaps, to give substance to his imperial vision and to
stamp his mark indelibly upon the Unionist alliance—no mean
prospect for a man of sixty-four, but recently rehabilitated from
the political wilderness.

The war, however, would not end. Not until 31 May 1902 was
peace concluded between the Boer leaders and an uncharacteristi-
cally persuasive and obliging Kitchener at Vereeniging in the
Transvaal. The clauses of the peace Treaty were as follows: the
Boers to lay down their arms and acknowledge King Edward VII
as their lawful sovereign; all prisoners, internees, and those at war
beyond the annexed republics' frontiers would be allowed to
return home, without loss of property or freedom, on making the
same acknowledgement; amnesty would be granted to all those
who surrendered, except those who had committed acts contrary
to the usages of war; the Boers could keep their weapons (i.e.
rifles), under licence, for personal protection; Dutch (Afrikaans)

would be taught in the state schools of the annexed republics where parents so wished, and could be used, where necessary for greater efficiency, in courts of law; military administration would be superseded at the earliest possible date by civil government which would in turn be superseded, as soon as possible, by representative institutions leading to self-government; the question of the 'Native franchise' (i.e. votes for non-Europeans in the Transvaal and the Free State) would be decided after the restoration of self-government; no special tax would be levied to cover the cost of the war; district commissions to be established to assist resettlement, to provide necessities lost in the war, and to honour bank or promissory notes issued by the two republics— for these ends the British Government would provide a free gift of £3,000,000, and loans at low rates of interest after two years and interest-free before then.

These were essentially reasonable terms. Though the two republics were confirmed as crown colonies under direct military rule, the vexed question of non-European enfranchisement was deferred until the white population achieved self-government. In effect, this concession (not a particularly painful one for the British Government) meant that the overwhelming Afrikaner majority in the Free State, and even the Afrikaner and British population of the Transvaal would in all probability keep the non-Europeans disenfranchised and firmly in their place. Kitchener also gave informal assurances that the Cape rebels would, at the worst, face a temporary loss of voting rights, not the firing squad.

Chamberlain and Milner had, at last, got the victory they wanted. Almost immediately, however, they began to lose the peace. This despite all Milner's efforts. Thwarted in his design forcibly to bring about a federation in South Africa, he did his best to ensure that British supremacy, so painfully asserted during the war, should be maintained in the foreseeable future. A customs union, including Rhodesia, was established between the four colonies in South Africa in 1903, and Milner tried his utmost to promote the English language and to saturate the local civil services with British citizens. But the floods of anticipated British immigrants did not arrive; British working men were not attracted to a labour market underpinned by the rock bottom wages paid to black workers. 'Milnerisation' (or Anglicisation) was a failure, and the political future of unified South Africa was destined to lie with the

new, enlightened Afrikaner leaders—men like Botha and Smuts
who were sympathetic to the imperial connection, and Hertzog
and Malan who were not.

Milner's stern and authoritarian rule in South Africa contrasted
with Chamberlain's more flexible approach to reconstruction.
Nonetheless the visit to Britain at the end of August 1902 of three
Boer generals (Botha, de la Rey and de Wet), who came to ask for
modifications in the terms of the treaty of Vereeniging, tried
Chamberlain's patience. Before meeting the generals, who
received a reception tantamount to a hero's welcome in London,
Chamberlain wrote an exasperated letter to his son Austen on 1
September:

> I am having trouble with the Boer generals. . . . I asked for
> details of the subjects they wished to discuss with me tomorrow.
> In return they sent me a list of 14 which together would consti-
> tute an entirely new argument in substitution for the terms of
> surrender. I have absolutely refused to re-open that argument
> & have postponed meeting them till they accept my conditions.
> I have come to the conclusion they are thoroughly untrust-
> worthy.
> We are ready to be friends but the friendship must be on
> both sides & frankly declared.
> With them it is all take & no give. I shall no doubt hear from
> them again today but I shall keep them kicking their heels in
> London till I have a satisfactory statement in writing as to their
> intentions.[388]

Balfour too thought the demands of the generals 'so impudent
that I feel tempted to think they wish to pick a quarrel.' Chamberlain finally dealt with the generals with a characteristic blend of
firmness and cajolement. At least, he was able to tell Balfour on 9
September that 'the demands of the Boer generals had fizzled out.'
Moreover, he had sounded out Botha 'as to the possibility of his
joining the Government. I have not yet received his reply but his
general tone was quite friendly.'[389] Although Botha refused the
offer of a seat on the Transvaal's proposed Legislative Council,
Chamberlain found, when he arrived in South Africa in December
1902 to see the situation at first hand, that the Boer leaders were
now reconciled to making the best of the treaty of Vereeniging.

The tensions in the Cape Parliament had also somewhat abated. Chamberlain's visit to South Africa, which lasted from 26 December 1902 to 25 February 1903, was no brash Roman triumph, a crowing over conquered foes. He desired to promote two themes, each of which he considered essential to the well-being and development of the Empire: Anglo-Afrikaner reconciliation, and practical colonial contributions to Britain's imperial burden. It was typical of his flair for political campaigning that he went off to meet his South African constituents face to face—unreconciled republicans, loyalists from Natal, Afrikaner 'hands-uppers', Uitlanders, suspicious Cape Dutch and truculent Cape Progressives. He was, in a sense, campaigning for votes for a pacified, unified South Africa to take its place within the British Empire.

The trail that Chamberlain stumped through South Africa was tortuous and difficult. In Natal he received a rapturous reception and the colonial Government's offer to shoulder nearly one million pounds in war expenditure which would otherwise have been Britain's responsibility. In Pretoria he wrangled once more with Boer leaders over the peace terms, while affirming his belief that 'before many years are over . . . we shall be a free people under one flag.' The Uitlander mining companies in Johannesburg agreed to put up £30,000,000 as Transvaal's contribution to the cost of the war. On the Rand, Chamberlain was confirmed in his belief that the Transvaal needed a period of crown colony Government before it could be granted self-governing institutions.

He also saw at first hand the problems in attracting white immigrants to an economy so heavily dependent upon cheap black labour, but was quite opposed to Milner's proposal to import Chinese indentured workers to plug the yawning gap in the gold-mining industry's work force, arguing that white South African opinion was against it, and that 'such action would be extremely unpopular and would raise a storm at home'—a prophecy which came home to roost with a vengeance during the 'Chinese Slavery' controversy of 1905–6. Chamberlain was anxious to offer economic inducements to coax black labour down the mines, but rejected outright a white delegation's plea that the flogging of Africans for minor offences should be introduced. In response to this request his old hatred of corporal punishment was rekindled, and he stated that 'if it is suggested that a Kaffir must be flogged for a breach of contract etc., then I protest against it as being contrary to the English character, unworthy of the English, and inhuman.'[390]

In the newly-annexed Orange River Colony, Bloemfontein's welcome was surprisingly warm, but in Government House members of an Afrikaner delegation presented a document which, among other things, accused the British Government of violating three of the terms of peace. Chamberlain turned in fury upon these critics and argued bitterly with their leader, General Hertzog, for over two hours. At one stage Hertzog, getting the worst of the encounter, said, 'We cannot expect that you will remain with us for ever to attend to these points', and Chamberlain replied bluntly, 'The British Government remains for ever'.

Cape Colony promised Chamberlain as stormy a ride as anywhere in South Africa. His chief task was to reconcile the stalwarts of the English-speaking Progressive party and of the Afrikaner Bond—if necessary by banging their heads together. As it happened the Bond, dominated by Hofmeyr, proved more amenable than the extremists among the Progressives, now under the leadership of Dr. Jameson who had arisen from the ashes of the raid and was bidding, in the immediate aftermath of Rhodes's death, for the premiership of the colony. Jameson was hostile to Chamberlain's message of reconciliation, calling him 'the callous devil from Birmingham'.[391] Though Chamberlain was unable to prise any financial contribution to the cost of the war out of Cape Colony, he did persuade the Prime Minister, John Gordon Sprigg, to hold elections as soon as possible, and cajoled the leadership of the Bond and the Progressives into issuing public statements of reconciliation. The Cape elections were in fact held in 1904 and, with the Cape rebels still disenfranchised, returned a Progressive Government with Jameson as Prime Minister.

Chamberlain's South African tour confirmed him in the belief that the Transvaal held the key to South Africa's future, but also convinced him that the bid to establish British supremacy in the long term was doomed to failure. In terms of giving substance to his plans for encouraging inter-imperial trade, the vast economic potential of South Africa made a profound impression upon him.

His wife, who had accompanied him throughout the arduous tour, gave her view of his achievements in a letter written on 2 March, while sailing back to Britain:

Joe's constant endeavour was to try to reconcile those who ought to be friends and to impress upon them that a new era was dawning in which they must take their part now, if in the future they were going to claim—as no doubt they would claim—their share in the councils of federated South Africa.

. . . . And so you see that the rock on which Joe feared his bark might strike [the tensions in the Cape] was safely weathered, and he could feel on leaving that the success of his mission had not been impaired by failure in Cape Colony.

. . . . Next morning [18 February] came our formal arrival in Cape Town. . . . A vast crowd gave Joe a mighty cheer.

. . . . It was a critical moment, for it was necessary to mask his sense of the unhappy condition of affairs, at the same time acknowledging the hospitality of the town. The speech was full of courage, tact and friendliness, and while he made no conceal-ment of his appreciation of the gravity of the situation, he did it in such a way that it elicited approbation instead of disap-proval.[392]

There was a banquet the night before leaving Cape Town, and Mrs. Chamberlain gave her somewhat relieved appraisal of her husband's performance:

It was a great speech, delivered as he only delivers it under the stress of important events.

. . . . It was the final success of the tour and it was a great satis-faction to him, as well as to me, to have it come at that moment— so the curtain was rung down and the audience went away well pleased with the chief actor, while I, his wife, laid my head down in peace that night, happy in the thought that his labour was finished in that arduous task, and proud in the belief that the work was truly and faithfully done.[393]

Chamberlain's South African tour took almost exactly two months. He and his wife visited twenty-nine towns; he delivered sixty-four speeches—nearly all of them vitally important to the task of reconstruction; he received eighty-seven deputations (some of which were downright difficult to handle) and gave 250 interviews.

Had it all been worth it? There was no magical metamorphosis in South Africa; English-speaking and Afrikaans-speaking citizens did not fall on each others' necks protesting their brotherly love.

Milner, who resigned from his onerous position in 1905 (to be
succeeded by Selborne whom Chamberlain told, in his letter of
congratulation, 'There are few positions I would sooner fill'),
believed towards the end of his term of office that 'we have turned
the corner here—economically. There is no mistake about it. . . .
Politically things are much as they always have been, & will be
for the next 10 years, or more.'[394]

In fact substantial political changes were already in train. A
representative constitution was granted to the Transvaal in 1905;
it was the work of Milner and Lyttelton (who had succeeded
Chamberlain as Colonial Secretary in September 1903). In
December 1905, however, the Unionist Government resigned.
Campbell-Bannerman became Prime Minister; in the election of
January 1906 the Liberals annihilated their opponents. In Feb-
ruary 1906 the Government announced, in the speech from the
throne, that self-government would be given forthwith to the
Transvaal and the Orange River Colony. In February 1907 elec-
tions for the Transvaal's new assembly gave an overall majority of
five seats to Het Volk, the Afrikaner party led by Louis Botha and
Jan Smuts. In March, Botha was installed as the first Prime
Minister of the self-governing colony of the Transvaal. The
Uitlanders, as unreliable after the war as before it, had split their
vote between the Progressive and Labour parties, and had thus
helped Het Volk to its victory. Soon afterwards the Afrikaner
Oranje Unie party predictably swept the board in elections in the
Orange River Colony.

Within two years a Bill for the Union of South Africa was
before the British Parliament, and on 1 January 1910 Botha
became the first Prime Minister of the new Union, which took its
place as a self-governing Dominion within the British Empire.

In March 1908 Chamberlain told Selborne that he had earlier
disapproved of the Transvaal's 1905 constitution: 'It went too
far, or not far enough, & I am not surprised that the present
Government when they came into office determined to make a
clean sweep of it.'[395] In the same letter Chamberlain expressed
his keen interest in the current plans for unifying the four self-
governing South African colonies.

The unification of South Africa, and the rise to power of
Afrikaner political moderates like Botha and Smuts, was some sort
of vindication for Chamberlain's earlier efforts in the cause of

reconciliation. Gold shares and British capital investment in South Africa were safe under Botha and Smuts. South Africa's place in the British Empire, moreover, was more easily assured under enlightened Afrikaner leadership than under the tutelage of Progressive party stalwarts like Jameson. Selborne, in 1908, put a not inaccurate gloss on the war and subsequent events when he told his old mentor, Chamberlain:

> The War, therefore was really fought on two immense issues. Was South Africa ever to become a united, progressive, modern State? Was it to remain part of the British Empire? . . . You and Milner and Roberts have done a work which nothing can undo. To put it tersely, you have created a new South Africa.[396]

Although in the long term Chamberlain's South African tour of 1902–3 helped to ripen some choice imperial fruit, in other ways it may be seen as a rash abandonment of domestic politics at a time of crucial importance for his plans to consolidate the imperial connection—particularly in the bid to establish the principle of reciprocal preferential tariffs.

Apart from the ending of the Boer War, 1902 was, in fact, an unhappy year for Chamberlain's ambitions. It was the year in which he abandoned his long-cherished hope of an Anglo-German alliance, and instead became an advocate of 'an "entente cordiale" with France, which is what I would now like.'[397]

Furthermore, in July 1902, Salisbury, no longer in control of all his faculties, resigned and was succeeded as Prime Minister by Balfour. This was a predictable progress, for whereas others who were less well-born had to contend with the slippery pole of political promotion, Balfour, with his Cecil blood and his intellectual distinction, was assured of preferment. Some of Chamberlain's less inhibited supporters bitterly regretted that their man had been passed over. In journals like the *Nineteenth Century*, the *National Review* and the *African Review* there had earlier been an enthusiastic advocacy of Chamberlain's claims for the premiership, the *African Review* arguing on 15 March that 'Mr. Chamberlain is no ephemeron, no mere man of the hour. He is the man of tomorrow and the day after tomorrow.'[398]

Chamberlain could, nonetheless, hardly hope to oust Balfour from his rightful inheritance. The bosses of the Conservative party would not stand for it, even though many rank-and-file Unionists recognised Chamberlain's vote-winning and organisational qualities. Chamberlain, moreover, believed he owed a debt of loyalty to Balfour for the latter's friendship and support that had been manifest since 1886. At the same time, it was impossible to believe that the man who had once said that the premiership was the only political position worth having had completely abandoned all ambition to inhabit 10 Downing Street. He was still a remarkably sprightly sexagenarian, his vigour apparently undimmed by the passing years.

It was perhaps in tacit recognition of Chamberlain's powerful political presence that Lord Salisbury chose to rush through his resignation while his Colonial Secretary was injured and confined to his bed. On 7 July Chamberlain was involved in a cab accident which cost him a pint of blood and left him with three stitches in a deep cut upon his right temple. The next day he was well enough to leave hospital (where he had characteristically refused an anaesthetic for his stitches) and returned to Prince's Gardens with a dapper black silk scarf covering the bandages on his hatless head. His doctors, however, insisted that he should cease all work and stay in bed for a fortnight.

Two days after Chamberlain left hospital, Salisbury wrote to him announcing his intention of resigning. The next day, 11 July, before Chamberlain had received this letter, Balfour was summoned to Buckingham Palace to form an administration. Before kissing hands Balfour prudently called upon Chamberlain, who had to be woken by his wife, and received the injured man's assurances of loyalty. Later that same day, with the matter settled beyond redemption Chamberlain wrote in reply to Salisbury's letter of 10 July:

My Dear Salisbury,
I thank you very much for your letter. When I spoke to Cranborne [Lord Salisbury's eldest son] some months ago, I had no anticipation of any early change, but the newspapers were saying silly things about me, and I wished you to know that, if at any time you contemplated retirement, my supposed ambition would not prevent me from giving to Arthur any support that it might be in my power to render.[399]

Not merely were Chamberlain's prospects of becoming Prime

Minister dramatically, and perhaps permanently, deferred during 1902, his overall schemes for greater imperial unity also suffered a considerable set-back. The Colonial Conference, which met as Chamberlain was recovering from his accident, produced no satisfactory response to the call for imperial federation and closer defence cooperation.

Serious difficulties also remained in the way of achieving an imperial *zollverein*. Discussions with the Canadian delegation, however, revealed a chink of light amid the gloom: the Canadian Government, building on their 1897 initiative, had in effect given British exports a tariff preference of thirty-three and a third per cent by 1900. On 14 April 1902 Hicks Beach, the Chancellor, had announced in his budget speech a revival of the registration duty of 3d. per cwt. on imported corn and 5d. per cwt. on imported meal and flour. The Canadian delegates at the Colonial Conference showed a distinct interest in the possibility of the new Corn Tax being remitted in their favour. Here, if Chamberlain could obtain Cabinet agreement, was a stealthy but effective way forward for the cause of reciprocal inter-imperial tariff concessions. Such a step would, however, deal a heavy blow at the holy sepulchre of free trade, and would establish a portentous fiscal precedent.

Even while Chamberlain was grasping at this particular opportunity, on another front the controversy over the 1902 Education Act was threatening to erode the remnants of his support among Nonconformist voters. The Education Act of 1902 was persuasively sponsored by Balfour in terms of a drive for national efficiency in education; putting an end to the outdated educational system that made England 'the laughing stock of every advanced nation in Europe and America'. These were reforming objectives that Chamberlain, the unwearying and articulate apostle of national efficiency, might have been expected warmly to advocate. The proposals of the Education Bill, however, amounted to a death sentence for the local school boards that had been set up under Forster's Act of 1870 largely to administer elementary education but now responsible for a good many secondary schools as well. These school boards, some 2,500 in number, were much cherished by Nonconformists throughout the country. The 1902 Bill by proposing to establish a state system of primary, secondary and technical schools, controlled centrally for policy and through local authorities for administration, would not only destroy the

independence of the board schools, but would also extend rate aid
to the voluntary (mainly Church of England) schools.

The Bill was bound to enrage Nonconformists, Radicals and
many Liberal Unionists—all past, or present, soul-mates of
Chamberlain. Buckling on the tarnished sword of the old Education
League, Chamberlain prepared to do battle once more with the
Anglican ogre in defence of the 1870 compromise. Circumstances,
however, had altered almost beyond recognition in the interim.
For one thing, the Conservatives had an overall majority in the
Commons and could simply pass the Bill—in buoyant contrast to
their apparently permanent minority status in 1870. For another,
Chamberlain was a senior Cabinet minister (co-Prime Minister
some said) not a provincial Radical with his name still to make.
Moreover, he owed his Cabinet rank to the Conservative party and
part, at least, of his influence to the cordial relationship he had
developed with Salisbury and, more especially, with Balfour, the
new Prime Minister and the moving spirit behind the proposed
Education Bill. It was, finally, downright inconsistent, if not
perverse, for Chamberlain to advocate, on the one hand, a more
efficient handling of empire or a rationalisation of Britain's commercial relations and, on the other, to cling to a cumbersome
dualist system of education.

Chamberlain had, in fact, lost the battle almost before it began.
When Robert Morant, the Bill's chief sponsor within the Education
Department, visited him at 'Highbury' in December 1902,
Chamberlain threatened him with the prospect of Nonconformist
rate-martyrs who would go to prison rather than subsidise Anglican
schools within the proposed system. Chamberlain also asked
Morant why voluntary schools should not get additional financial
aid from central state funds rather than from the rates, only to
receive the unanswerable reply, 'Because your War has made
further recourse to State grants impossible.'

Eventually Chamberlain managed to extract the major concession that the granting of rate aid to voluntary schools should be
left to the discretion of local authorities. Even this concession was
to be rescinded before the Bill was guillotined through in December
1902 amid an outraged Nonconformist and Liberal clamour.

The 1902 Education Bill controversy revealed Chamberlain as a
man desperate to salvage votes for the Unionist alliance and to
preserve the Liberal Unionist organisation as a viable power base.

The impassioned educational reformer of the late 1860s and early 1870s had been largely transformed into a party manager and election winner, anxious to find a convenient loophole or two in the Bill. Chamberlain's deportment was in marked contrast to that other senior Liberal Unionist the Duke of Devonshire who, ponderous of thought and action and, as Lord President of the Council, nominally in charge of educational matters, fought resolutely for the Bill at all its stages simply because he had come to believe in it.

Chamberlain summed up his real anxieties over the Bill when he told Sandars, Balfour's private secretary, on 9 October 1902 that if the Prime Minister persisted in nailing his educational colours to the mast, 'I consider the Unionist cause is hopeless at the next election, and we shall certainly lose the majority of the Liberal Unionists once and for all.'[400]

As it was, Chamberlain had to make the best of a bad job. He proceeded to force the bulk of his Birmingham supporters to swallow the bitter medicine of the Bill, and to disentangle himself from the whole imbroglio as expeditiously as possible. There was no doubt, however, that Nonconformist Liberal Unionists would desert the Unionist alliance in droves as a result of the Education Bill row. Perhaps even his own Birmingham support, apparently successfully rallied in October 1902, would continue to be eroded in the emotive wake of the Education Bill.

Chamberlain needed a new cause to revitalise Unionism and to refurbish his own electoral appeal. As 1902 drew towards its close there was only one apparent hand-hold—tariff reform or, more specifically, reciprocal imperial preference. Lord George Hamilton, Secretary of State for India from 1895–1903 and a convinced free trader, no doubt put it too crudely when he later wrote, 'If we had had no Education Bill of 1902, we should have had no Tariff Reform in 1903.'[401] Nonetheless, Chamberlain, by the autumn of 1902, had latched firmly onto tariff reform as both beneficial to Britain and the empire and restorative for his own political fortunes. By so doing he was about to plunge the nation into a controversy as damaging to party loyalties as the Home Rule crisis of 1885–6.

ELEVEN

ANOTHER OLD MAN IN A HURRY?
THE TARIFF REFORM CAMPAIGN
1903–6

Joe—the ever youthful—has started a new hare, and we are all running about in different ways after it. Like every other new idea, it is proclaimed the "ruin of the Empire". He himself is entirely confident of success with the constituencies, and he is reputed a good judge.

C. F. Moberly Bell, manager of *The Times*, 1903

CHAMBERLAIN UNDERTOOK his tour of South Africa in November 1902 in the belief that the Cabinet had agreed to make a remission on the corn tax in favour of the self-governing colonies in the next budget. On 21 October he had proposed this step at a meeting of the Cabinet, where it had received a generally favourable reception. Balfour wrote at once to Edward VII saying, 'There is a very great deal to be said in favour of this proposal. . . . But it raises very big questions indeed—colonial and fiscal—and the Government which embarks upon it provokes a big fight. On the whole Mr. Balfour leans towards it; but it behoves us to walk warily.'[402]

The proposal to remit the corn tax had not come like a bolt from the blue. When the Chancellor of the Exchequer, Hicks Beach, had announced in his budget of April 1902 the imposition of a corn registration tax to raise revenue to pay for the Boer War, Wilfrid Laurier, the Canadian Prime Minister, had promptly claimed that 'a step had . . . been taken that would make it possible to obtain preference for Canadian goods.'[403] A way now existed, in other words, to give a belated reward for the raising of Canadian tariffs against foreign manufactures in 1897 and 1900, which had in effect made Britain the gift of a thirty-three and a third per cent preference. In return, Canadian wheat could now be allowed to enter Britain without being subject to the new corn tax; an exchange of fiscal gifts was at last possible.

On 16 May 1902, moreover, Chamberlain had taken speculation a stage further by announcing:

If by adherence to economic pedantry, to old shibboleths, we are to lose opportunities of closer union which are offered us by our colonies . . . if we do not take every chance in our power to keep British trade in British hands, I am certain that we shall deserve the disasters which will infallibly come upon us.[404]

In this context 'economic pedantry' could only mean free trade. Moreover, Chamberlain was bound to take the opportunity of the 1902 Colonial Conference to reiterate the case for imperial preference—and this time the corn tax would provide something to surrender as part of a bargain. On 30 June, furthermore, Gerald Balfour, President of the Board of Trade and Arthur Balfour's younger brother, had presented a comprehensive document entitled 'Memorandum on Preferential Trade Arrangements with the Colonies'. The document had cautiously reiterated the familiar arguments against an imperial *zollverein*, notably that imperial trade only accounted for a comparatively small proportion of the British total. How would Britain find compensation for the losses in foreign trade which would certainly accompany a policy of protection? But, more controversially, the memorandum suggested that Britain 'for the sake of the Imperial idea . . . might . . . concede reciprocity on existing duties or upon duties in the future imposed for revenue purposes.'[405]

Chamberlain's discussions at the Colonial Conference in July 1902 had revealed that serious difficulties remained in the way of achieving an imperial *zollverein*. Anxious to retain their protectionist defences, and unwilling to lower their duties on British goods, the best that the self-governing colonies seemed able to offer were the advantages resulting from still higher tariffs against the foreigner. The Canadian delegation in particular showed interest in concluding a limited reciprocal agreement, which could now include Britain's remission of the corn tax.

On Lord Salisbury's resignation from the premiership in July, however, Hicks Beach had left the Exchequer. His place was taken by C. T. Ritchie, who had earlier been associated with the 'fair trade' movement in the 1880s and 1890s, but who proceeded to fall under the influence of his officials upon taking office and to adopt an orthodox Treasury stance in defence of free trade. Nonetheless the Cabinet agreed in November 1902 to the Chamberlainite principle of remitting the corn tax in favour of the colonies, though, ominously, Ritchie argued that he could not commit the Treasury to such a policy so long before the next budget. Despite Ritchie's delaying tactics, Chamberlain left for his South African tour convinced that the Chancellor was now obliged to introduce the recommended fiscal preference in the following spring.

When Chamberlain arrived back from South Africa, inspired by much of what he had seen but also 'listless and irritable', he discovered that a fortnight before his return Ritchie had brought off a *coup* by telling Balfour that he could not be responsible for a budget which introduced a measure of imperial preference, and that he furthermore demanded the abandonment of the corn tax. He had threatened resignation unless he had his way. Rather than lose Ritchie a few days before the budget (though Gerald Balfour urged this course) Balfour surrendered, but only after two Cabinet meetings had discussed the matter. The budget of 23 April 1903 swept away the corn tax. Ritchie and free trade orthodoxy had apparently triumphed.

Chamberlain had every reason to feel betrayed. Ritchie had been in a minority of two when the Cabinet had agreed in November 1902 to introduce a preference on corn. Now he had employed the crudest methods of political bludgeoning to avoid implementing this decision. Admittedly the Cabinet had not been exact about details, but the spirit had been clear. Balfour, towards the end of his life, admitted that:

> Joe was ill-used by the Cabinet. We had discussed the principle of taxing food-stuffs before he left the country, and he certainly had a right to suppose that the bulk of the Cabinet were in favour of a shilling duty on corn, or some analogous small tax. That was my impression, and I was perfectly horrified at what happened.[406]

To have been out-manoeuvred by the second-rate Ritchie was a humiliation for Chamberlain. On the other hand, he had helped to bring it upon himself by absenting himself from Britain—in the crucial period before the presentation of the budget. Given Chamberlain's reputation for sharp political infighting, his decision to abandon the corn tax to a possible Ritchie counter-attack seems positively naïve. Perhaps he relied too much on Balfour's friendship and support to sustain the Cabinet decision of November 1902. If this is so, it was to prove merely the beginning of a process of disillusionment with Balfour—a disillusionment arising chiefly from the pitfalls and betrayals that marked the tariff reform controversy.

The miserable failure of Chamberlain's corn tax initiative merely emphasised his perilous and uncertain political status early in 1903. The 1902 Education Act had ravaged his Liberal Unionist political power-base and full-scale repairs appeared to be impossible. The phantom of Irish Home rule seemed temporarily exorcised, thus further undermining the historic justification of the Conservative and Liberal Unionist alliance. Lord Salisbury was gone, Balfour was proving to be a shifting and unreliable colleague, and apart from his son Austen, who held the junior post of Postmaster-General, Chamberlain had no real allies in the Cabinet. The Boer War had stirred up as many problems as it had solved. Chamberlain's more grandiose schemes for fostering imperial unity had been wrecked upon the rocks of colonial self-interest and indifference.

Nor had Chamberlain been able to shrug off these disappointments by introducing a set of social reforms that would permanently bind enough of the working classes to Unionism to guarantee its future. The Unionist Government's record in the field of social reform since 1895 had been virtually non-existent. Even old age pensions seemed as out of reach as ever. In 1898 the Rothschild Committee's report had uncovered a hornet's nest of difficulties to be overcome before old age pensions could be introduced. A year later a Parliamentary Committee, chaired by Henry Chaplin, had argued that the only feasible source of the money to finance an old age pension scheme would be revenue raised from some sort of tariff reform policy. Chaplin, the spokesman for the protectionist agricultural lobby within the Tory party, thus proposed a solution to the problem that was much to Chamberlain's taste. But though the Chaplin Committee recommended a minimum pension of 5s. per week for all needy and deserving persons over the age of sixty-five, there seemed no immediate prospect of implementing such a reform. Quite apart from Lord Salisbury's coolness towards the project, the Boer War had put a heavy burden on the Exchequer; the money, quite simply, was not there.

Chamberlain was thus caught in a snare of his own making: 'Chamberlain's War' was a major stumbling-block in the way of Chamberlainite social reform; indeed revenue for all Government spending was in short supply. Since the raising of the level of income tax was not acceptable to him, nor to the vast bulk of the Unionist party, there was no other way to turn except to tariff reform. But tariff reform itself was likely bitterly to divide the party. It was clear that until the party was converted to tariff reform, old age pensions would have to wait.

By the end of 1902, therefore, tariff reform had become the key with which Chamberlain might open many doors: he could promote an old age pension scheme; he could confirm his hold over the industrial West Midlands and hope to build up a new power base in the constituencies; if successful, he would be the obvious man to lead a Government committed to the revision of free trade. Tariff reform was to become the obsession of Chamberlain's last years of public life; a goal to be pursued with all his verve and power, and with relentless consistency. In the process, old age pensions virtually ceased to be a Chamberlainite preoccupation; the means became more important than the ends, and finally were transformed into the ends themselves. Winston Churchill has left a record of Chamberlain's wholehearted commitment to tariff reform as early as April 1902. Churchill was a member of a small Parliamentary society nicknamed 'The Hughligans', which dined every Thursday at the House of Commons and invited a distinguished guest on each occasion. Recalling that in April, Chamberlain dined as their guest, Churchill wrote in *My Early Life*:

> As [Chamberlain] rose to leave he paused at the door, and turning said with much deliberation, "You young gentlemen have entertained me royally, and in return I will give you a priceless secret. Tariffs! They are the politics of the future, and of the near future. Study them closely and make yourself masters of them, and you will not regret your hospitality to me."[407]

Quite apart from the personal political advantages to be gained from leading a successful movement for tariff reform, Chamberlain was convinced that an adjustment of the fiscal system that would at the same time consolidate the imperial connection was necessary for the future well-being of the nation. Believing (not altogether accurately) that the future belonged to great empires not to little states, Chamberlain was determined to guarantee the British Empire a profitable place in the twentieth-century sun.

The need for some sort of action was evident enough. Although the value of British exports had begun to rise again between 1899 and 1902, for nearly thirty years previously there had been alarming fluctuations. By the end of the nineteenth century, furthermore, the once acknowledged industrial supremacy of Britain had been seriously challenged. Not only had the United States and Germany taken tremendous strides in industrial expansion, they had also been quick to avail themselves of new techniques, which were often the products of intensive scientific research. Ominously, by 1900, Germany's steel production had outstripped Britain's.

On all sides, foreign salesmen were successfully contesting traditional markets with Britain, and even in the industrial Midlands German buttons and screws competed with their Birmingham equivalents. By 1900, moreover, Germany, France, the United States, Italy, Austria-Hungary and Russia had erected substantial tariff walls behind which their expanding industries could flourish. Despite this, Britain clung to her free trade principles; indeed the progress of mid-Victorian England had seemed to spring from the abandonment of protection in the 1840s. Britain had subsequently bought food for her increasing population and raw materials for her booming industries at the lowest price she could get. She had correspondingly sold her manufactured goods for the best possible price to whoever would buy them. Free trade seemed to be inextricably associated with commercial success, and even the periods of economic stagnation in the last third of the century had not shaken the Liberals or the great majority of Conservatives from their faith. Nor had bouts of unemployment destroyed the working man's belief that free trade ensured cheap food. Long memories reached back to the 'hungry forties', to the great famine, to protection and widespread suffering and hardship.

Chamberlain was not simply advocating a return to protection. He was prepared to see tariffs on imported food stuffs to benefit the colonies, and to introduce retaliatory tariffs against the foreigner—thus forcing them to open up their markets to the unrestricted entry of British exports. He was also prepared to use tariffs as a deterrent against the 'dumping' of foreign goods. Selective import controls were to be more characteristic of Chamberlain's tariff reform scheme than full-blooded protection. Indeed it was necessary to steer between the two extremes of free trade and

protection in order to bring Chamberlain's hopes for greater
imperial unity to consummation. Tariff reform meant what it
said; it was a pragmatic, though radical, proposal, not a narrow,
doctrinaire panacea for Britain's ills. A response to the Empire as
it was, and an indication of what it might become.

Despite Chamberlain's claim that the Empire 'If we chose . . .
might be self-sustaining', it was doubtful that an imperial free
trade area was within the realm of practical politics—at least in the
foreseeable future. Indeed, within the markets of the Empire,
British trade was actually losing ground. Between 1881 and 1900
British possessions had increased their overall purchases by 17
per cent, but during the same period the *volume* of British exports
to these territories had decreased by 1 per cent. By 1901, moreover, foreign imports into the self-governing colonies were worth
nearly £50 million, and were increasing. In India, Canada, the
Australian colonies, and British South Africa, on the other hand,
the proportion to total imports of imports *from* the United Kingdom had fallen substantially between 1881 and 1900. In 1901
Britain's trade with foreign countries amounted to some £592
million, while only £210 million was carried on with British
possessions.

Chamberlain was to argue, in his speech at Glasgow on 6
October 1903, that there was one favourable offsetting trend: that
over the previous thirty years the United Kingdom's trade with
British possessions had greatly increased. This assertion led him
into a lengthy private correspondence with Sir Robert Giffen—
who had been a permanent official at the Board of Trade during
Chamberlain's tenure of the Presidency of that department between 1880–5. Giffen flatly disputed Chamberlain's statistical
evidence, declaring himself 'quite bewildered', and pointing out
that 'your figures are quite different from those in the Monthly
Trade and Navigation Accounts'.[408] Giffen went on to argue
that Chamberlain had included *all* of South Africa, including the
booming economy of the Transvaal (an independent republic
until 1900), in his trade statistics. In a letter of 4 December 1903,
Chamberlain privately recanted, agreeing that if South Africa was
excluded from the trade figures, Britain's exports to British
possessions between 1888 and 1902 had increased by only £4
million, from £77 million to £81 million, but arguing that this
increase represented a bigger proportion than an equivalent £4

million increase to foreign countries between 1888 and 1902.[409] Giffen was not able to agree with this assertion, either, claiming that, in fact, between 1888 and 1902 the United Kingdom's exports to foreign countries had increased in value from £150 million to over £174 million—a bigger proportional increase than in British exports to the Empire, *excluding* South Africa.[410]

This correspondence between Chamberlain and Giffen was an early indication of the scholastic pitfalls that awaited the chief advocate of tariff reform, and Chamberlain tried to shrug off his difficulties by telling Giffen: 'The further I go in this matter the more I recognise the difficulty of arguing from figures alone, and the more I am inclined to depend upon certain great principles which affect human action and national policy.'[411] At the same time, Chamberlain revealed his hope that 'When we get any kind of commercial bond we should probably start with a Council to consider from time to time all the points connected with it. Beginning with commercial matters we might refer other questions to the same or a similar body, and ultimately rise by slow degrees to a full Imperial Council.'[412]

On 15 May 1903 Chamberlain began his bid for tariff reform, and for personal and national salvation in a controversial speech delivered from the citadel of Birmingham's town hall. Still smarting from his mauling at the hands of Ritchie, he called, with his customary eloquence, for a new definition of free trade. In his speech Chamberlain deplored the fate of the corn tax and, while denying that he was a protectionist, he argued that the British people faced an entirely new economic situation. The choice before them was whether 'it is better to cultivate the trade with your own people or to let that go in order that you may keep the trade of those who . . . are your competitors.'[413]

This speech created a tremendous stir. Leo Amery, who had served with Milner in South Africa, and was to become one of Chamberlain's most ardent supporters, called the speech 'a challenge to free thought as direct and provocative as the theses which Luther nailed to the church door at Wittenberg.'[414] The Liberals were also delighted, though for different reasons; their divided party would now be able to rally to the sacred cause of free trade. Asquith, indeed, thought the speech 'wonderful news . . . it is only a question of time when we shall sweep this country.'[415]

Chamberlain put his cards plainly upon the table later in May, when, taunted by Lloyd George in the Commons with abandoning old age pensions, he eventually said, 'Therefore we must come to this—if you are to give a preference to the colonies . . . you must put a tax on food. I make hon. gentlemen opposite a present of that.' The prospect of dearer food prices was seen by Unionist free traders as electoral suicide. Winston Churchill and Hugh and Robert Cecil were among those appalled by the implications of tariff reform; they began badgering Balfour to resist Chamberlain's proposals, and Churchill was eventually to cross the floor of the House in 1904.

Balfour was in deep and dangerous waters. Though he had no personal disinclination to review the nation's fiscal policy, he was also obliged to keep the Unionist alliance together. The ghost of Sir Robert Peel, and memories of the Conservative split over the 1846 repeal of the corn laws and the subsequent ending of protection, were sufficient to make Balfour seek for compromise. His true position on the tariff reform issue was a cultured agnosticism; he was also well aware that the new political initiative that Chamberlain was about to take might indeed appeal to a wide public and revitalise the flagging cause of Unionism. In short, he had to keep open the option of embracing tariff reform if it proved to be a runaway success, and at the same time had to try and avoid alienating the party's dedicated free traders. Balfour therefore proposed that the Cabinet should devote the summer to an investigation of the fiscal problem.

Such gentlemanly restraint did not, however, commend itself to Chamberlain who was actively contemplating an early election which would provide a verdict on the tariff question. Balfour saw his party breaking open at the seams during the summer of 1903. Within the Cabinet a head-on collision could hardly be avoided between Chamberlain and the irreconcilable free traders, Ritchie, Lord George Hamilton and Balfour of Burleigh. Moreover, there was Devonshire, whose ponderous, respectable and comforting presence Balfour wished to retain, but who might jib at the prospect of overhauling free trade.

In the country, Unionist free traders and tariff reformers were already staking out their positions. On 1 July fifty-four Unionist M.P.s inaugurated the Free Food League. Although this organisation was essentially weak and lacking in funds, it had fervour, and at least put pressure on Balfour. On 16 July he wrote to his cousin Lord Hugh Cecil, one of the leaders of the Free Food League, telling him that 'the serious mistake into which I think you have fallen is that of supposing that the Unionist Party were put into office for the purpose of preserving, in every particular, a version of Free Trade doctrine which . . . I, at all events, have never accepted.'[416]

In contrast to Balfour's bid for the middle ground, the Tariff Reform League was decidedly and pugnaciously evangelical. The League held its first meeting on 21 July, three weeks after the foundation of its rival, the Free Food League. Nothing could have been more striking than the contrasting organisation of the two Leagues. The Free Fooders were a committed but poorly organised group. The Tariff Reform League, however, soon marshalled within its ranks captains of industry, aristocratic Tory landlords, the bulk of the Unionist M.P.s, and survivors of the protectionist National Fair Trade League. The League was supported by the *Daily Express*, the *Daily Mail*, the *Standard*, and had sympathisers like Amery of *The Times* and Garvin of the *Daily Telegraph*; in 1905 Harmsworth bought the *Observer* for the cause, and the *Spectator* was left as the only leading Unionist free-trade journal. Not only did the League have the money to launch a lavish campaign to convert trade union leaders and workers, it also had the inspiration of Chamberlain, and after his resignation from the Cabinet in September, his full-time leadership.

Balfour could not remain inert while the free trade and tariff reform stalwarts fought for control of the party. In a memorandum entitled *Economic Notes on Insular Free Trade*[417] which he put before the Cabinet on 1 August 1903, Balfour tried to paper over the widening cracks in his ministry. Hoping to demonstrate his basic independence of both groups of campaigners, Balfour plumped for the comparatively uncontroversial policy of retaliation. Retaliation involved taking discriminatory fiscal measures to protect British trade from the coercive commercial activities of foreing countries—particularly the erection of high tariff barriers. This proposal did not involve the electoral peril of food taxes, and at the same time was a modification of free trade principles.

A policy of retaliation, however, was more likely to send the electorate to sleep than set them afire with enthusiasm. It was all too plainly a device, a fig leaf to hide Balfour's embarrassment.

Unfortunately the fig leaf was transparent, and Chamberlain predictably found the policy feeble and half-hearted.

The Government's fiscal inquiry during the summer of 1903 could not be prolonged indefinitely. The Cabinet met on 13 August, but failed to reach agreement; a final decision was postponed until the next meeting, due on 14 September. What Balfour would have preferred would have been for Chamberlain to modify his stance on tariff reform sufficiently to keep the bulk of the Cabinet, especially the Duke of Devonshire, happy. The extreme free trade ministers would probably leave the Government, or be forced to resign, and this would at least exorcise one quarrelsome faction. Indeed it is evident that Balfour was prepared to provoke a show-down with the free traders by putting before the Cabinet on 13 August two documents: one was the Prime Minister's own memorandum *Economic Notes on Insular Free Trade*, which contained some vaguely radical fiscal views; the other was a Treasury memorandum which examined the advantages of pref-erential tariffs and food taxes, though without clearly recommend-ing them.

The Cabinet meeting of 14 September was therefore preceded by some urgent stocktaking on the part of the free trade ministers. On 9 September Chamberlain took dramatic action. He wrote a letter of resignation to Balfour explaining that ever since his speech of 15 May, he had been endeavouring to raise 'a question of the greatest national and Imperial importance'. While ritually deplor-ing the subsequent show of faction in the Unionist party, Chamber-lain argued that, while remaining absolutely loyal to Balfour's Government, he could best promote his heart-felt cause from out-side the Cabinet.[418]

Balfour made haste to do a deal. An hour before the Cabinet meeting of 14 September he contrived to meet Chamberlain, and gathered that the Colonial Secretary would certainly go if all hope of preferential tariffs vanished. For his part, Balfour still felt that a food tax was not practical politics.[419] The two men then proceeded to rig up a formula by which Chamberlain would leave the Government to lead a grass roots tariff reform crusade, and that Austen Chamberlain should be promoted to the key post of Chancellor of the Exchequer. If all went well with the campaign, Balfour could then lead the loyalist bulk of the Unionist party along the pathway that Chamberlain had blazed. The plan held considerable advantages for both men: Balfour would keep control of the party; Chamberlain would be able to revitalise Unionism and to convince the country that tariff reform offered economic salvation.

The Cabinet meeting of 14 September became Balfour's 'day of the long knives'. First Chamberlain announced his intention of resigning. Since his colleagues had become accustomed to such demonstrations from the Colonial Secretary, this threat left them comparatively unmoved. Some took him to be serious, some did not. Balfour did nothing to dispel the confusion; he made no mention of Chamberlain's letter of resignation, thus keeping his colleagues in ignorance. He then rounded on Ritchie and Balfour of Burleigh and more or less sacked them from the Cabinet for the unrepentant free trade memoranda they had submitted. On 15 September, Lord George Hamilton also resigned. Three days later, Balfour announced the resignations not only of Ritchie and Hamilton, but also of Chamberlain. Balfour of Burleigh's resignation was made known later. The free trade ministers were naturally outraged that they had not been informed of Chamberlain's letter of resignation. Their position had been utterly undermined by Balfour's silence. At any rate, he had got rid of them, even though he still hoped to keep the Duke of Devonshire. But the Duke wavered, uncertain what to do. He resigned, then withdrew his resignation when he knew that Chamberlain had gone, only to resign finally at the beginning of October after Balfour had explained his cautiously reformist fiscal policy in a speech at Sheffield on 1 October. The Duke's final desertion irritated Balfour, who had gone to some lengths to retain him.

Balfour's Cabinet was now a poor thing, bereft of Chamberlain's energy and charisma and the Duke of Devonshire's solid respectability. The informal pact between Balfour and Chamberlain offered the only credible way forward for Unionism, but even that pathway was strewn with daunting obstacles. Free fooders, tariff reform 'whole hoggers', and Balfourites of 'unsettled convictions' could not be restrained from inflicting serious wounds upon each other and the party as they snapped and snarled over the tariff controversy. Balfour, moreover, stood in deadly peril if the tariff reform campaign did succeed in sweeping the country. Chamberlain could hardly be denied, at least in the long term, the leadership of a party which even by October 1903 was broadly sympathetic to tariff reform—the annual meeting of the National

Union of Conservative Associations had revealed majority support
for Chamberlain's campaign, and Chamberlain himself managed
to assert his dominance of the Liberal Unionist organisation in the
months after the Duke of Devonshire's resignation.

In fact Balfour managed to stay in power until December 1905,
enduring a good deal of humiliation and abuse in the process, and
prompting Campbell-Bannerman to remark as early as November
1903, 'The contemptible person is the 1st L. of Treasury [Balfour]
—never was anything more immoral, dishonest and unconsti-
tutional, than the rigging up of retaliation as a formal policy while
proclaiming adhesion to Joe's.'[420] Balfour's determination to
hang on to the premiership was partly due to his desire to super-
vise certain vital changes in the fields of defence (such as the
establishment of the Committee of Imperial Defence) and of
foreign policy (notably the *entente* with France and the renewal of
the 1902 Anglo-Japanese alliance). But there was one other over-
riding need—the need to thwart a Chamberlainite takeover of the
party. Hence Balfour's refusal to rush into an early General
Election which would almost certainly have confirmed Chamberlain as the effective master of Unionism. As it happened, Balfour's
labyrinthine defences were sufficiently resilient to hold off the
Chamberlainite flood tide, though in the process the Prime
Minister's ambiguous and semi-philosophical utterances provoked
John Morley to challenge anyone to summarise his fiscal policy
on 'a sheet of notepaper'.

In the aftermath of his resignation from the Cabinet, Chamberlain flung himself into a tremendous demagogic campaign to sell
tariff reform to the nation. Chamberlain was not only backed by
the bulk of the Unionist press, but also by distinguished academics
like Professor W. A. S. Hewins of the London School of Economics,
and flattered by Rudyard Kipling's *Things and the Man*:

> The peace of shocked Foundations flew
>   Before his ribald questionings.
> He broke the Oracles in two,
>   And bared the paltry wires and strings.
> He headed desert wanderings;
>   He led his soul, his cause, his clan
> A little from the ruck of Things.
>   *Once on a time there was a Man.*

Anxious to allay the fears of working men that food taxes meant dearer food, the tariff reformers eventually hit upon the slogan 'Tariff Reform Means Work for All'. An enormous flood of leaflets and pamphlets were produced, and doorstep canvassers argued the League's case from house to house. The overflowing funds of the campaign were reflected in the dispatch of Chamberlain's recorded voice into hundreds of small halls and meeting houses. Tariff reform songs enlivened the music halls, and the public was regaled with verses of undisputed vigour but doubtful quality:

> When wealth and mirth refill the earth,
> Let each man tell his neighbour,
> All this we owe to Chamberlain!
> Hurrah! Hurrah! Hurrah!

The Tariff Reform League's grass-roots, democratic style of campaigning owed much to the example of America, where Grover Cleveland had earlier made successful use of the gramophone to spread his message to the people. But the tariff reform campaign, despite its funds and efficiency, needed the prodigious powers of Radical Joe to launch itself with full effect at the Edwardian public.

On 6 October 1903 Chamberlain made the opening speech of his campaign at Glasgow. He then addressed packed meetings at Greenock, Newcastle, Liverpool and Leeds. Mrs. Chamberlain has left an admiring account of these first shots of the campaign:

6 October 1903 [After the speech at Glasgow.]

I think that many people must have felt something of the emotion which it gave me, and one knew that all who heard it must go away convinced of his absolute and unselfish earnestness.

11 October [After the speech at Greenock.]

The speech was very different but also full of the best elements of oratory, and as I listened to that, and compared it to the night before, I came to the conclusion that in the years that I have known him he has made a great advance in the force of speaking, and that certainly he rises to heights which he could not then reach, for I think one can fairly call him now an orator.

30 October [After Liverpool meetings.]

I really was lost in admiration of Joe's "infinite variety", for though there was but one text, he contrived to make each speech different from the last and all interesting.[421]

In these speeches Chamberlain met the issue of food taxes head-on, demanding that his audiences looked further ahead than the 'small loaf' as opposed to the 'large loaf'. Imperial preferences would prepare the way for Britain to take full advantage of all the resources and business opportunities that her world-wide Empire offered. Only by such far-sighted planning could Britain's great power status be guaranteed. Nor did Chamberlain dodge the protectionist bogey. Indeed he presented the necessity for the protection of British industry in terms strong enough to delight his supporters, vex Balfour, and horrify his enemies:

> Free imports . . . have destroyed sugar-refining for a time as one of the great staple industries of the country, which it ought always to have remained. They have destroyed agriculture. . . . Agriculture, as the greatest of all trades and industries of this country, has been practically destroyed. Sugar has gone; silk has gone; iron is threatened; wool is threatened; cotton will go! How long are you going to stand it? At the present moment these industries, and the working men who depend upon them, are like sheep in a field. One by one they allow themselves to be led out to slaughter, and there is no combination, no apparent prevision of what is in store for the rest of us. . . . What is the remedy? . . . Let us claim some protection like every other civilised nation.[422]

At Newcastle on 20 October Chamberlain went on to argue that the short supply of wheat and corn, not any tax that he had ever suggested, would cause the dearer loaf:

> There is only one remedy for short supply. It is to increase your sources of supply. You must call in the new world, the Colonies, to redress the balance of the old. Call in the Colonies, and they will answer to your call with very little stimulus and encouragement. They will give you a supply which will be never-failing and all-sufficient.[423]

On 27 October Chamberlain spoke at Liverpool in Tory Lancashire. The rain poured down as he arrived at the station and clattered off with an escort of mounted police through dense, cheering crowds. 'Radical Joey', slight and spruce, with his astrakhan-collared travelling coat, eyeglass and orchid had come to town to preach his new gospel. The Liverpool speech was particularly important since it was delivered at the request of the Conservative Working Men's Association, and Chamberlain, stepping forward and grasping the lapel of his frock-coat amid a roaring six minutes' welcome, used it as an opportunity to reassure the working-class electorate:

> What is the whole problem as it affects the working classes of this country? It is all contained in one word—employment. Cheap food, a higher standard of living, higher wages—all these things, important as they are, are contained in the word "employment". If this policy [tariff reform] will give you more employment, all the others will be added unto you. If you lose your employment, all the others put together will not compensate you for that loss. [424]

He was also, on other occasions, to ridicule the notion that working men rendered unemployed by foreign competition could quite easily find alternative means of livelihood:

> I believe that all this is part of the old fallacy about the transfer of employment. . . . It is your fault if you do not leave the industry which is falling and join the industry which is rising. Well, sir, it is an admirable theory; it satisfies everything but an empty stomach. Look how easy it is. Your once great trade in sugar refining is gone; all right, try jam. Your iron trade is going; never mind, you can make mousetraps. The cotton trade is threatened; well, what does that matter to you? Suppose you try doll's eyes. . . . But how long is this to go on? Why on earth are you to suppose that the same process which ruined the sugar refining will not in the course of time be applied to jam? And when jam is gone? Then you have to find something else. And believe me, that although the industries of this country are very various, you cannot go on for ever. You cannot go on watching with indifference the disappearance of your principal industries. [425]

Despite Chamberlain's capacity to appeal persuasively to different sections of the nation ('bribing each class of the community in turn' so Lord Robert Cecil thought) he faced a tremendously difficult task. For one thing, his recipe for curing Britain's economic ills and for binding the Empire more closely together was, as he openly admitted, only to be achieved some time in the future and at the cost of some immediate sacrifices. This spartan, futuristic programme could hardly be considered as an ideal appeal to the electorate. Moreover, the rigour of Chamberlain's demands upon the public's understanding, and the scorching intensity of his search for economic salvation, were not necessarily comfortable enough qualities for the arm-chair voters. Given his reputation for single-minded and ruthless politics, a future dominated by Chamberlain and his allies, the great captains of industry, had a steely, almost authoritarian, quality about it.

Another problem that Chamberlain faced was that his analysis of industrial and economic decline was clearly open to dispute. Despite his attempts, like the fat boy in *Pickwick Papers*, to make his audiences' flesh creep, it was by no means evident that something like an economic crisis gripped Britain, or, even if that were so, that it was caused by a flood of unfair foreign competition. Cotton did not 'go', though exports tended to decline as more of the world supplied their own cotton goods; woollen textiles, and boots and shoes, actually increased their exports during the Edwardian age; shipbuilding remained a strong industry, and a good deal of success attended engineering manufactures. Where there were faltering industries like iron and steel, coal, chemical engineering, or the manufacturing of tools and armaments, it was not self-evident that the cause was simply foreign competition— poor management, indifferent salesmanship, or inferior workmanship were all, or severally, equally likely to be responsible.

Also, by a cruel quirk of fate for Chamberlain, the opening of the tariff reform campaign coincided with a clearly defined upswing in world trade, from which British industry naturally benefitted. This had the effect of allaying the fears of at least some of those who had earlier clamoured for a policy of protection. It also meant that the Edwardian working man was likely to take less seriously the dire warnings of the tariff reformers, and to listen instead to the free trade orthodoxy of most of his trade union leaders. If the working class could not be won over for tariff reform, then Chamberlain's platform became decidedly rickety. Indeed, as the tariff reform campaign ground on, Chamberlain made a determined, and unsavoury attempt to whip up working class anxiety at foreign immigration, especially into the East End of London. Many of the immigrants were Jews fleeing from persecution in Russia and Poland. Despite Chamberlain's bizarre offer in 1903 of Uganda as a Jewish homeland, he was not above anti-semitic sentiment, telling H. Wickman Steed, 'There is, in fact, only one race that I despise—the Jews, sir. They are physical cowards.' Speaking at Limehouse in December 1904 he rubbed his audience's noses in the controversy over unrestricted alien (mainly Jewish) immigration, hoping to convince them of the emotive equation between foreign imports, foreign immigrants and British unemployment:

> You are suffering from the unrestricted imports of cheaper goods. You are suffering from the unrestricted immigration of the people who make these goods. (Loud and prolonged cheers.) . . . The evils of this immigration have increased during recent years. And behind those people who have already reached these shores, remember there are millions of the same kind who . . . might follow in their track, and might invade this country in a way and to an extent of which few people have at present any conception. . . . If sweated goods are to be allowed in(to) this country without restriction, why not the people who make them? Where is the difference? . . . It all comes to the same thing—less labour for the British working man.(Cheers).[426]

Despite such questionable appeals, however, the prospect of 'stomach taxes' was likely to drive large numbers of working men towards the Labour groups and the Liberal party. At the same time, Chamberlain's espousal of imperial consolidation had a disappointing impact upon imperialists outside of the Unionist alliance. The Lib-Imps did not jostle to follow him; Asquith, Grey, Haldane, even Rosebery, were, it seemed, Liberals first and imperialists second. After all, the assault on free trade had united the party and looked likely to help it to an overdue electoral triumph. The Lib-Imps had been as long without office as those in the centre and on the left of Liberalism; Asquith, indeed, went out of his way to dog Chamberlain's campaign, following him round the country and addressing free trade meetings in halls that were scarcely cold from the clamour and fire of tariff reform gatherings.

Chamberlain's apostolic fervour was, however, marvellous to behold, and on 3 November his son Neville wrote admiringly from Rome, ' "Nil Admirare" is an old shibboleth! At any rate we, although we have had some experience of you, can't help being amazed at your proceedings. Gout & headache & cold only seem

to bring out your speeches in greater number and with greater
vigour than ever.' His audiences, too, got their money's worth, and
Mrs. Chamberlain relayed to her mother an anecdote of a conversation between two Bristol men:

> *First Man:*   I'm a poor man and I can't afford to pay 10*s.* for
> a seat in the gallery.
> *Second Man:* It's worth paying a guinea just to see him say
> "Free Fooder".

In fact, Chamberlain's strenuous campaigning was soon to have
repercussions upon his health. His gout and his frequent headaches
were both symptoms of circulatory problems. In January 1904 he
had a bad attack of gout and neuralgia and medical examinations
revealed, in his own words, that he 'had overdone matters and had
got something a little wrong with my heart.' Though his doctors
pressed the need for a four months' holiday, he refused to accept
their advice, though agreeing to take two months off from 11
February. In June 1905 he was, in Mrs. Chamberlain's words
'stricken. . . . He was ordered to cancel the St. Helens meeting.
He replied: "If I don't do it I shall never speak again. I must and
will." He did.'[427] In August of the same year he left for Aix-les-
Bains to restore his health, but on arriving there 'he complained of
giddiness, but though we begged him to lie down he refused.[428]
   A more prudent spirit would have heeded these warning signs
more seriously than Chamberlain chose to. But, though approaching his seventieth year, the cause of tariff reform possessed him
like a demon. On 4 July 1904, Austen Chamberlain told his step-
mother, 'Father dined with me tonight . . . & though he would talk
of nothing but the political situation I think he rested. . . . I should
like to have got his mind on other subjects but that was evidently
impossible.'[429] In February 1906 amid the debris of the Unionist
electoral débâcle Gerald Balfour considered that Chamberlain 'has
become a monomaniac and is ready to sacrifice everything to his
policy of Tariff Reform.'[430]
   Chamberlain had good cause to fret and toil as his campaign
ploughed on into 1904. Balfour, despite their earlier understanding,
was plainly trying to wriggle away from the more Chamberlainite
implications of his Sheffield speech of October 1903. In March
1904 Chamberlain wrote to Austen from his restorative holiday:

Balfour has plainly pledged himself to go to the country on Retaliation & *nothing more*.

Well! I think he is wrong but I do not care. In the circumstances the best thing that can happen is that we should be beaten whenever the General Election does come for *our* position would be intolerable if we won & then found that we were as far off our Imperial policy as ever.[431]

Balfour, of course, had no intention of making an early appeal to the country. By-election results during 1904 were uniformly bad, in contrast to those of the previous year. Throughout 1904 the Prime Minister struggled to avoid making any meaningful commitment to the Chamberlainite cause, while former colleagues like Lord George Hamilton gloomily prophesied that when the election came 'the heaviest defeat on record awaits the Unionist Party.' In March 1904, Chamberlain wrote to Neville from Palermo analysing the recent crop of unfavourable by-election results and also predicting electoral disaster:

> The simple fact is that the . . . swing of the pendulum against us is not to be materially affected *either* way by the fiscal question or any other new issue. We have lost the impetus of the feeling against Home Rule & the constituencies have forgiven the pro-Boerism & Little Englanderism of our opponents. It is unsatisfactory, but it is no use blinking the facts: & Education, Temperance, Chinese Labour, & the general desire for a change & belief that the Government is worn out accounts for the débâcle. Fiscal Reformers should recognise this & should understand that our time has not yet come & that we should look forward to the future.[432]

How could the future be guaranteed for Chamberlain and the tariff reform movement? Recognising that Balfour would not go one inch beyond his Sheffield policy, and observing that to him 'naturally this is worse than nothing', Chamberlain plainly stated that:

> I am obliged therefore, without publicly separating myself from Balfour, to hope that he will fail; & I have not the least doubt that he *will* fail. I see no advantage in postponing the general election much longer, both because I think the longer it is delayed the worse will be the result & because every month

spent now in fighting against overwhelming chances is a month more to wait before we can come to close quarters on our question.[433]

Chamberlain thought that the predictable 'Radical interregnum' would allow the Unionist party to heal its differences and would open the eyes of the electorate to 'the serious dangers that a Radical administration would involve'. It was clear that Chamberlain envisaged that a reunited Unionist party would be committed to tariff reform, purged of the free fooders, and, very probably under his leadership not Balfour's:

> All that Chamberlainites have to hope & struggle for is that when the Radical reaction is over this may be a clear issue between ourselves & the Free Traders. But this is the delicate point & the difficulty of the situation. Are we to work for the success of the Unionist Party & then find the Balfourites in command of the ship feebly steering her on the course of a partial & half-hearted retaliation? And how are we to present this without quarrelling politically with Balfour? It needs careful management.
>
> Our first step is clear. The Free Traders are *common* enemies. We must clear them out of the party & let them disappear or go to the Radicals. They vote against the Government. They oppose us at elections—they are our greatest weakness & danger.[434]

The next step to guarantee the future was to persuade the Liberal Unionist and Conservative associations to commit themselves to the principle of reciprocal imperial preference. Failing this, 'we must have a local association of our own, & we must arrange that every Unionist candidate shall be asked by some influential local elector whether he will accept or favourably consider my proposals.'[435] Here was the real danger for Balfour and the Cecil oligarchy—the establishment of vigorous local Tariff Reform League branches striving to draw the life-blood of constituency support away from non-Chamberlainite Liberal-Unionist and Conservative local associations. By the end of 1904, not only was the Liberal Unionist association under Chamberlain's control, but Tariff Reform League branches in the constituencies were indeed challenging the Conservatives' National

Union. Chamberlain even suggested, though without success, that a representative of the Tariff Reform League should be placed in Central Office.

Throughout 1904, therefore, and during 1905 as well, Balfour squirmed to avoid the suffocating embrace of Chamberlain's national movement. In the late summer of 1904 he entered into a scholastic disputation with his Chancellor, Austen Chamberlain, over the latter's proposal to bridge the awkward gap between Chamberlainites and Balfourites by planning in terms of winning the election after next, and by the Prime Minister announcing that, if returned to power, he would summon a conference of colonial and Indian delegates to discuss the reform of imperial trade. To reinforce his case Austen added, almost poignantly:

> You encouraged my father to go out as "a pioneer"; you gave your blessing to his efforts for closer union with the colonies; you assured us who remained that we too thus served the interests of Imperial union & we were thus induced to leave him for the time almost single-handed in his herculean task.[436]

Balfour demurred, stuck firmly to his Sheffield programme, and tried to minimise the differences that all too obviously existed between himself and Chamberlain. On 3 October the Prime Minister made a public pronouncement at Edinburgh where he fundamentally reiterated the Sheffield programme and threw in the innovation of his own double election plan. The double election plan was an exercise in optimism as well as delay; it proposed that the Unionists should go to the polls without any precise fiscal policy, but pledged to summon a full and free Colonial Conference if they were returned to power.

Though fundamentally disappointed by the Edinburgh speech, the Chamberlains put up a bold front, claiming that the pronouncement was simply Balfour's first step towards accepting a fully-fledged programme of tariff reform.

By May 1905, however, a new crisis was reached between Chamberlain and Balfour. At one stage, the latter seemed willing to drop the 'double election' plan, to treat the impending Colonial Conference of 1906 as the opportunity to discuss tariff reform, and to follow the Conference by a General Election. On the basis of this apparent agreement, Chamberlain offered to return to the

Government as a minister without portfolio and to support tariff reform from within the administration.

This agreement was soon to crumble in Chamberlain's hands. Faced with a Unionist free trade revolt in the Commons which threatened to bring down the Government, Balfour backtracked, and added insult to injury by telling the Chamberlains that he now no longer intended to remain in office until the autumn of 1906— an essential feature of the recent agreement.

Both Austen and Joseph Chamberlain proceeded to badger Balfour until finally he made a tortuous concession, relayed via Alfred Lyttelton, who had succeeded Chamberlain at the Colonial Office in 1903:

> If by "Colonial Preference" is meant (as I suppose it is) closer commercial union with the Colonies (as per "half sheet of note-paper"), and if by "first item in my programme" be meant (as I suppose it is) that I regard it as the most important part (though the most difficult) of fiscal reform, and fiscal reform itself as the most important part of the Unionist policy, why should I not give the assurances asked for?—and why should any colleagues resign? . . . "First item" must not of course be understood as meaning necessarily *first carried out*, because "preference" requires a conference, while retaliation does not. But on this I suppose all agree.[437]

This was a dry bone tossed to the Chamberlains, not a juicy morsel. Though Chamberlain made the best of it, he ignored Balfour's plea for unity at the party conference on 15 November 1905, and a week later in Bristol called for an aggressive campaign for tariff reform.

Almost directly afterwards, Balfour's Government resigned on 4 December. Campbell-Bannerman took office and immediately asked for a dissolution. The election campaign now began, absorbing the tariff reform campaign in the process.

Polling began on 12 January 1906. The early results indicated an anti-Unionist landslide. Among the first results announced was Balfour's defeat in East Manchester by some 2,000 votes. An avalanche of Unionist losses followed, with Cabinet ministers falling like ninepins in the rout. Chamberlain, whose Birmingham citadel held firm (returning seven tariff reformers, several with increased majorities), had predicted a Liberal majority of not more than eighty. But there was a national swing of around nine per cent towards the Liberals; Tory Lancashire was almost wiped out, and in London savage losses were sustained.

The Unionist split over imperial preference had merely accentuated electoral disenchantment with a party that had been in power since 1895 and had recently done little in the way of social reform, apart from the Unemployed Workmen Act. Nor had the 1905 Aliens Immigration Act, which Chamberlain had enthusiastically advocated, assuaged working-class discontent on any significant scale. Thus, though the Unionist vote rose from 1,676,020 in 1900 to 2,463,606 in 1906, the combined Liberal and Labour vote soared from 1,520,285 in 1900 to a total of 3,111,929 in 1906. Among all classes the vote had swung against the Unionists and annihilated them. In the Commons the Liberals had an overall majority of eighty-four and with the Irish Nationalist and Labour vote, a majority of 356. The Unionists were reduced to a scant 157 seats.

The election results fulfilled Robert Cecil's fears that Balfour would be defeated and that Chamberlain would be victorious. Cecil saw this as the 'greatest electoral disaster' in view of his low opinion of the Chamberlains: 'It is not by any means only the Fiscal Question upon which I differ from them. It is their whole way of looking at politics. It appears to me to be utterly sordid and materialistic, not yet corrupt but on the high road to corruption.'[438]

Chamberlain now mounted a tremendous challenge to the unseated Balfour. Of the 157 Unionist M.P.s, at least seventy-nine and possibly 102 were Chamberlainites. While Balfour searched for a safe seat, who else could lead them but Chamberlain? It was, moreover, clear that Chamberlain would demand some concession to his tariff reform views in return for continuing to sustain Balfour. The old guard of the Conservative leadership was now within a hair's breadth of that democratisation of the party that Chamberlain's methods had long since threatened.

Chamberlain pressed home his tactical advantage by calling for a meeting of the party on 15 February. Such a meeting could easily become a confrontation between himself and Balfour, and the party might well throw over their defeated leader for Chamberlain. A meeting early in February between Balfour and Joseph and Austen Chamberlain, as recounted by Betty Balfour (the wife of

Gerald Balfour), revealed the hardline that Chamberlain now felt able to pursue:

> Joe sticks to an immediate calling of a party meeting to decide at once between the two policies and says if A. J. [Balfour] refuses this he will call a meeting of his own followers. He says whatever the result he will not lead the Conservative Party— but if a majority are with Arthur, he will split off with his own section! G. [Gerald Balfour] still thinks the great majority of the party will refuse to leave Arthur for Joe. He says of Joe—it is the action of a madman—he has become a monomaniac and is ready to sacrifice everything to his policy of Tariff Reform; and the machinery by which he could have carried it—namely the Conservative Party—he is actually going to shatter. A. J. told him [Gerald] that he, Joe, Austen and Mrs. Joe sat on discussing the matter at the dinner table and that Joe and even Austen were "nasty" and that he, A. J., kept his temper "like an angel" & that Mrs. Joe at the end was almost in tears! . . . I think if Joe is able to be so unreasonable the time has come when it will be better for him to break with Arthur—even if temporarily it is disastrous to the party.[439]

Balfour had little choice but to do a deal with Chamberlain. He hastened to surrender something more to Chamberlain over tariff reform, realising that such a concession could at least keep the party machinery in his own hands and buy off a Chamberlainite take-over. Accordingly, on 14 February a truce was arranged between the two men. In return for a promise of support, Balfour produced yet another verbal concession. In these 'Valentine letters' Balfour wrote:

> I hold that Fiscal Reform is, and must remain, the first constructive work of the Unionist Party. That the objects of such reforms are to secure more equal terms of competition for British trade, and closer commercial union with the Colonies.[440]

Chamberlain graciously accepted Balfour's concession, even though, with the free trade Liberals unassailably entrenched in power, tariff reform had been deferred to an uncertain future. While still pressing home his newly-won advantages, Chamberlain attained his seventieth birthday on 8 July. All Birmingham turned out to acclaim their most famous citizen: for several days there were official luncheons, cavalcades, tours of the city, public addresses, thousands of congratulatory telegrams, bands playing patriotic tunes, and, everywhere, tens of thousands of people lining the streets and packing the parks to see Joey Chamberlain.

On 10 July Chamberlain made an impassioned and characteristically comprehensive speech, defending the apparent changes of direction that had marked his public life as occasioned by consistency of principle, upholding his Radical aspirations, advocating tariff reform, and appealing, once more, for the unity of the Empire.

The next day Chamberlain, who had eaten and drunk with his customary freedom during his birthday celebrations, returned to London. On 13 July he attended a meeting of the Tariff Commission in the morning, where he confessed to W. A. S. Hewins, 'I am a wreck'. After lunch he was tired, and, unusually for him, flushed.

That evening he and his wife were due to dine at Lady Cunard's house in Grosvenor Square. Though Mrs. Chamberlain was ready when the carriage arrived, he did not appear. Going to the bathroom, which he used as a dressing room, she discovered that the door was locked. She called out, and heard the faint reply, 'I can't get out'. While waiting for a footman to arrive to break the door down, Chamberlain managed to turn the handle from the inside. Mrs. Chamberlain found him lying exhausted on the floor. A stroke had paralysed his right side and he was almost helpless.

TWELVE

PROMETHEUS IN CHAINS
1906–14

> . . . his ardent spirit should have gone to heaven in a chariot of fire and not in a bath chair.
>
> John Morley on Chamberlain, 1909.

CHAMBERLAIN'S PARALYTIC stroke ended his active public life at one blow. On 13 July 1906, he was still a political colossus, towering above his colleagues in the Unionist party, armed with the sharp weapons of his intellect and oratory, and bearing aloft the dented but still bright shield of the tariff reform movement. The next day Chamberlain the King-maker was an old, broken man confined to his bed, unable to walk and with his faculties of speech and sight tragically impaired.

For a month Chamberlain lay in a darkened room at Prince's Gardens. On 14 August he was at last able to walk a few steps. Three days later he managed to struggle downstairs, and sub-sequently began to make painful progress towards recovering a fraction of his old physical powers. In the middle of September he returned to Birmingham and at 'Highbury' began to take an interest in his surroundings once more, especially in the shrubbery garden and its growth. Mrs. Chamberlain recorded that on 19 September he 'came down about 1 o'clock and walked to the end of the terrace and back—then as soon as he had had his lunch went into his new chair, which proved very handy . . . he stayed out till nearly 5 o'clock. . . . By 9.40 after his cigar with Austen and Neville he was quite ready for bed'.[441]

Believing, on medical advice, that he could master his infirmities, Chamberlain pitted his formidable will against apparently hopeless odds. By the end of the year he had in fact made some progress. His mind had been unaffected by the stroke, and generally he began to feel stronger. His sight improved a little, but reading was a painful process and his huge appetite for the printed word had to be satisfied by others reading to him. His speech, which had at first been thick and slurred, also recovered enough for him to talk in terse, clipped staccato sentences—a far cry indeed from the precise diction and polished phrases of his heyday. His physical movements were also greatly restricted. He could walk with a stick and the support of a friendly arm, but his right foot dragged pitifully behind him. Nor did he have any movement in his right arm. For the most part, the indefatigable political campaigner and man of action was obliged to travel short distances in a wheel chair.

His characteristic fight back against the odds represented Chamberlain's last real chance of any meaningful recovery. It failed to do more than ameliorate his condition. Holidays at Cannes on the French Riviera and an attempted cure at Aix-les-Bains were unlikely to restore his health. His own hopes for a substantial recovery waxed and waned with the years. In May 1907 the signs were relatively hopeful and he told Henry Chaplin in a dictated letter from France that 'Complete recovery will however be slow and I am still very lame and have not yet recovered the use of my right hand although in both respects I am much better than when I left England. I shall keep quiet at Highbury for this summer, and then I hope that I may again be in my place at the beginning of next year.[442] By 1910, however, he seemed reconciled to the fact that he could expect death rather than recovery. Mrs. Asquith left an account of visiting Chamberlain on 10 February 1910:

I was welcomed on my arrival by the lovely Mrs. Chamberlain and found her husband sitting erect in his arm-chair near the tea-table; his hair was black and brushed, and he had an orchid in his tightly-buttoned frock coat. . . .

My host's speech was indistinct but his mind was alert. . . . Wanting to show him some of the compassion I felt for him, I told him before leaving that I also had had a nervous breakdown, and added:

"You know, Mr. Chamberlain, I was *so* ill I thought that I was done", to which he answered:

"Better to *think* it Mrs. Asquith, than to *know* it."[443]

Chamberlain's family attended to his needs with a fierce protective care. His wife was constantly supportive, his sons kept in close contact with him, and his daughters also attended him faithfully,

Ida acting as his amanuensis and shorthand writer. Medical advice was sought from various specialists, and in April 1909 Mrs. Chamberlain was troubled that one consultant had suggested that if his opinion had been sought earlier Chamberlain would have stood a better chance of recovery. Austen, who had developed a close and loving relationship with his step-mother, wrote re-assuringly:

> Meanwhile you must not dwell on lost opportunities. Honestly I do not feel any great confidence that things would have been different even if you had seen [the specialist] earlier. . . . Father has had all the loving care that you could give & all the skill that you could secure. The skill has meant much but you have meant more. You kept him well in spite of his work for so long, & you have done everything to make life yield all it can to him since his illness[444]

The details of Chamberlain's physical collapse were kept from the public for as long as possible. After the stroke of 13 July 1906 the press was simply informed that he was ill. Suspicions were aroused, however, when he was absent from Austen's wedding to Ivy Dundas eight days later. The family flung a cloak of secrecy round the true nature of the illness, which was described as gout; friends ridiculed the idea of a paralytic stroke. When he returned to Birmingham in September it was announced that he had had to be conveyed from the train to his carriage in a wheel-chair and that the fingers of his right hand were so cramped that he could not write with comfort.

After going to his home in Birmingham he was kept shrouded from the outside world for six weeks. In March 1907 he travelled to London in secrecy, a compartment being reserved for him under an assumed name. When he then proceeded to cross the Channel en route for the Riviera, a fellow passenger who saw him said that he was so changed as to be almost unrecognisable. In June he returned to Britain and was seen several times on railway stations as he travelled between London and Birmingham. Observers noticed how slowly he walked, even with support, and how the spectacles he now wore instead of the famous eye-glass quite altered his appearance.

On 16 February 1910 Chamberlain made his first visit to the

House of Commons since his stroke. He came to be sworn-in to the new House following the recent General Election. The Commons was almost empty when an old, broken man came slowly from behind the Speaker's chair, leaning on a stick in his left hand and putting his right foot stiffly down on the heel; Austen Chamberlain supported him on the right side and the Liberal Unionist Whip was ready to aid him at his other elbow. His right arm was held closely to his breast; his eyes were dull, and spectacles gave a familiar face a strange almost disguised appearance. Onlookers felt a shock of sorrow when in the stricken, helpless man they recognised Radical Joe who had inspired and dominated Parliament. Chamberlain was assisted to a convenient place on the Treasury Bench, a copy of the oath was held before him; he recited its terms as they were read out, phrase by phrase, by his son, his voice being quite audible but his articulation indistinct. Austen signed the roll on his behalf, the invalid confirming the signature by formally touching the pen. 'Mr. Chamberlain West Birmingham Sir', announced the Clerk of the House with evident emotion in his voice as he presented the newly sworn-in member to the Speaker.

Mr. Lowther, leaning from his chair, grasped the left hand which was offered while he whispered, 'How do you do? Glad to see you again'. Having taken the oath, Mr. Chamberlain could be 'paired' in the divisions with an absentee on the other side, his 'pair' was his only part in the proceedings of the short Parliament elected in January 1910.

Long before this poignant reappearance in the House of Commons, Chamberlain's friends and enemies had realised the extent of his disability. Balfour's private secretary Sandars had taken a photograph of Chamberlain to a doctor for his opinion and had learnt that he 'must have had a severe hemiplegia (paralysis of one side of the body) and that, having regard to the length of time which has elapsed since the stroke, recovery must be *very, very* doubtful.'[445] Balfour could thus rest secure in the leadership of the party, for the time being at least.

Chamberlain's fellow-apostle of tariff reform, W. A. S. Hewins, visited him in February 1908 and claimed that 'He looks better than before his illness. He is fatter in the face and body, and his left hand with which he gave me a good grip, has grown quite plump. He looks as well groomed and young as ever'. Hewins also noticed Chamberlain's deterioration of speech:

His voice has lost all its old ring and is not exactly thick but dull. He speaks very slowly and articulates with evident difficulty. It is as though, the old ringing human voice had quite gone and he had been fitted with some clumsy mechanical contrivance as a substitute. But I had no difficulty in understanding him. He laughed several times and shrugged his shoulders in the old manner.[446]

In July 1909, Edward VII visited Chamberlain at Prince's Gardens and afterwards 'told J[ohn Morley] that it was painful because of C[hamberlain's] inability to *speak* plain. J. M. says that his ardent spirit should have gone to heaven in a chariot of fire not in a bath-chair.'

For all his courage, for all his patience and resilience, Chamberlain's fate was a pitiful one. It was almost as if the gods had decreed an exquisite torture for one who had offended them: Chamberlain's robust activity had been replaced by physical incapacity; the prodigious writer of letters could not even hold a pen in his right hand; the persuasive and eloquent speech-maker could only jerk out slurred words and phrases; the man who constantly made plans and proposed solutions could not follow any of them through; the political artificer could no longer dominate the Birmingham machine or play even a trivial part in the life of Parliament.

Chamberlain was virtually a spent force. The vigorous dictated correspondence he maintained with his contemporaries, the pressure he exerted to achieve his ends, could not carry the same authority and power as previously. He could no longer work tirelessly to cajole, explain and browbeat; any sanctions or threats he might once have employed now had an empty, hollow ring. He could not sit on committees, or even easily read their reports.

Nonetheless, Chamberlain had Austen as his standard-bearer. Austen received a steady stream of letters written by Mrs. Chamberlain, and beginning, 'Your father says to tell you. . . .', or 'Your father thinks that. . . .'. Though he took Chamberlain's place on the Liberal Unionist Council and in the Tariff Reform League, Austen, no matter how hard he struggled, could not command the respect and devotion, nor the hatred, that his father had inspired. The wilder spirits of the tariff reform movement were soon chafing at Austen's leadership and calling for a show-down with the free fooders within the party. Austen was evidently not an inspiration, and F. E. Smith was very near the mark when he said 'Austen always played the game and always lost it'.

Despite Austen's deficiencies the tariff reform movement flourished within Unionism in the years after 1906. In part this was due to the early spade work of Chamberlain's great campaign of 1903–6, and in part it reflected the ability of his most enthusiastic supporters, men like Leopold Amery, Leo Maxse, Hewins, and a Scots-Canadian iron-master named Andrew Bonar Law. The Tariff Reform League itself was still a mighty apparatus: its funds grew steadily, its propaganda continued unabated, and converts entered its ranks.

Tariff reform's success within the ranks of Unionism was chiefly the result of the party having no other credible electoral alternative (save backwoods obscurantism) to a variety of challenges between 1906 and 1914. The growth of socialism among the working class, the confiscatory taxation proposed by the 'Peoples' Budget' of 1909, the faltering of the economy after 1908, the need to provide funds to finance social reform and to pay for the naval armaments necessary to meet Germany's battleship-building programme—tariff reform, it was argued, could provide a solution to such problems or be an obstacle to such trends.

Even Balfour came to assume a shallow enthusiasm for tariff reform, calling, in November 1907, for a Chamberlainite programme of social reform, including old age pensions, going far in his support for imperial preference, and telling the tariff reformers that time was on their side. On 22 September 1909, faced with the allegedly 'socialist' features of Lloyd George's budget, Balfour at last decided to go the whole hog for tariff reform. Speaking at Bingley Hall in Birmingham (a singularly appropriate venue for a recantation) he stated that the nation had a simple choice before it: to be dragged down in the 'bottomless confusion of socialist legislation', or to advance with the 'hopeful movement of tariff reform'. After the speech Balfour stayed at 'Highbury', hoping that he had won Chamberlain's approval. After a day or two, Chamberlain eventually said, 'On thinking it over, I have come to the conclusion that Balfour played up very well'.

Balfour's hold upon the party was to end in 1911. His tactics during the Parliament Bill controversy had enraged many aristocratic Tories, and even free fooders; the tariff reformers were sceptical as to his apparent conversion to their cause. At first the leadership struggle seemed to be between Austen Chamberlain and the Tory traditionalist Walter Long. Deadlock resulted in them both standing down for Bonar Law. Though a protectionist and an admirer of Chamberlain, Law did not achieve the premiership until 1922, and tariff reform could hardly be introduced in the interim.

Indeed, in 1913 the movement suffered a prodigious set-back when Law was obliged by constituency and party pressure to abandon the principle of food taxes which was the essential prerequisite to the introduction of tariff reform. This was a bitter blow to Chamberlain, but he made it clear that he would never surrender his commitment to his last great cause—a cause that had to wait until 1932 for the tardy introduction of imperial preference at the Ottawa Conference. But even though Neville Chamberlain, as Chancellor of the Exchequer, supervised Britain's role in these bilateral trading agreements between different parts of the Empire, the Ottawa Conference did not herald the dawn of a new age of imperial unity: the Dominions still effectively protected their industries and Britain still steered clear of food taxes. Hardheaded bargaining had characterised the negotiations, not dewy-eyed imperial sentiment. In the midst of a global commercial crisis, Britain and the Dominions had thought of their own interests first and had subsequently added the gloss of Empire harmony.

By 1914 Joseph Chamberlain's condition was visibly deteriorating. Neville Chamberlain has left an unadorned account of his father's last months:

"I thought the work might kill me, but I never expected this", he said to me pathetically one evening and many times he must have wished to be dead. He who had been so self reliant was now dependent upon a woman for every common act of life. Yet he submitted with amazing patience and allowed himself to be dragged out to walk his daily round, panting and sweating with the exertion, to be thrust into his coat and piled up with rugs on the hottest day, to have his gloves pulled on and off, to have his cigars cut down and to be sent to bed early, in short to endure humiliations and discomforts without end every day of his life. His only real pleasure was in watching his grandchildren. He could not even talk to them. He could only make uncouth noises which often frightened them, and it was touching watching his efforts to attract them.[447]

In January, Chamberlain announced his decision not to seek re-election for Birmingham West, and Austen was adopted as his successor. The announcement was almost like a death-knell, and the press responded with a number of articles and assessments that were redolent of the obituary columns. Jesse Collings also made public his decision to stand down at the next election.

On 30 June, Chamberlain suffered a slight heart attack at his London home and was obliged to stay in bed. On the night of 1 July, Mrs. Chamberlain heard noises and went into his bedroom to see how he was. Standing over him, she realised that he was making a speech in his sleep; he was replying to Asquith as he had done a decade before during the tariff reform campaign.

The next day, 2 July, he appeared to be a little better. Mrs. Chamberlain read to him from *The Times*, which carried an article on the murder of the Archduke Franz Ferdinand at Sarajevo, but he did not let her get far in the account before stopping her.

That afternoon he had a second, more serious heart attack, and the family were summoned to his bedside. In the evening his breathing grew fainter. He never regained consciousness, and died tranquilly in his wife's arms.

For a man who had aroused so much antagonism and violent controversy in his lifetime it was wholly fitting that he should die peacefully in the bosom of his family. He and his wife had celebrated their silver wedding the year before his death, and on the first anniversary of her marriage during her widowhood Mrs. Chamberlain provided a passionate epitaph for her dead husband, telling her eldest step-son, 'Oh Austen what a Father you had! And what a husband I had! We may well be thankful for such a privilege.'[448]

Messages of condolence and sorrow poured in from all over the world; the telegram from King George V said simply, 'I deeply regret the loss of one for whom I had the greatest admiration and respect'. In the House of Commons, Balfour supplemented Bonar Law's tribute by saying that Chamberlain had been 'a great statesman, a great friend, a great orator, a great man'; Asquith, the Prime Minister, rose to greater heights when he claimed that 'in that striking personality, vivid, masterful, resolute, tenacious, there were no blurred or nebulous outlines, there were no relaxed fibres, there were no moods of doubt and hesitation, there were no pauses of lethargy or fear.'

The Dean of Westminster offered burial at the Abbey, but the offer was refused. A Unitarian funeral in Chamberlain's political heartland was far more appropriate. In the early hours of Sunday morning, 5 July, his body was taken to Paddington Station and then conveyed to Birmingham. On 6 July there was a service of stark simplicity at the Church of the Messiah, and his coffin was then carried through the crowded streets of Birmingham to be buried at the Key Hill Cemetery. Only the immediate family stood at the graveside as Joseph Chamberlain was laid to rest not far from his father and beside his first and second wives.

NOTES

CHAPTER I

1. Louis Creswicke, *The Life of Joseph Chamberlain*, vol. 1, pp. 15–16.
2. A. Mackintosh, *Joseph Chamberlain: an Honest Biography*, p. 2.
3. N. Murrell Marris, *Joseph Chamberlain: the Man and the Statesman*, p. 8.
4. J. L. Garvin, *The Life of Joseph Chamberlain*, vol. 1, pp. 16–18.
5. Walter Wilson, *History and Antiquities of Dissenting Churches in London*. Quoted in Garvin, vol. 1, p. 44.
6. Letter from Hon. W. Porter, quoted in Garvin, vol. 1, p. 44.
7. Murrell Marris, p. 11.
8. *Ibid.*, p. 12.
9. *Ibid.*, p. 13.
10. *Ibid.*, pp. 13–14.
11. Garvin, vol. 1, p. 30.
12. Creswicke, vol. 1, p. 19.
13. Murrell Marris, p. 17.
14. *Ibid.*, p. 18.
15. Creswicke, vol. 1, pp. 21–2.
16. John Morley, *Recollections*, vol. 1, pp. 148–9.
17. Garvin, vol. 1, p. 39.
18. Fanny Martineau, quoted in Garvin, vol. 1, p. 32.

CHAPTER 2

19. Asa Briggs, *History of Birmingham*, vol. 2.
20. G. C. Allen, 'The Industrial Development of Birmingham', *Journal of the History of Ideas*, 9, 1948.
21. Quoted in Harry Browne, *Joseph Chamberlain, Radical and Imperialist*, p. 4.
22. *Ibid.*
23. Garvin, vol. 1, p. 56.
24. Birmingham University Library, Chamberlain papers, JC 1/18/2. Joseph Chamberlain's business notebook, 1866–74.
25. *Ibid.*
26. Marris, p. 41.
27. Creswicke, vol. 1, p. 29.
28. Marris, p. 43.
29. Garvin, vol. 1, p. 66.
30. Marris, p. 28.
31. *Ibid.*, p. 30.
32. Chamberlain papers, JC 1/1/2, Joseph Chamberlain, to mother, 19 June 1860.
33. *Ibid.*, JC 1/14/1.
34. T. Anderton, in *Midland Counties Herald*, quoted in Marris, p. 53.

35. Chamberlain papers, JC 1/14/2.
36. Quoted in Marris, p. 49.
37. *Ibid.*, pp. 51–2.
38. Quoted in Garvin, vol. 1, pp. 59–60.
39. *Ibid.*, pp. 59–61.
40. Chamberlain papers, JC 1/1/10, Joseph Chamberlain to mother, 11 February 1861.
41. Chamberlain papers, JC 1/1/1, Joseph Chamberlain to mother, 27 August 1857.
42. *Ibid.*, JC 1/1/3, J.C. to mother, 2 August 1860.
43. Ellen Preston to Fanny Martineau, 7 July 1857, quoted in Garvin, vol. 1, p. 71.
44. Chamberlain papers, JC 1/1/10, J.C. to mother, 11 February 1861.
45. Quoted in Garvin, vol. 1., p. 79.

CHAPTER 3
46. Marris, p. 60.
47. R. Shannon, *The Crisis of Imperialism*, pp. 14–15.
48. D. G. Wright, *Democracy and Reform*, 1815–85, p. 69.
49. J. Thorold Rogers (ed.), *Speeches on Questions of Public Policy by John Bright, M.P.*, vol. 2, p. 175.
50. Garvin, vol. 1, pp. 87–8.
51. Quoted in Marris, p. 65.
52. *Ibid.*, pp. 67–8.
53. *Ibid.*, pp. 70–1.
54. *Ibid.*, p. 74.
55. Garvin, vol. 1, pp. 92–3.
56. Marris, pp. 75–6.
57. *Ibid.*, pp. 77–8.
58. Quoted in Peter Fraser, *Joseph Chamberlain*, p. 7.
59. Chamberlain papers, Joseph Chamberlain to George Dixon, 3 March 1870.
60. C. E. Mathews, speaking at the West Birmingham Liberal Unionist Club, 2 May 1891, quoted in Garvin, vol. 1, p. 113.
61. Garvin, vol. 1, p. 113.
62. Chamberlain papers, Joseph Chamberlain to George Dixon, 16 July 1870.
63. Marris, pp. 82–3.
64. *Ibid.*, p. 83.
65. *Birmingham Daily Post*, 4 July 1914.
66. Chamberlain papers, JC1/7/2, Joseph Chamberlain to Carrie Kenrick, 19 July 1868.
67. John Morley, *Recollections*, vol. 1, p. 155.
68. *Ibid.*, letter to Austen Chamberlain enclosed with JC/1/7/2 above.
69. Sir Charles Petrie (ed.), *The Life and Letters of the Right Hon. Sir Austen Chamberlain*, vol. 1.
70. Morley, *Recollections*, vol. 1, pp. 151–3.
71. *National Review*, February 1933, p. 249.

72. Garvin, vol. 1, p. 161.
73. *Fortnightly Review*, September 1873.

CHAPTER 4
74. Garvin, vol. 1, p. 186.
75. *Ibid.*, p. 187.
76. Marris, p. 101.
77. *Ibid.*
78. *Ibid.*, p. 125.
79. *Ibid.*, p. 116.
80. B.M. Add. MS. 44125, Joseph Chamberlain to Gladstone, 9 December 1880 and 16 April 1881.
81. Marris, p. 101.
82. B.M. Add. MS. 43885, Joseph Chamberlain to Dilke, 29 January 1876.
83. Marris, p. 113.
84. Speech at Ratepayers' Meeting, 13 April 1874, quoted in Garvin, vol. 1, pp. 189–90.
85. Marris, p. 114.
86. *Ibid.*, p. 117.
87. Garvin, vol. 1, p. 192.
88. Marris, pp. 104–5.
89. C. W. Boyd (ed.), *Mr. Chamberlain's Speeches*, vol. 1, pp. 43–4.
90. Marris, p. 119.
91. Quoted in Peter Fraser, *Joseph Chamberlain*, p. 23.
92. Garvin, vol. 1, p. 199.
93. Chamberlain Papers, Joseph Chamberlain to Jesse Collings, 26 April 1875.
94. Marris, p. 108.
95. Chamberlain Papers, Joseph Chamberlain to Jesse Collings, 6 June 1876.
96. Marris, p. 127.
97. Garvin, vol. 1, p. 208.
98. Chamberlain Papers, JC 1/5/1.
99. *Ibid.*, Joseph Chamberlain to John Morley, 7 December 1875.
100. Marris, pp. 88–9.
101. *Ibid.*, pp. 89–90.
102. *Ibid.*
103. *Ibid.*, p. 106.
104. *Ibid.*, p. 107.
105. Garvin, vol. 1, p. 205.
106. *Punch*, 14 November 1874.
107. *Fortnightly Review*, October 1874.
108. B.M. Add. MS. 43885, Joseph Chamberlain to Dilke, 17 March 1874.
109. *Ibid.*, Dilke to Joseph Chamberlain, 15 March 1874.
110. Chamberlain Papers, Joseph Chamberlain to Morley, 23 August 1873.

111. B.M. Add. MS. 43885, Joseph Chamberlain to Dilke, 17 March 1874.
112. *Ibid.*, Dilke to Joseph Chamberlain, March 1874.
113. *Ibid.*, 3 November 1875.
114. Chamberlain Papers, Jesse Collings to Joseph Chamberlain, 31 May 1875.
115. *Ibid.*, Joseph Chamberlain to Collings, 26 May 1876.
116. B.M. Add. MS. 43885, Joseph Chamberlain to Dilke, 24 January 1876.
117. Garvin, vol. 1, p. 228.
118. *Ibid.*, p. 230.
119. Beatrice Webb's diary, 1 January 1901.

CHAPTER 5
120. Marris, p. 142.
121. Garvin, vol. 1, p. 231.
122. B.M. Add, MS. 43885, Joseph Chamberlain to Dilke, 27 July 1876.
123. Chamberlain papers, JC L. add. 275, Joseph Chamberlain to Walter Wren, 11 April 1878.
124. *Ibid.*
125. B.M. Add. MS. 43885, Joseph Chamberlain to Dilke, 7 December 1876.
126. Garvin, vol. 1, p. 240.
127. Chamberlain papers, Joseph Chamberlain to Morley, 6 February 1877.
128. B.M. Add. MS. 44125, Joseph Chamberlain to Gladstone, 16 April 1877.
129. *Ibid.*, 24 May 1877.
130. *Ibid.*, 16 April 1877.
131. Garvin, vol. 1, pp. 232–3.
132. Hansard, 3rd Series, vol. 231, 4 August 1876, col. 542.
133. B.M. Add. MS. 43885, Joseph Chamberlain to Dilke, 7 December 1876.
134. See Hansard 3rd Series, 1876–80.
135. *Ibid.*, vol. 247, 17 June 1879, cols. 45–6.
136. Chamberlain papers, JC 1/9/2, Joseph Chamberlain to H. Lee-Warner, 8 April 1879.
137. Chamberlain papers, AC 4/1/1149, Austen Chamberlain to Mary Chamberlain.
138. Garvin, vol. 1, p. 223.
139. *Ibid.*
140. Hansard, 3rd Series, vol. 234, 7 May 1877, col. 454.
141. *Ibid.*, vol. 244, 27 March 1879, cols. 1912–13.
142. Garvin, vol. 1, p. 224.
143. Hansard, 3rd Series, vol. 234, 9 April 1878, cols. 982–3.
144. Garvin, vol. 1, p. 234.
145. *Ibid.*, p. 280.
146. Iain Macleod, *Neville Chamberlain*, p. 20.

147. Austen Chamberlain, *Down the Years*, pp. 270–1.
148. Chamberlain papers, AC 1/4/4a/5, Joseph to Austen Chamberlain, 15 May 1875.
149. *Ibid.*, AC 1/4/4a/7, 13 June 1875.
150. *Ibid.*, AC 1/4/4a/3, April 1875.
151. Quoted in Sir Charles Petrie, *The Chamberlain Tradition*, p. 130.
152. *Ibid.*
153. Chamberlain papers, AC 4/1/1149, Austen Chamberlain to Mary Chamberlain.
154. Garvin, vol. 1, p. 273.
155. Chamberlain papers, Joseph Chamberlain to John Morley, 3 October 1877.
156. Memorandum by Chamberlain, quoted in Garvin, vol. 1, p. 274.
157. Garvin, vol. 1, p. 274.
158. B.M. Add. MS. 43885, Joseph Chamberlain to Dilke, 5 November 1879.
159. Chamberlain papers, Joseph Chamberlain to Jesse Collings, 28 March 1880.
160. Quoted in Garvin, vol. 1, p. 280.
161. Chamberlain papers, Joseph Chamberlain to Morley, 25 January 1880.

CHAPTER 6
162. B.M. Add. MS. 43885, Joseph Chamberlain to Dilke, 4 April 1880.
163. *Ibid.*, Dilke to Chamberlain, 5 April 1880.
164. Garvin, vol. 1, p. 294.
165. B.M. Add. MS. 43885, Dilke to Joseph Chamberlain, 24 April 1880.
166. Chamberlain papers, Joseph Chamberlain to Collings, 27 April 1880.
167. *Diaries of John Bright*, p. 439.
168. C. H. D. Howard (ed.), Joseph Chamberlain, *A Political Memoir*, *1880–1892*, p. 3.
169. G. E. Buckle (ed.), *The Letters of Queen Victoria*, second series, vol. 3, p. 91.
170. Chamberlain papers, JC 1/3/1, Joseph Chamberlain to Clara Chamberlain, 4 May 1880.
171. *Ibid.*
172. K. Feiling, *The Life of Neville Chamberlain*, p. 7.
173. *A Political Memoir*, p. 4.
174. Garvin, vol. 1, p. 409.
175. *Ibid.*, p. 410; speech of 26 December 1880.
176. P.R.O. Cab. 37/5/No. 12, 3 June 1881.
177. P.R.O. Cab. 37/7/No. 13, 16 February 1882.
178. Hansard, 3rd series, vol. 277, 19 March.
179. B.M. Add. MS. 44125, Joseph Chamberlain to Gladstone, 15 August 1883.
180. *Ibid.*, Joseph Chamberlain to Gladstone, 6 March 1884.
181. *Ibid.*, 4 October 1881.
182. Hansard, 3rd series, vol. 260, 12 August 1881, col. 1803.

183. Dilke's *Life*, vol. 1, p. 401.
184. B.M. Add. MS. 44125, Joseph Chamberlain to Gladstone, 25 July 1883.
185. *Ibid.*, copy of speech delivered at Birmingham on 26 October 1880.
186. *Ibid.*, Joseph Chamberlain to Gladstone, 16 November 1880.
187. *Ibid.*, Joseph Chamberlain to Gladstone, 22 December 1880.
188. P. Fraser, p. 37.
189. Garvin, vol. 1, p. 345.
190. B.M. Add. MS. Joseph Chamberlain to Gladstone, 25 April 1882.
191. *A Political Memoir*, p. 62.
192. B.M. Add. MS. Joseph Chamberlain to Gladstone, 2 May 1882.
193. Garvin, vol. 1, p. 366.
194. B.M. Add. MS. 43885, Dilke to Chamberlain, 8 May 1882.
195. Quoted in *A Political Memoir*, p. 58. Gladstone to Morley 11 August 1888.
196. *Ibid.*, p. 60. Chamberlain to Morley, 16 August 1888.
197. Garvin, vol. 1, p. 439.
198. *Ibid.*, p. 490.
199. *Ibid.*, p. 445.
200. Lord Edmond Fitzmaurice, *Life of Lord Granville*, vol. 2, p. 265.
201. Garvin, vol. 1, p. 451.
202. *Pall Mall Gazette*, 1 December 1884.
203. Speech at Birmingham, 5 January 1885. Garvin, vol. 1, pp. 549–51.
204. B.M. Add. MS. 44126, Joseph Chamberlain to Gladstone, 28 December 1884.
205. Chamberlain papers, Joseph Chamberlain to Morley, 2 February 1885.
206. Garvin, vol. 1, p. 622.

CHAPTER 7
207. D. Hamer (ed.), *The Radical Programme, with a preface by J. Chamberlain, 1885*.
208. Garvin, vol. 2, p. 63.
209. Lord Milner, and others, *Life of Joseph Chamberlain*, p. 164.
210. W. Tuckwell, *Reminiscences of a Radical Parson*, p. 59.
211. B.M. Add. MS. 43887, J. C. to Dilke, 31 October 1885.
212. *Birmingham Daily Post*, 22 May 1885.
213. Chamberlain papers, J.C. to Frank Harris, 18 June 1885.
214. Quoted in P. Fraser, p. 70.
215. A. Ramm (ed.), *Correspondence of Gladstone and Granville*, vol. 2; pp. 366–7.
216. *A Political Memoir*, p. 167.
217. Garvin, vol. 2, p. 108.
218. Lord Edmond Fitzmaurice, *Life of the Second Earl Granville*, vol. 2, p. 465.
219. Garvin, vol. 2, p. 112.
220. *Ibid.*, p. 108.

221. *Cornhill Magazine*, September 1914.
222. *A Political Memoir*, p. 164.
223. B.M. Add. MS. 44126, Gladstone to J. C., 25 October 1885.
224. *Ibid.*, J. C. to Gladstone, 26 October 1885.
225. B.M. Add. MS. 43887, J. C. to Dilke, 26 October 1885.
226. *Ibid.*, J. C. to Dilke, 4 November 1885.
227. P. Fraser, p. 74.
228. Chamberlain papers, J. C. to Lady Dorothy Nevill, 4 December 1885.
229. B.M. Add. MS. 43887, J. C. to Dilke, 16 December 1885.
230. Garvin, vol. 2, p. 140.
231. B.M. Add. MS. 43887, J. C. to Dilke, 17 December 1885.
232. *Ibid.*
233. B.M. Add. MS. 44126, J. C. to Gladstone, 18 December 1885.
234. B.M. Add. MS. 43887, J. C. to Dilke, 18 December 1885.
235. Garvin, vol. 2, p. 162. J. C. to Harcourt, 6 January 1886.
236. B.M. Add. MS. 43887, J. C. to Dilke, 26 December 1885.
237. Garvin, vol. 2, p. 172.
238. *Ibid.*, p. 177.
239. *A Political Memoir*, pp. 189–90.
240. P.R.O. Cab. 37/18/22/140; memorandum 'Land Purchase', by J. C. 15 February 1886.
241. *A Political Memoir*, p. 190.
242. P.R.O. Cab. 37/18/22/140.
243. *A Political Memoir*, p. 193.
244. *Ibid.*, pp. 193–4.
245. Chamberlain papers, JC 5/11/5, J. C. to Arthur Chamberlain, 8 March 1886.
246. B.M. Add. MS. 44126, J. C. to Gladstone, 27 March 1886.
247. Chamberlain papers, J. C. to J. T. Bunce, 17 March 1886.
248. *Ibid.*
249. P. Magnus, *Gladstone*, p. 348.
250. Garvin, vol. 2, p. 177.
251. *Life of Joseph Chamberlain*, pp. 116–17.
252. Chamberlain papers, JC 5/11/5, J. C. to Arthur Chamberlain, 8 March 1886.
253. Roy Jenkins, *Sir Charles Dilke*, p. 218.
254. *Ibid.*, p. 355.
255. B.M. Add. MS. 43885, Dilke to J. C. 14 September 1881.
256. *Ibid.*, J. C. to Dilke, 6 December 1882.
257. *Ibid.*, 12 September 1882.
258. B.M. Add. MS. 43887, J. C. to Dilke, 20 February 1885.
259. See Chamberlain papers AC 35/1/38, Neville to Austen Chamberlain, 22 August 1927; NC 1/27/95, Austen to Neville, 29 August 1927; also H. Harrison, *Parnell, Joseph Chamberlain and Mr. Garvin*, for a discussion of the evidence.
260. *A Political Memoir*, p. 208.

CHAPTER 8

261. Chamberlain papers, NC 1/27/90, A. J. Balfour to Lord Salisbury 22 March 1886.
262. *Ibid.*
263. *Ibid.*
264. Chamberlain papers, JC 5/11/8, J. C. to Arthur Chamberlain, 1 May 1886.
265. Quoted in P. Fraser, p. 100.
266. Chamberlain papers, JC 5/11/11, J. C. to Arthur Chamberlain, June 1886.
267. *Ibid.*, JC 5/11/13, J. C. to Arthur Chamberlain, 9 June 1886.
268. R. Shannon, *The Crisis of Imperialism*, p. 227.
269. Garvin, vol. 2, p. 212.
270. Chamberlain papers, speech at Birmingham 2 July 1886.
271. Blanche Dugdale, *Arthur James Balfour*, vol. 1, pp. 103–4.
272. W. Tuckwell, *Reminiscences of a Radical Parson*, pp. 59–60.
273. B.M. Add. MS. 44126, J. C. to Labouchere, 2 May 1886.
274. A. G. Gardiner, *Harcourt*, vol. 2, pp. 24–9.
275. B.M. Add. MS. 43541, Morley to Ripon, 19 January 1887.
276. Chamberlain papers, AC 1/4/5/5 J. C. to Austen Chamberlain, 1 January 1887.
277. Chamberlain papers, JC L. Add. 272, J. C. to Walter Wren, 18 January 1887.
278. *Ibid.*
279. P. Fraser, p. 134.
280. Chamberlain papers, J. C. to Trevelyan, 9 March 1887.
281. B.M. Add. MS. 43541, Morley to Ripon, 7 February 1887.
282. Lady Stanley's Diary, 5 February 1887, quoted in Garvin, vol. 2 p. 299.
283. Garvin, vol. 2, p. 306, J. C. to Dr. Dale, 12 July 1887.
284. *Ibid.*, p. 313.
285. Chamberlain papers, JC 1/2/5, J. C. to Beatrice Chamberlain, December 1887.
286. *Ibid.*, JC 1/2/7, J. C. to Beatrice Chamberlain, 15 December 1887.
287. *Ibid.*, JC 1/2/8, J. C. to Beatrice Chamberlain, 28 December 1887.
288. *Ibid.*
289. *Ibid.*, JC 1/2/9, J. C. to Beatrice Chamberlain, 3 January 1888.
290. *Ibid.*, JC 1/2/17, J. C. to Beatrice Chamberlain, 24 February 1888.
291. *Ibid.*, JC 1/2/9, J. C. to Beatrice Chamberlain, 3 January 1888.
292. *Ibid.*, JC 1/2/5, J. C. to Beatrice Chamberlain, 2 December 1887.
293. *Ibid.*, JC 1/2/10, J. C. to Beatrice Chamberlain, 13 January 1888.
294. *Ibid.*, JC 1/2/6, J. C. to Beatrice Chamberlain, 9 December 1887.
295. All quoted in Garvin, vol. 2, pp. 365–7.
296. *Ibid.*, p. 367.
297. Margaret Cole (ed.), *Diaries of Beatrice Webb*, p. 316.
298. Beatrice Webb, *My Apprenticeship*, pp. 108–9.
299. Beatrice Webb's Diary, quoted in P. Fraser, p. 119.
300. P. Fraser, p. 117.

301. *Ibid.*, pp. 117–18.
302. Quoted in Garvin, vol. 2, p. 372.
303. *Ibid.*, p. 373.
304. Chamberlain papers, JC 5/12/1, J. C. to Austen Chamberlain, 16 July 1887.
305. Bodleian, Selborne papers, J. C. to Wolmer (Selborne), 25 January 1892.
306. Chamberlain papers, JC 1/2/13, J. C. to Beatrice Chamberlain, 3 February 1888.
307. Garvin, vol. 2, p. 356.
308. Bodleian, Selborne papers, J. C. to Wolmer, 13 March 1888.
309. Chamberlain papers, J. C. to Dr. Dale, 1 May 1891.
310. Lady Stanley's Diary, 5 February 1887, quoted in Garvin, vol. 2, p. 299.
311. Frank Harris, *My Life and Loves*, p. 416.
312. Quoted in P. Magnus, *Gladstone*, p. 348.
313. Garvin, vol. 2, p. 364.
314. Quoted in R. Shannon, p. 229.
315. Hansard, 4th series, vol. 15, 27 July 1893.
316. Chamberlain papers, NC 1/6/9/20, J. C. to Neville Chamberlain, 4 March 1894.
317. Garvin, vol. 2, p. 594.
318. Chamberlain papers, memo by J. C., 13 November 1894.
319. *Ibid.*
320. Chamberlain papers, *The Game of Politics.*
321. Bodleian, Selborne papers, J. C. to Wolmer, 12 October 1894.
322. *Ibid.*, Wolmer to J. C., 25 October 1894.
323. Quoted in Garvin, vol. 2, pp. 333–4.
324. Chamberlain papers, JC 5/12/10, J. C. to Austen Chamberlain, 30 December 1889.
325. *Ibid.*, NC 1/6/9/25, J. C. to Neville Chamberlain, 7 April 1895.
326. *Ibid.*, NC 1/6/9/26, 25 April 1895.

CHAPTER 9
327. Garvin, vol. 3, p. 5.
328. Chamberlain papers, NC 1/19/170, Neville to Austen Chamberlain, 5 November 1895.
329. Garvin, vol. 3, p. 11.
330. *Ibid.*, p. 16.
331. Speech at Walsall, 15 July 1895, quoted in Garvin, vol. 3, p. 19.
332. Garvin, vol. 3, p. 22.
333. *Ibid.*, pp. 23–4.
334. *The Echo*, 4 December 1895.
335. *The Times*, 7 November 1895.
336. Garvin, vol. 3, pp. 28–9.
337. Chamberlain papers, JC L. add. J. C. to H. W. Massingham, 29 March 1897.
338. Garvin, vol. 3, p. 50.

339. Salisbury papers, Christ Church, Box 3, Wallet 1, Balfour to Salisbury, 10 April 1897.
340. Garvin, vol. 3, p. 114.
341. *Ibid.*, p. 111.
342. Jean van der Poel, *The Jameson Raid.*
343. Chamberlain papers, JC 5/5/65, J. C. to Balfour, 2 February 1896.
344. *Ibid.*
345. Bodleian, Selborne papers, J. C. to Selborne, 23 December 1896.
346. *Ibid.*, J. C. to Selborne, 12 December 1896.
347. *Ibid.*, J. C. to Selborne, 6 January 1897.
348. *Ibid.*, J. C. to Selborne, 30 December 1896.
349. *Ibid.*
350. Garvin, vol. 3, p. 125.
351. Bodleian, Selborne papers, J. C. to Selborne, 20 December 1895.
352. *Ibid.*, J. C. to Selborne, 21 December 1895.
353. *Ibid.*, Selborne to J. C., 1 September 1896.
354. *Ibid.*, J. C. to Selborne, 21 September 1897.
355. *Ibid.*, J. C. to Selborne, 12 September 1897.
356. *Ibid.*, J. C. to Selborne, 1 December 1897.
357. B.M. Add. MS. 49691, Salisbury to Balfour, 9 April 1898.
358. *Ibid.*, Balfour to Salisbury, 14 April 1898.
359. *Ibid.*
360. Chamberlain papers, JC 5/5/70, J. C. to Balfour, 3 February 1898.
361. Whittingehame, J. C. to Balfour, 23 August 1898.
362. Chamberlain papers, NC 1/6/10/11, Austen Chamberlain to J. C., 3 January 1891.
363. *Ibid.*, NC 1/6/9/7, J. C. to Neville Chamberlain, 5 January 1892.
364. *Ibid.*, JC 5/5/24, Balfour to J. C., 27 November 1895.
365. *Ibid.*, JC L. add. 74, J. C. to Richard Cadbury, 13 January 1899.
366. Bodleian, Selborne papers, J. C. to Selborne, 11 December 1896.
367. *Daily Mail*, 23 June 1897.
368. Colonial Conference 1897, Cmd. 8/596.
369. Chamberlain papers, J. C. to Devonshire, 4 July 1897.
370. Bodleian, Selborne papers, Selborne to J. C., 6 October 1896.
371. *Ibid.*, J. C. to Selborne, 14 October 1896.
372. *Ibid.*, Selborne to J. C., 18 October 1896.
373. Christ Church, Box 3, Wallet 1, Balfour to Salisbury, 10 April 1897.

CHAPTER 10
374. Whittingehame, Wyndham to Balfour, 7 October 1899.
375. Chamberlain papers, JC 5/15/83, J. C. to Balfour, 3 October 1899.
376. Speech at Trinity College, Dublin, 18 December 1899. Quoted in Garvin, vol. 3, p. 526.
377. J. C. to Minto, 26 October 1899. Quoted in Garvin, vol. 3, p. 533.
378. B. M. Add. MS. 49774, J. C. to Balfour, 9 September 1902.
379. *Ibid.*, copy of a memorandum by J. C., 6 November 1902.
380. Hansard, 4th series, vol. 78, 5 February 1900, cols. 609–24.

381. Chamberlain papers, NC 1/6/9/32, J. C. to Neville Chamberlain, 10 February 1900.
382. Quoted in Garvin, vol. 3, p. 597.
383. Whittingehame, J. C. to Balfour, 21 October 1900.
384. *Ibid.*, Salisbury to Balfour, 9 October 1900.
385. W. S. Churchill, *My Early Life*, p. 365.
386. Hansard, 4th series, vol. 88, 6 December 1900, cols. 128–9.
387. *Ibid.*, 10 December 1900, cols, 125–7.
388. Chamberlain papers, J. C. to Austen, 1 September 1902.
389. B.M. Add. MS. 49774, J. C. to Balfour, 9 September 1902.
390. Amery, vol. 4, p. 333.
391. *Ibid.*, p. 375.
392. Chamberlain papers, JC 23/2/3, Mary Endicott Chamberlain to her mother, 2 March 1903.
393. *Ibid.*
394. B.M. Add. MS. 49697, Milner to Balfour, 19 December 1904.
395. Bodleian, Selborne papers, J. C. to Selborne, 24 March 1908.
396. *Ibid.*, Selborne to J. C., 24 February 1908.
397. Chamberlain papers, J. C. to Austen C., 9 January 1903.
398. *African Review*, 15 March 1902.
399. Quoted in Amery, vol. 4. p. 403.
400. *Ibid.*, p. 500.
401. Lord George Hamilton, *Parliamentary Reminiscences and Reflections*; p. 315.

CHAPTER II
402. Quoted in Blanche Dugdale, *Arthur James Balfour*, vol. 1, pp. 339–340.
403. *The Times*, 12 May 1902.
404. *Ibid.*, 17 May 1902.
405. P.R.O. Cab. 37/62/120.
406. B. Dugdale, vol. 1, p. 345.
407. W. S. Churchill, *My Early Life*, p. 378.
408. Chamberlain papers, JC L. Add. 49a, Robert Giffen to J. C., 26 October. 1903.
409. *Ibid.*, JC L. Add. 53a, J. C. to Giffen, 4 Dec. 1903.
410. *Ibid.*, JC L. Add. 50a, Giffen to J. C., 2 November 1903.
411. *Ibid.*, JC L. Add. 53a, J. C. to Giffen, 4 December 1903.
412. *Ibid.*
413. *The Times*, 16 May 1903.
414. A. M. Gollin, *Balfour's Burden*, p. 38.
415. R. Jenkins, *Asquith*, p. 137.
416. B.M. Add. MS. 49759, Balfour to Hugh Cecil, 16 July 1903.
417. P.R.O. Cab. 37/65/47, 1 August 1903.
418. *The Times*, 18 September 1903. J.C.'s letter of resignation.
419. P.R.O. Cab. 37/66/60.

420. B.M. Add. MS. 41214, Campbell-Bannerman to John Ellis, 10 November 1903.
421. Chamberlain papers, Mary Endicott Chamberlain to her mother.
422. Amery, vol. 6, pp. 471–2. J. C.'s speech at Greenock, 11 November 1903.
423. *Ibid.*, p. 484, J. C.'s speech at Newcastle, 20 October 1903.
424. C. W. Boyd (ed.), *Mr. Chamberlain's Speeches*, vol. 2, p. 201.
425. *Ibid.*, p. 428.
426. *Ibid.*, pp. 462–6.
427. Chamberlain papers, Mary Endicott Chamberlain to her mother, 1 June 1905.
428. Amery, vol. 6, p. 732, from Neville Chamberlain's recollections.
429. Chamberlain papers, AC 4/1/51, Austen to Mary Endicott Chamberlain, 4 July 1904.
430. Whittingehame, Betty Balfour to Alice Balfour, 4 February 1906.
431. Chamberlain papers, AC 4/5/32, J. C. to Austen, 11 March 1904.
432. *Ibid.*, NC 1/6/9/36, J. C. to Neville, 25 March 1904.
433. *Ibid.*
434. *Ibid.*
435. *Ibid.*
436. B.M. Add. MS. 49735, Austen Chamberlain to Balfour, 24 August 1904.
437. *Ibid.*, 49775, Balfour to Lyttelton, 27 May 1905.
438. *Ibid.*, 49737, Robert Cecil to Balfour, 25 January 1906.
439. Whittingehame, Betty Balfour to Alice Balfour, 4 February 1906.
440. *The Times*, 15 February 1906.

CHAPTER 12
441. Chamberlain papers, Mrs. Mary Endicott Chamberlain to Mrs Endicott, 19 September 1906.
442. Amery, vol. 6, p. 919, letter from J. C. to Chaplin, 25 May 1907.
443. *Autobiography of Margot Asquith*, part 2, p. 133.
444. Chamberlain papers, AC 4/1/425, Austen to Mrs. Chamberlain, 20 April 1909.
445. B.M. Add. MS. 49765, Sandars to W. M. Short, 4 March 1907.
446. W. A. S. Hewins, *Apologia of an Imperialist*, vol. 2, pp. 220–2.
447. Amery, vol. 6, p. 986.
448. Chamberlain papers, AC 42/2/13, Mrs. Mary Endicott Chamberlain to Austen, 16 November 1914.

BIBLIOGRAPHY

I   MANUSCRIPT SOURCES

(The author has used the description of 'British Museum' rather than that of the subsequently-designated 'British Library').

a   The papers of Joseph, Austen and Neville Chamberlain, deposited in the Main Library, University of Birmingham.
b   W. E. Gladstone's and Herbert Gladstone's papers deposited at the British Museum.
c   Dilke papers (British Museum).
d   Balfour papers (British Museum & Whittingehame, East Lothian).
e   Campbell-Bannerman papers (British Museum).
f   Morley papers (British Museum).
g   Ripon papers (British Museum).
h   Salisbury papers (Christ Church Library, Oxford; now in Hatfield House).
i   Selborne papers (Bodleian Library, Oxford).
j   Asquith papers (Bodleian).
k   Bryce papers (Bodleian).
l   Milner papers (Bodleian—but owned by New College, Oxford).
m   Monk Bretton papers (Bodleian).

II   PARLIAMENTARY PAPERS AND OFFICIAL DOCUMENTS
a   The Public Record Office's collection of Cabinet papers.
b   Hansard's Parliamentary Debates.
c   Proceedings of the Colonial and Imperial Conferences of 1887, 1897, 1902, 1907, 1911, 1932.
d   Reports of Royal Commissions and Government Committees.
    i. The Royal West India Commission, P.P. 1897 (C 8655).
    ii. The Royal Commission on the War in South Africa (Elgin Report), P.P. 1904 (Cd. 1789).

III   JOURNALS AND NEWSPAPERS
a   *The Fortnightly Review.*
b   *Pall Mall Gazette.*
c   *Birmingham Daily Post.*
d   *Cornhill Magazine.*
e   *The Times.*
f   *The Daily News.*
g   *The Daily Mail.*

IV   SPEECHES, ARTICLES AND OTHER WORKS BY JOSEPH CHAMBERLAIN

Lucy, Henry W. (ed.) *Speeches of J. Chamberlain* (1885).
—*Imperial Union and Tariff Reform*; speeches delivered *15 May–4 November, 1903*, (1903)
Boyd, C. W. (ed.) *Mr. Chamberlain's Speeches* (vols. 1 & 2, 1914).

'The Manufacture of Iron Wood Screws', in *The Resources, Products and Industrial History of Birmingham* . . . (ed. S. Timmins), 1866.
'The Educational Policy of the Government from a Nonconformist Point of View', *National Education League*, 1872
'The Liberal Party and its Leaders', *Fortnightly Review*, September 1873.
'The Next Page of the Liberal Programme', *Fortnightly Review*, October 1874.
'The Right Method with Publicans', *Fortnightly Review*, May 1876.
'A Visit to Lapland, with Notes of Swedish Licensing', *Fortnightly Review*, December 1876.
'Free Schools', *Fortnightly Review*, January 1877.
'Municipal Public Houses', *Fortnightly Review*, February 1877.
'A New Political Organization', *Fortnightly Review*, July 1877.
'The Caucus', *Fortnightly Review*, November 1878.
'Land Nationalization', *Pall Mall Gazette*, 24, 29 January 1882.
'Labourers' and Artisans' Dwellings', *Fortnightly Review*, December 1883.
'The Radical Platform', 1885.
'The Radical Programme', 1885.
'A Radical View of the Irish Crisis', *Fortnightly Review*, February 1886.
'A Unionist Policy for Ireland', *National Radical Union*, 1888
'Shall we Americanize our Institutions?' *Nineteenth Century*, December 1890.
'Speeches on the Irish Question', 1890
'Favourable Aspects of State Socialism', *North American Review*, May 1891.
'Old Age Pensions', *National Review*, February 1892.
'Municipal Institutions in America and England', *Forum*, November 1892 (New York).
'Pauperism and Old Age Pensions', letters between Chamberlain & C. S. Loch, 1892
'The Labour Question', *Nineteenth Century*, November 1892.
'A Bill for the Weakening of Great Britain', *Nineteenth Century*, April 1893.
'The Case against Home Rule', *Pall Mall Gazette*, 8 August 1893.
'The Home Rule Campaign', *National Review*, May 1894.
'Municipal Government', *New Review*, June 1894.
'Old Age Pensions and Friendly Societies', *National Review*, January 1895.
'The New Democracy: Its Wants, Its Claims, Its Rights', *National Liberal Federation*, 1895.
'Patriotism': Rectorial Address to the students of Glasgow University, November 1897.
'The Policy of the United States', *Scribner's Magazine*, December 1898.
'Nelson's Year and National Duty', *Outlook*, 11 March 1905.

Chamberlain, J. *A Political Memoir* (edited from Chamberlain's manuscript by C. H. D. Howard, who chose the title; published in 1953).

V SELECT   ARTICLES,   CHAPTERS   AND   TRACTS   RELATING   TO
CHAMBERLAIN'S LIFE AND CAREER

Alderman, G. 'Joseph Chamberlain's attempted reform of the British
Mercantile Marine', *Journal of Transport History*, N.S. 1:3 (1972)

Baylen, J. O. 'W. T. Stead's *History of the Mystery* and the Jameson Raid',
Journal of British Studies, 4:1 (1964).

Bradley, I. 'Joseph Chamberlain', *Central Literary Magazine*, vol. XI, no. 8
(1914).

Drus, E. 'The Question of Imperial Complicity in the Jameson Raid', *English
Historical Review*, (October 1950).

Dumett, R. E. 'Joseph Chamberlain, imperial finance and railway policy in
British West Africa in the late nineteenth century', *English Historical Review*,
90 (1975).

Dutton, D. 'Unionist Politicians and the Aftermath of the General Election of
1906', *Historical Journal*, 22 (1979).

—'Life Beyond the Political Grave: Joseph Chamberlain 1906–14', *History
Today*, 4 (1984).

Egerton, H. E. 'Chamberlain, Joseph', *Dictionary of National Biography*:
Twentieth Century 1912–21 (1927).

Fraser, D. 'Joseph Chamberlain and the Municpal Ideal', *History Today*, 37
(1986).

Fraser, P. 'The Liberal Unionist Alliance: Chamberlain, Hartington and the
Conservatives, 1886–1904', *English Historical Review*, 76:1 (1962).

—'Unionism and Tariff Reform: the Crisis of 1906', *The Historical Journal*, 5:2
(1962).

Galbraith, J. S. 'The British South Africa Company and the Jameson Raid',
Journal of British Studies, 10 (1970).

Gardiner, A. B. 'Joseph Chamberlain' in *Pillars of Society* (1913).

Garson, N. G. 'British Imperialism and the Coming of the Anglo-Boer War',
South Africa Journal of Economics, 30:2 (1962)

Garvin, J. L. 'Imperial Reciprocity; a Study of Fiscal Policy,' *Daily Telegraph*
(1903).

Griffiths, P. 'Pressure Groups and Parties in Mid-Victorian England; the
National Education League', *Midlands History*, 3 (1976).

Green, C. 'Birmingham's Politics, 1873–1891: the Local Basis of Change',
Midland History, 2:2 (1973).

Hardy, S. M. 'Joseph Chamberlain and some problems of the "Underdeveloped Estates" ', *University of Birmingham Historical Journal*, 11 (1967–
8).

Harries, F. J. *The Rt. Hon. Joseph Chamberlain* (1913).

Howard, C. H. D. 'Joseph Chamberlain and the Unauthorized Programme',
English Historical Review, 65 (1950).

—'Select Documents, XXI. Joseph Chamberlain, W. H. O. O'Shea, and
Parnell, 1884, 1891–2', *Irish Historical Studies*, 13:1 (1962).

—'Joseph Chamberlain & the Irish "Central Board" scheme, 1884–5' *Irish
Historical Studies*, 8 (1952–3).

Hurst, M. 'Joseph Chamberlain and West Midland Politics, 1886–1895',
Dugdale Society Occasional, Papers, 15 (1962).

—'Joseph Chamberlain and Late-Victorian Liberalism', *Durham University Journal*, 66 (1973).

James, Robert Rhodes, 'Radical Joe', *History Today*, 7 (1957).

Judd, D. 'Pioneers of the Welfare State; Radical Joe Chamberlain', *New Society*, 28 October 1982.

Loughlin, J. 'Joseph Chamberlain, English Nationalism and the Ulster Question', *History*, 77 (1992).

Lubenow, W. C. 'Irish Home Rule and the Great Separation in the Liberal Party in 1886', *Victorian Studies*, 26 (1983).

Marsh, P. 'Joseph Chamberlain', *Dictionary of Business Biography*, vol. 1, A–C (1943).

Porter, A. N. 'Lord Salisbury, Mr. Chamberlain and South Africa, 1895–1899', *Journal of Imperial and Commonwealth History*, 1:1 (1972).

—'In Memoriam Joseph Chamberlain: A Review of Periodical Literature, 1960–73', *Journal of Imperial and Commonwealth History*, 3:2 (1974).

Quinault, R. 'John Bright & Joseph Chamberlain', *Historical Journal*, 28, (1985).

—'Joseph Chamberlain: a reassessment', in T. R. Gourvish & A. O'Day (eds.), *Later Victorian Britain* (1988).

Saul, S. B. 'The Economic Significance of "constructive imperialism" ', *Journal of Economic History*, 17:2 (1957).

Shannon, C. 'The Ulster Liberal Unionists and Local Government Reform, 1885–98', *Irish Historical Studies*, 18 (1973).

Simon, A. 'Joseph Chamberlain and Free Education in the Election of 1885', *History of Education*, 2 (1973).

Snowden, P. 'The Chamberlain Bubble'. Tract publishd by the Independent Labour Party, 1903.

Strauss, W. 'Joseph Chamberlain and the Theory of Imperialism', *Public Affairs* (1942).

Tholfsen, T. R. 'The Origins of the Birmingham Caucus', *Historical Journal*, 2:2 (1959).

Vince, C. A. 'Chamberlain Souvenir', pamphlet (1906).

Wilde, R. H. 'Joseph Chamberlain and the South African Republic 1895–1899', *Archives Yearbook for South African History*, 1 (1956).

—'Canada, the 1902 Conference and Chamberlain's Preference Campaign', paper presented at the Institute of Commonwealth Studies, London, 28 October 1965.

Will, H. A. 'Colonial Policy and Economic Development in the British West Indies, 1895–1903', *Economic History Review*, 23:1 (1970).

Zebel, S. H. 'Joseph Chamberlain and the Genesis of Tariff Reform', *Journal of British Studies*, 7:1 (1967).

VI SELECT BIOGRAPHIES AND STUDIES OF CHAMBERLAIN'S LIFE AND CAREER

Browne, H. *Joseph Chamberlain; Radical and Imperialist* (1974).

Balfour, M. *Britain and Joseph Chamberlain* (1985).

Creswicke, L. *Life of Joseph Chamberlain*, vols. 1–4 (1904).

Elletson, D. M. *The Chamberlains* (1966).

Fraser, P. *Joseph Chamberlain* (1966).

Bibliography

Garvin, J. L. *The Life of Joseph Chamberlain*, vols. 1–3, and Amery, J. vols. 4–6 (1932–69).

Griffiths, G. *With Chamberlain Through South Africa: a narrative of the Great Trek* (1903).

Gulley, E. C. *Joseph Chamberlain and English Social Politics* (1926).

Hurst, M. *Joseph Chamberlain and Liberal Reunion: the Round Table Conference of 1887* (1967).

Jay, R. *Joseph Chamberlain; a Political Study* (1981).

Jeyes, S. H. *Mr. Chamberlain: his Life and Public Career*, vols. 1–2 (1904).

Kubicek, R. V. *The Administration of Imperialism: Joseph Chamberlain at the Colonial Office* (1969).

Leech, H. J. *The Right Honourable Joseph Chamberlain, M.P., a Political Biography* (1885).

Mackintosh, A. *Joseph Chamberlain: an Honest Biography* (1906).

—*The Story of Mr. Chamberlain's Life* (1914).

Marris, N. M. *Joseph Chamberlain: the Man and the Statesman* (1900).

Mee, A. *Joseph Chamberlain: a Romance of Modern Politics* (1901).

Milner, A., Spender, J. A., *et al.*, *Life of Joseph Chamberlain* (1912).

Pedder, H. C. *Right Hon. Joseph Chamberlain* (1902).

Petrie, C. A. *The Chamberlain Tradition* (1938).

—*Joseph Chamberlain* (1940).

Powell, E. *Joseph Chamberlain* (1977).

Robertson, J. M. *Chamberlain: a Study* (1905).

Skottowe, B. C. *The Life of Joseph Chamberlain* (1885).

Smith, B. *Chamberlain and Chamberlainism* (1903).

Stead, W. T. *Joseph Chamberlain: conspirator or statesman?* (1900).

Strauss, W. L. *Joseph Chamberlain & the Theory of Imperialism* (1971).

VII BOOKS
(The following books are those which the author has found particularly useful. The list does not pretend to be a comprehensive bibliography of the period. Books which have been acknowledged in the endnotes are not necessarily included in this list)

Amery, L. S. *My Political Life*, vols. 1&2 (1953).

Ashworth, W. *An Economic History of England, 1870–1939* (1960).

Barker, M. *Gladstone & Radicalism: the Reconstruction of Liberal Policy in Britain, 1885–1894* (1975).

Beloff, M. *Imperial Sunset*, vol. 1 (1969).

Blake, R. *The Conservative Party from Peel to Thatcher* (1985).

Bernstein, G. L. *Liberalism and Liberal Politics in Edwardian England* (1986).

Bogdanor, V. *Devolution* (1979).

Briggs, A. *The History of Birmingham*, vol. 2 (1952).

Bunce, J. T. *History of the Corporation of Birmingham*, vol. 2 (1885).

Chamberlain, A. *Down the Years* (1935).

—*Politics from the Inside* (1936).

Churchill, R. S. *Winston S. Churchill*, vol. 1 (1966), vol. 2 (1967).

Churchill, W. S. *Great Contemporaries* (1949 ed.).

Coetzee, F. *For Party or Country: Nationalism and the Dilemmas of Popular Conservatism in Edwardian England* (1990).

Cole, M. *Beatrice Webb* (1945).

Cooke, A. B. & Vincent, J. R. *The Governing Passion; Cabinet Government and Party Politics in Britain 1885–86* (1974).

Cunningham, W. *Alien Immigration to England* (1987).

Daunton, M. J. *House and Home in the Victorian City: Working Class Housing 1850–1914* (1983).

Dennis, R. *English Industrial Cities of the Nineteenth Century* (1984).

Dilks, D. *Neville Chamberlain*, vol. 1, 1869–1929 (1984).

Dugdale, B. *Arthur James Balfour*, vols. 1 & 2 (1936).

Dutton, D. *Austen Chamberlain* (1985).

—*Simon; a Political Biography of Sir John Simon* (1992).

Egremont, M. *Balfour* (1980).

Ensor, R. C. K. *England, 1870–1914* (1936).

Feuchtwanger, E. J. *Gladstone* (1975).

—*Democracy and Empire: Britain 1865–1914* (1985).

Fieldhouse, D. K. *Economics and Empire* (1973).

Flint, J. E. *Cecil Rhodes* (1976).

Fraser, D. *Power and Authority in the Victorian City* (1979).

Friedberg, A. L. *Weary Titan; Britain and the Experience of Relative Decline, 1895–1905* (1988).

Garvin, T. *The Evolution of Irish Nationalist Politics* (1981).

Gollin, A. M. *The Observer and J. L. Garvin* (1960).

—*Proconsul in Politics: Milner* (1964).

—*Balfour's Burden* (1965).

Gourvish T. R & O'Day, A. (eds.) *Later Victorian Britain 1867–1900* (1988).

Green, M. *Dreams of Adventure, Deeds of Empire* (1980).

Grenville, J. A. S. *Lord Salisbury and Foreign Policy* (1964).

Grigg, J. *The Young Lloyd George* (1973).

—*Lloyd George; the People's Champion, 1902–11* (1978).

Gwynn, S. & Tuckwell, G. M. *Life of Sir Charles Dilke*, 2 vols. (1917).

Hamer, D. A. *Liberal Politics in the Age of Gladstone and Rosebery* (1972).

Harrison, H. *Parnell, Joseph Chamberlain and Mr. Garvin* (1938).

Hennock, E. P. *Fit and Proper Persons: Ideal and Reality in Nineteenth Century Urban Government* (1973)

Hewins, W. A. S. *Apologia of an Imperialist*, 2 vols. (1929).

Hobson, J. A. *The Psychology of Jingoism* (1901).

—*Imperialism; a study* (1902).

James, R. Rhodes, *The British Revolution*, vol. 1 (1976).

Jenkins, R. *Sir Charles Dilke; a Victorian Tragedy* (1958).

—*Asquith* (1964).

Jenkins, T.A. *Gladstone, Whiggery and the Liberal Party, 1874–86* (1988).

Judd, D. *Balfour and the British Empire* (1968).

—*Lord Reading* (1982).

Kendle, J. E. *The Colonial and Imperial Conferences, 1887–1911* (1967).

Kennedy, P. *The Rise of Anglo-German Antagonism, 1860–1914* (1980).

Kennedy, P. & Nicholls, A. (eds.) *Nationalist & Racialist Movement in Britain & Germany Before 1914* (1981). See Mock, W. on Chamberlain.

Kirkby, M. W. *The Decline of British Economic Power Since 1870* (1981).

Koss, S. *Asquith* (1976).

Langton, J. & Morris, J. R. (eds.) *Atlas of Industrialising Britain, 1780–1914* (1986).

Le May, G. H. *British Supremacy in South Africa, 1899–1907* (1965).

Lewis, J. *Women in England, 1870–1950* (1984).

Longford, E. *Jameson's Raid* (2nd edition 1980).

Low, D. A. *Lion Rampant: Essays in the Study of British Imperialism* (1973).

Lubenow, W. C. *Parliamentary Politics and the Home Rule Crisis* (1988).

Maccoby, S. *English Radicalism, 1886–1914* (1953).

Mackay, R. *Balfour; Intellectual Statesman* (1985).

Mackenzie, J. M. (ed.) *Propaganda and Empire* (1984).

—(ed.)*Imperialism and Popular Culture* (1986).

Magnus, P. *Gladstone* (1954).

—*Edward VII* (1964).

Mansergh, N. *The Irish Question, 1840–1921*, 3rd edition (1975).

—*The Commonwealth Experience*, 2 vols., 2nd edition (1982).

Marais, J. S. *The Fall of Kruger's Republic* (1961).

Matthew, H. C. G. *The Liberal Imperialists* (1973).

Matthews, R. C. O., Feinstein, C. H. & Odling-Smee, J. C. (eds.) *British Economic Growth* (1982).

Maycock, W. *With Mr. Chamberlain in the United States and Canada, 1887–88* (1914).

Meintjes, J. *President Paul Kruger* (1974).

Morgan, K. O. *Lloyd George* (1974).

—*Keir Hardie* (1975).

Morley, J. *Recollections*, 2 vols. (1917).

Muggeridge, K. & Adams, R. *Beatrice Webb* (1967).

O' Day, A. *Parnell and the First Home Rule Episode* (1986).

—(ed.) *Reactions to Irish Nationalism* (1987).

—(ed.) *The Edwardian Age* (1979).

Pakenham, T. *The Boer War* (1979).

—*The Scramble for Africa* (1991).

Payne, P. L. *British Entrepreneurship in the Nineteenth Century* (1974).

Pelling, H. *Popular Politics and Society in Late Victorian Britain* (1968).

Porter, B. *Critics of Empire* (1968).

—*The Lion's Share* (1975).

Porter, A. N. *The Origins of the South African War* (1980).

Price, R. *An Imperial War and the British Working Class; Working Class Attitudes and Reaction to the Boer War 1899–1902* (1972).

Read, D. *Edwardian England* (1972).

—*England 1868–1914* (1979).

Rempel, R. A. *Unionists Divided: Arthur Balfour, Joseph Chamberlain and the Unionist Free Traders* (1972).

Robbins, K. *Sir Edward Grey* (1971).

—*The Eclipse of a Great Power; Modern Britain, 1870–1975* (1983).

Russell, A. K. *Liberal Landslide; the General Election of 1906* (1973).

Robinson, R. & Gallagher, J. *Africa and the Victorians: the Official Mind of Imperialism* (1961).

Searle, G. R. *The Quest for National Efficiency* (1971).

Semmel, B. *Imperialism and Social Reform* (1967).

Shannon, R. *The Crisis of Imperialism* (1974).

Smith, P. *Disraelian Conservatism and Social Reform* (1967).

Stokes, E. *The Political Ideas of Imperialism* (1960).

Sykes, A. *Tariff Reform in British Politics, 1903–13* (1979).

Taylor, A. J. P. *Essays in English History* (1976).

Taylor, R. *Salisbury* (1974).

Thorton, A. P. *The Imperial Idea and its Enemies* (1959).

Vincent, J. R. *The Formation of the British Liberal Party* (1966).

Webb, B. *My Apprenticeship* (1926).

Weiner, M. J. *English Culture and the Decline of the Industrial Spirit, 1850–1980* (1981).

Weintraub, S. *Victoria: Biography of a Queen* (1987).

Wilson, J. *C-B: a Life of Sir Henry Campbell-Bannerman* (1973).

Young, K. *Arthur James Balfour* (1965).

Zebel, S. H. *Balfour* (1973).

INDEX

(Joseph Chamberlain is shown as JC throughout the index)

sanctioned by Gladstone, 81, 98; dominance of Birmingham men, 82; JC as President, 82; and the 1880 election, 95, 98; Gladstone and its growing power, 98; and Merchant Shipping Bill, 107; supports Gladstone on Home Rule, 146, 153; JC's estrangement from, 153

National Radical Union, 157, 171; founded by JC., 153-4

National Reform Union, 37

National Review, 233

National Union of Conservative Associations, 249-50, 258-9

Nettlefold and Chamberlain, screw manufacturers, 17, 18, 38, 86, 107, 191; success of firm, 18, 20, 33, 51-2; Chamberlain family sells out, 52

Nettlefold family, 7, 22-3

Nettlefold, John Sutton, and screw industry, 14, 17

Nettlefold, Joseph, 17

Nettlefold, Martha (*née* Chamberlain), aunt of JC, 14

Nevill, Lady Dorothy, 131, 170

New Meeting House, Birmingham, 22; JC married at (1861), 32

New South Wales Lancers, 218

New Zealand, payments for upkeep of Royal Navy, 208

'Newcastle programme', radical, 179

Niagara Falls, JC walks under, 165

Nigeria, 203

Nineteenth Century, 233

No Rent Manifesto (Ireland, 1882), 112

Nolan, Major, Irish Nationalist M.P., 94

Nonconformists: and Church schools, 44, 48, 55; and licensing of alcohol, 85-6; vote in 1880 election, 95; JC speaks nationally for them, 98; and 1902 Education Bill, 235-7

Norman, Sir Henry, 206

Observer, 247

Old age pensions, 241, 262, 269; JC and, 3, 178, 224, 241, 246

Olney, Richard, 203

Omdurman, battle of (1898), 188, 217-18

Orange Free State, 193, 195, 221, 227; joins Transvaal in South African War, 215

Orange River Colony, 230; self-government (1906), 232

Oranje Unie party, 232

O'Shea, Mrs. Katharine, 145

O'Shea, Capt. W. H., 112; divorce case, 145

Ottawa, JC visits, 164, 165

Ottawa Conference (1932), 270

Paardeberg, battle of, 219

Pace, Charlotte, JC's school teacher, 1, 4-6

Pall Mall Gazette, 103, 153

Palmerston, Visct., 11, 12, 29, 30, 73; death, 35, 36

Parliament Bill (1911), 269

Parliamentary reform: demand for, 24, 35-8; failure of Liberals' Bill (1866), 36; public demonstrations, 37-8; extension of rural franchise, 104, 116

see also Reform Bills (1832), (1867), (1884)

Parnell, Charles Stewart, 54, 93, 110-11, 119, 125, 133, 138, 145, 156; meeting with JC (1879), 94; JC's description of him, 94; in Kilmainham Gaol, 111; 'Kilmainham treaty', 112; released from gaol, 112; and Phoenix Park murders, 112; brings down Gladstone's administration, 120, 121; meeting with Lord Carnarvon (1885-6), 125-6, 130; talks with Gladstone, 126, 130, 132; advises his English supporters to vote Conservative, 130; and O'Shea divorce case, 145

Patents Bill (Act) (1883), 107